A BRAND-NEW YEAR—
A PROMISING NEW START

With expert readings and forecasts, you can chart a course to romance, adventure, good health, or career opportunities while gaining valuable insight into yourself and others. Offering a daily outlook for 18 full months, this fascinating guide shows you:

- The important dates in your life
- What to expect from an astrological reading
- How the stars can help you stay healthy and fit
  And more!

Let this sound advice guide you through a year of heavenly possibilities—for today and for every day of 2011!

SYDNEY OMARR'S® DAY-BY-DAY
ASTROLOGICAL GUIDE FOR

ARIES—March 21–April 19
TAURUS—April 20–May 20
GEMINI—May 21–June 20
CANCER—June 21–July 22
LEO—July 23–August 22
VIRGO—August 23–September 22
LIBRA—September 23–October 22
SCORPIO—October 23–November 21
SAGITTARIUS—November 22–December 21
CAPRICORN—December 22–January 19
AQUARIUS—January 20–February 18
PISCES—February 19–March 20

IN 2011

SYDNEY OMARR'S®

DAY-BY-DAY ASTROLOGICAL GUIDE FOR

CAPRICORN

DECEMBER 22–JANUARY 19

2011

by Trish MacGregor
with Rob MacGregor

A SIGNET BOOK

SIGNET
Published by New American Library, a division of
Penguin Group (USA) Inc., 375 Hudson Street,
New York, New York 10014, USA
Penguin Group (Canada), 90 Eglinton Avenue East, Suite 700, Toronto,
Ontario M4P 2Y3, Canada (a division of Pearson Penguin Canada Inc.)
Penguin Books Ltd., 80 Strand, London WC2R 0RL, England
Penguin Ireland, 25 St. Stephen's Green, Dublin 2,
Ireland (a division of Penguin Books Ltd.)
Penguin Group (Australia), 250 Camberwell Road, Camberwell, Victoria 3124,
Australia (a division of Pearson Australia Group Pty. Ltd.)
Penguin Books India Pvt. Ltd., 11 Community Centre, Panchsheel Park,
New Delhi - 110 017, India
Penguin Group (NZ), 67 Apollo Drive, Rosedale, North Shore 0645
New Zealand (a division of Pearson New Zealand Ltd.)
Penguin Books (South Africa) (Pty.) Ltd., 24 Sturdee Avenue,
Rosebank, Johannesburg 2196, South Africa

Penguin Books Ltd., Registered Offices:
80 Strand, London WC2R 0RL, England

First Printing, June 2010
10 9 8 7 6 5 4 3 2 1

First published by Signet, an imprint of New American Library,
a division of Penguin Group (USA) Inc.

Copyright © The Estate of Sydney Omarr, 2010
All rights reserved

Syndey Omarr's is a registered trademark of Writers House, LLC.

Sydney Omarr® is syndicated worldwide by Los Angeles Times Syndicate.

 REGISTERED TRADEMARK—MARCA REGISTRADA

Printed in the United States of America

PUBLISHER'S NOTE
While the author has made every effort to provide accurate telephone numbers
and Internet addresses at the time of publication, neither the publisher nor the
author assumes any responsibility for errors, or for changes that occur after publication. Further, publisher does not have any control over and does not assume
any responsibility for author or third-party Web sites or their content.

CONTENTS

CHAPTER 1

Transition in 2011

Our lives are marked by transitions. We make the *transition* from adolescence to adulthood, from dependent to independent, from being single to being married, from youth to middle age to old age, from life to death. These transitions are often marked by rituals—diplomas, ceremonies—that recognize our rites of passage.

In astrology, we have similar transitions, but they are triggered by the movement of the outer planets—Jupiter, Saturn, Uranus, Neptune, and Pluto. These planets are the slowest moving, so they exert the most impact on our lives. The lineup this year makes 2011 a time of transition from chaos to the paradigm shift that will occur in 2012.

So now you're asking *how it is going to affect you?* That depends on the angles these slower-moving planets make to your sun sign—and on your attitudes and deepest beliefs. After all, the planets only depict possible patterns that may occur. We are the scriptwriters. We have free will, the ability to make choices. Astrology simply provides information that makes those choices easier. To be informed is to be empowered.

Now let's take a closer look.

Welcome to Pluto

Transition from and to—what?

Since 2008, it seems that the world has been in a constant state of chaos, rather like a dysfunctional family whose daily life is riddled with one disaster and shock after another. Bank failures and bailouts, housing and financial meltdowns, the spike and fall in oil prices, upheavals in the health-care, banking, and insurance industries, loss of jobs, rise in unemployment and homelessness, two wars, a recession that some economists call the worst since the great depression. It's all part of a global eruption that will culminate in 2012, with what many believe will be a massive paradigm shift.

If you Google Mayan calendar 2012, more than six hundred thousand hits come up, many of them doom and gloom, predicting end times, the apocalypse, that we're done, cooked. But a more likely scenario is that we're learning that the old way of doing things no longer works, so we have to come up with viable options. A greener world, alternative fuels, universal health care, more regulation in the banking and insurance industries, the right to unionize—well, you get the idea, right?

All of this chaos is a hallmark of powerful Pluto, the snail of the zodiac. It takes 249 years to go through the twelve signs. It symbolizes profound transformation, collapses what no longer works, and then asks that we rebuild from the ashes. It rules the political and economic realities of our world, death and sex, life after death, reincarnation, taxes, insurance, mortgages. It entered Capricorn in 2008, turned retrograde, and in mid-June 2008 moved back into Sagittarius for a last fling. In late November 2008 it entered Capricorn again, where it will be until 2024. To gain some perspective on the patterns we might expect until 2024, let's take a brief foray back in time.

Pluto's last transit through Capricorn occurred between November 1762 and December 1, 1778. Unrest and outright rebellion and revolution were evident during much of this period in Europe and in the colonies. Spain acquired Louisiana from France; Catherine the Great became queen and presided over wars with the Ottoman Empire; Britain struck a deal with Spain to exchange Cuba for Florida. The first partition of Poland also happened during this period, and that country was divided into three areas owned by Russia, Prussia, and Austria. The Quartering Act was passed, requiring the housing of British troops in private homes. Parliament passed the Stamp Act—its first serious attempt to assert governmental authority over its North American colonies. It was intended to pay for the huge national debt Britain had incurred during the Seven Years War, but created a serious threat of revolt. The Boston Tea Party also occurred during Pluto's last passage through Capricorn.

Capricorn, among other things, represents government, authority figures, the consensus belief system, corporate entities that are too big to fail. Combine these qualities with Pluto, and here we are, in 2011, the year of transition.

Of course, Pluto is only part of the picture. There are some other major cycles occurring this year involving Jupiter, Saturn, Uranus, and Neptune. But we'll get to those in a later chapter. Right now let's focus on Pluto and find out what this transitional year means for each sign, in broad strokes. If you have a copy of your natal chart, check to see where Capricorn is found. If you don't have a copy of your chart, go to www.astro.com to get one. It will prove invaluable. But you'll need your exact time of birth—preferably from your birth certificate.

If you don't know your time of birth, then use the guidelines below. In this system, your sun sign is placed on the ascendant, which erects a solar chart. Yet natally, your ascendant—the sign rising at your birth—might be in Gemini or Cancer, which would change the layout of the chart. In other words, the solar chart isn't as accurate as your birth chart.

Under the title for each sign, you'll find that sign's element—fire, earth, air, or water—and it's quality—cardinal, fixed, mutable. We'll discuss this in more depth in a later chapter.

Aries ♈

(fire, cardinal)

Okay, down to brass tacks, Aries. You like everything up front and direct—spare the adjectives. So let's take a glimpse at how the transition of 2011 may affect you.

Regardless of what your natal ascendant or rising sign is, Aries and Capricorn form a challenging 90-degree angle to each other called a square. It's a source of tension that prompts you to take action (something you're good at) by initiating projects, relationships, communication, whatever it takes. When you want something, you tend to be focused and determined, and in 2011, you're reaching for the new, the untried, the unexplored. You're reaching with passion and resolve, and you aren't easily intimidated when you encounter obstacles. In fact, you refuse to recognize obstacles and barrel right through anything that's blocking you from what you desire.

Aries is terrific at launching projects, but not as good at completing them. That could change this year. Pluto in Capricorn demands that you bring your ideas down to earth and express them in terms that other people will understand. You're after what's practical, grounded, efficient. You're looking for new solutions that work. You're the trailblazer, the entrepreneur, the maverick, the explorer. You're forging new paths through the unknown.

In your solar chart, Capricorn falls in your career area,

so that will be the focus for the year. During Pluto's long transit through this sign, your career will undergo profound and irrevocable change. You may, for instance, change careers, suddenly and without apology or explanation. Equally possible, you may fall from power or enjoy a rapid ascension in terms of promotions, salary, recognition. Again, it all depends on your intent, emotions, beliefs.

Taurus ♉

(earth, fixed)

You're known for your resoluteness, your ability to finish what you start, for your stubbornness and fixed opinions. But you're also known for your sensuality and that sensuality extends to all things—sex, foods, art, music, the entire spectrum of human experience.

In your solar chart, Pluto in Capricorn changes your worldview at profound and irrevocable levels. If, for instance, you were brought up in a household that adhered to traditional religious views, then you may become, during this long transit, the complete opposite. A Buddhist, a Sufi, a spiritualist, an agnostic, an atheist. Another area that will undergo transformation is your attitudes or beliefs about foreigners, foreign countries, the global economy.

Let's say that you grew bitter during the years that Pluto was in Sagittarius—1995 to 2008. You lived through Clinton to Bush to Obama and witnessed 9/11 and the terrible divisiveness that grew in this country. Maybe your beliefs went from one extreme to another, or you were among the fortunate few who found a middle ground with which you could live. Well, now you begin to understand the true meaning of a Pluto transit to your ninth house. Your beliefs must be your own—not those you've adopted from parents, teachers, friends. Your philosophy during this transit will be evolving, changing, becoming more holistic, more integrated into who you are.

Other areas that may go through change: publishing, higher education, professional goals, your attitude and beliefs about the law. If you're self-employed, your product or services could expand to overseas markets, and you'll reap the benefits. Pluto's transit is apt to bring travel abroad too, but not for the usual reasons. You may be on a quest of some kind, trying to fulfill a need you may not fully understand. Ashram? Yoga retreat? A second home in a country that is the locus of your soul?

Gemini ♊
(air, mutable)

Yes, we all know about your communication skills, your ability to make friends with anyone, to strike up a conversation with even the strangest of strangers. It's your defense, your gift, your reason for being. We all know you're capable of changing your mind about anything anywhere, anytime. You figure it's your birthright. Others may think you're stretching the truth to accommodate your vision of reality, but you really aren't. So here's the deal. Until 2024, you're compelled to deal with what is, as it is. The present moment and all that.

What does this mean? Until 2024, you're delving into everything that goes bump in the night—ghosts, hauntings, reincarnation, communication with the dead, divination systems. But you're also dealing with mortgages, loans, insurance, taxes, inheritances, lawyers—all that Woody Allen stuff that may drive you completely nuts. But you find that you're up to the task, that you can do whatever is required. One possible repercussion of Pluto in Capricorn is that your partner's income experiences precipitous ups and downs until she really understands her beliefs about money.

If you read about sun signs, Geminis are often depicted as "flaky, shallow, flighty, unreliable," and a host of other unflattering adjectives. If you know people who think of you in those terms (and let's hope they aren't family members or friends), then Pluto's transit prompts them to change their minds and to see you in a much more positive light. Of course, by the time they come around, you've moved on to people who have appreciated your gifts from the start.

As you proceed through this Pluto transit, your beliefs about the universe and about what is possible are transformed at the most fundamental and profound levels. If you started out as a skeptic about metaphysical ideas, you end up as a believer because you've had too many experiences to think otherwise.

Cancer ♋
(water, cardinal)

Gentle Cancer. Life for you is a subjective dream, in which nearly everything you experience is filtered through your emotions and intuition. It isn't that you're a solipsist. You really don't believe you're the center of the universe. But when you experience something, your emotions and intuition act as your barometers of how true or genuine the experience is.

During Pluto's transit through Capricorn, your opposite sign, you may have to revamp your attitude about relationships and power issues. You'll have to change your MO! Instead of trying to push other people to act in ways that don't suit them, against which they resist, you'll learn to back off and let things take their own course. You'll learn that each of us has our own barometers to measure our individual experiences, and that each of us must find our own path.

If, during this transit, you realize that someone else

7

is trying to manipulate you in some way, then perhaps you have emitted a signal that attracts that experience. Life is about vibration and frequency, and if your signal attracts what you don't want, then you'll have to change the signal. You're extremely ambitious during this transit and can achieve just about anything you reach for if you can avoid opposition from people in authority. And this means any authority—from the government to a boss, partner, parent, or anyone else who tries to manipulate or cajole you into doing something that you feel isn't right for you or is flat-out wrong.

Your intuition will deepen considerably during this transit. Listen to that inner voice. Heed its guidance. Meaningful coincidence will proliferate during this transit, but only if you recognize the phenomenon isn't random, that there's an underlying order in the universe that can be your greatest ally.

Leo ♌

(fire, fixed)

Applause. Recognition. They say it's what you live for, what you crave, that it's your reason for being. While it's true that Leos can excel in any profession they enter, not every Leo hungers for the limelight. Some work tirelessly behind the scenes, drawing their satisfaction from the way they change other people's lives through their work for a particular cause or belief.

During Pluto's transit of Capricorn, you will discover new depths in your daily work, new ways of tackling old issues and challenges, and nothing will be business as usual. You will be called upon to make your ideas and actions tangible, solid, grounded, practical. When others ask you to explain what you mean, you'll have to spell it out, a challenge for someone who often explains on the spur of the moment. You won't be able to get by on just your charm, your flair for drama, your wit and talent. You'll have to produce what others can sink their teeth into.

Pluto in Capricorn, an earth sign. Uh, right? Earth is not your favorite element. Earth suffocates fire, kills it. And yet even for you, Leo, earth serves a purpose. It urges you to decompress, to pay attention to the minutiae of your daily life—grocery store runs, cooking, what you eat and when you eat it, whether you're getting enough exercise and are taking care of yourself. There could be health issues under this transit—or at least the propensity for such—but it's mitigated by your awareness of your body. Read Louise Hay's *You Can Heal Your Body*. You will never again feel the same about what causes physical discomfort, illness, or disease.

The other possible ramifications of this transit are more subtle and concern your career. In a time of transition, with Pluto forming a beneficial angle to your professional area, it's possible that you may change careers in midstream. Just when you seem to be on a winning path, you switch. Don't obsess too much about it. Things are unfolding as they are intended to for your greater enrichment and evolution.

Virgo ♍

(earth, mutable)

You're the perfectionist of the zodiac, the one who attempts to make every experience something so perfect that it will shine like a jewel in memory. You quickly discover that this shine is not endemic to every jewel and that life isn't that perfect either. But hey, you're actually an optimist—something you won't find in most descriptions of your sign, which seem to equate Virgo with the kiss of death. You really desire life to be a fairy tale, in some form or other, and if you're persistent, which many of you are, you'll gradually learn that you're the script-writer of your life.

Pluto's transit of Capricorn, a fellow earth sign, should be beneficial for you—profound and transformative but beneficial. Your love life, your creativity, your relationship with your children, if you have any, and everything you do for fun and pleasure will be vastly changed by 2024. You might argue, justifiably so, that change is inevitable over the course of the next thirteen years. But with Pluto, the change is deep and irrevocable. Pluto in Capricorn urges you to explore in a focused, directed way the parameters of your creativity, your worldview and spiritual beliefs, your romantic expectations and needs in personal relationships. And because Capricorn is involved in this equation, your career is part of the larger picture. What is it that you really want to do?

Pluto brings personal power and an awareness of your own place in the universe. Heady stuff, for sure. But you, Virgo, integrate this knowledge into who you are, how you act, and what you think. You figure out that our realities are a reflection of our deepest beliefs, that we create our lives from the inside out.

Libra ♎

(air, cardinal)

You're the peacemaker of the zodiac—the one who dislikes confrontation, aggression, disharmony, war. You aren't the type who draws lines in the sand and dares some abstract enemy to cross it. You aren't, never were, and never will be a bully. Your soul gravitates toward beauty in the arts, music, theater, photography, literature. Ultimately, you seek balance and harmony, the very qualities that may elude you.

As Pluto transits Capricorn and your solar fourth house, you will find that your home and family life, your domestic environment, undergo deep, transformative changes. You may start a family—or get divorced; you and your significant other buy a home or property together—or part ways; your parents find a path to independent living or move in with you. The idea here is that the choices are either/or, without nuances or gray areas. These possibilities are only that. The transit may unfold quite differently for you. The choices are difficult but you make them because you must.

A move is possible under this transit. But then again, over a period of thirteen years, most of us might move once. Yet this move, if you make it, will be transformative. You might find the neighborhood, city, or country that speaks to your soul. You might meet your soul mate, if you haven't already. There will be changes within your home life. While all of this is occurring, other indicators suggest expansiveness in your love life, creativity, with your children, and with what you do for fun and pleasure. In other words, astrology isn't about just one transit, one influence, a singular energy. It's about how all these energies mesh and interact with your birth chart.

In the end, Libra, you're the one who chooses what's right for you. You're the one who creates your life—not the stars, not some amorphous influence somewhere—but you. That's what Pluto's transit through Capricorn teaches you.

Scorpio ♏

(water, fixed)

As the most emotionally intense and psychic sign of the zodiac, little escapes you. You're the type who walks into a room filled with strangers, your psychic antennae twitch a couple times, and you're immediately inundated with a flow of intuitive information about the people around you. This can happen on a conscious or unconscious level, but either way, you'll find whatever you need to know to work the room. Or the entire conference. Or the university. Or the world.

Pluto's transit of Capricorn will benefit you. Earth (Capricorn) mixes with water (your sign). This transit occurs in your solar third house of communication, your daily conscious world, your neighborhood and community, your relationships with relatives. It impacts how you communicate. Even though you often hold back, maintaining your own space, your own counsel, you certainly don't mince words once the dam opens. And with Pluto moving through the communication sector, you're primed for change, bottom lines, investigation and research, and psychic development.

During this transit, your relationship with your siblings will change considerably. If there has been injury in these relationships, you have a chance to heal the relationship. If there has been misunderstanding, you have an opportunity to put things right again. If you want to move from your current neighborhood, you have opportunities to do that too. The point with this Pluto transit is that you become aware of how powerful you are as an individual, and that if you wield this power in a judicious way, so that everyone around you benefits, you win the day.

During this transit, it's important that you heed any and all synchronicities that you experience. These events are signposts of intuitive guidance—messages from the universe that you're on the right path.

Sagittarius ♐
(fire, mutable)

Ah, gregarious Sadge. You're the life of every party; you have a vast network of friends and acquaintances. People genuinely enjoy your company and the diversity of your intellect. You enjoy travel, the more exotic the better, and can talk with ease about the places you've been. You're a storehouse of information.

Pluto's journey through Capricorn and your solar second house will impact your values and your finances. There will be opportunities to structure your finances in such a way so that you accumulate money. Perhaps you'll learn to pay yourself first from every paycheck. Or you might decide to invest in land, property, or precious metals like gold and silver. It will be important to you that the way you earn your living is in line with your beliefs. If you're antiwar, for example, then you won't be working at the Pentagon! Or for a corporation that profits from war. If you've gone green, you won't be working for an oil company.

Pluto's job is to transform at profound levels, so if there are lessons you need to learn about money, you'll learn them during this transit. If you're a profligate spender, Pluto will tighten the financial reins. If you believe that money is good (as opposed to the belief that money is the root of all evil), then Pluto will bring you more money. It's a black-and-white world with this little powerhouse of a planet, and you'll quickly learn that what comes around goes around. Work with your deepest beliefs during this transit. Be positive. Nurture what Esther and Jerry Hicks call "rampaging appreciation" so that Pluto brings you even more to appreciate!

Capricorn ♑

(earth, cardinal)

You're the classic type-A personality who finds it challenging to relax. You're constantly moving, doing, your mind focused on several tasks at once. You're the one who usually assumes full responsibility for anything and everything at work. You may find it difficult to delegate.

You are the leader everyone turns to for answers and guidance.

During Pluto's transit of your sign, just about everything in your life will undergo a profound transformation. It won't all happen at once. It's not as if you'll wake up one morning and find yourself inside a Stephen King novel. But when, in 2024, you look back, you might not recognize the life you're living now. Possibilities? Your career path could change. You might go to graduate school for an advanced degree in an area about which you feel passionate. You could live abroad, join an ashram, get married or divorced, or start a family. You could inherit money, earn a fortune, or lose a fortune. You could build a home, buy a home, land the job of your dreams. What you experience during this transit will depend on what you've been doing with your life up until now.

Here are several tools that will prove invaluable during this transit: cultivate a positive attitude; live in the now; be grateful and express that gratitude whenever and wherever you can; reach for what you desire with the trust and faith that you will attain it. Books that will help you do this include anything by Esther and Jerry Hicks, *The Power of Now* by Eckhard Tolle, *You Can Heal Your Life* by Louise Hay. Another great navigational tool is to probe into any meaningful coincidence you experience. What's the message? Meaningful coincidences or synchronicities often hold messages about guidance.

Aquarius ≈
(air, fixed)

Now that we're in the Age of Aquarius, you should be feeling right at home. After all, you're the paradigm buster. You set out to find your own truth. Or you don't like what you see and set out to change it. Or you find a better way of doing something. You're the true visionary of the zodiac.

During Pluto's transit through Capricorn and your solar twelfth house, your inner world will experience profound transformation. This can include a spiritual quest, an intense exploration of your personal unconscious, traditional therapy, the study of shamanism, Wicca, of some other nontraditional belief system, the study of your own dreams, an exploration of the world of synchronicity or your past lives. It can take virtually any form and, because you are an Aquarian, it won't be ordinary! If you don't blog already, then you may start blogging about this journey, could write a book about it, or use your discovery for some other form of creative self-expression.

During this long transit, you'll have to bring your ideas into concrete, tangible forms that others understand—that's the Capricorn part of the equation. You'll be urged to build upon the knowledge that you uncover and to communicate it to others through writing, teaching, or some other venue.

Your prime directive, first and foremost, is the freedom to explore whatever interests you, and during this transit, you will value that freedom even more deeply. Nothing and no one will deter you from a path you choose to follow.

Pisces)(

(water, mutable)

There's a reason that your sign is symbolized by a pair of fish swimming in opposite directions. Your talents are many and your conflicts often center around which talent to express. Are you the writer today or the artist? Are you the filmmaker or the psychic? The parent or the kid? Some consider you to be the dreamer of the zodiac; others label you the healer. In truth, you're both.

Pluto's journey through Capricorn impacts your solar eleventh house, which governs friendships, group associations, and your wishes and dreams. This transit will help you to concentrate on one of your talents, develop and nurture it, and to build something with it. Your prodigious imagination will be more focused. You'll be able to tune in to information you need, when you need it, and then transform the information into something concrete that others can understand.

Anyone who knows you understands how rich your inner life is. With Pluto's transit in Capricorn, you'll now have a chance to share that inner wealth through a creative venue of some kind. It will be easier to manifest your deepest desires and to build on them. Your intuition undoubtedly plays an important part in your life already, but with this transit, it proves immensely valuable. You'll be able to size up a situation or individual in seconds flat, and know whether to go forward. Group involvement of any kind will prove to be beneficial, and it doesn't matter what sort of group it is. You'll be reaching out more frequently to others through sites like Facebook and Twitter, MySpace and Plaxo, thus creating a network, a community, of people who share your passions.

Now that you've got the larger picture of how this transition will work for you, let's take a look at some astrological basics.

CHAPTER 2

Star Stuff

How much do you know about the day you were born?
What was the weather like that day? If you were born
at night, had the moon already risen? Was it full or the
shape of a Cheshire cat's grin? Was the delivery ward
quiet or bustling with activity? Unless your mom or dad
has a very good memory, you'll probably never know
the full details. But there's one thing you can know for
sure: On the day you were born, the sun was located in
a particular zone of the zodiac, an imaginary 360-degree
belt that circles the earth. The belt is divided into twelve
30-degree portions called signs.

If you were born between March 21 and April 19, then
the sun was passing through the sign of Aries, so we say
that your sun sign is Aries. Each of the twelve signs has
distinct attributes and characteristics. Aries individuals,
for example, are independent pioneers, fearless and passionate. Virgos, born between August 23 and September
22, are perfectionists with discriminating intellects and
a genius for details. Geminis, born between May 21 and
June 20, are networkers and communicators.

The twelve signs are categorized according to element
and quality or modality. The first category reads like a
basic science lesson—fire, earth, air, and water—and describes the general physical characteristics of the signs.

Fire signs—Aries, Leo, Sagittarius—are warm, dynamic
individuals who are always passionate about what they do.

Earth signs—Taurus, Virgo, Capricorn—are the builders of the zodiac, practical and efficient, grounded in everything they do.

Air signs—Gemini, Libra, Aquarius—are people who live mostly in the world of ideas. They are terrific communicators.

Water signs—Cancer, Scorpio, Pisces—live through their emotions, imaginations, and intuitions.

The second category describes how each sign operates in the physical world, how adaptable it is to circumstances. Cardinal signs—Aries, Cancer, Libra, Capricorn—are initiators. These people are active, impatient, restless. They're great at starting things, but unless a project or a relationship holds their attention, they lose interest and may not finish what they start.

Fixed signs—Taurus, Leo, Scorpio, Aquarius—are deliberate, controlled, resolute. These individuals tend to move more slowly than cardinal signs, are often stubborn, and resist change. They seek roots and stability, and they are always in the game for the long haul. They aren't quitters.

Mutable signs—Gemini, Virgo, Sagittarius, Pisces—are adaptable. These people are flexible, changeable, communicative. They don't get locked into rigid patterns or belief systems.

SUN SIGNS

Sign	Date	Element	Quality
Aries	March 21–April 19	Fire	Cardinal
Taurus	April 20–May 20	Earth	Fixed
Gemini	May 21–June 21	Air	Mutable
Cancer	June 22–July 22	Water	Cardinal
Leo	July 23–August 22	Fire	Fixed
Virgo	August 23–September 22	Earth	Mutable
Libra	September 23–October 22	Air	Cardinal
Scorpio	October 23–November 21	Water	Fixed
Sagittarius	November 22–December 21	Fire	Mutable

Sign	Date		Element	Quality
Capricorn	December 22–January 19		Earth	Cardinal
Aquarius	January 20–February 18		Air	Fixed
Pisces	February 19–March 20		Water	Mutable

The Planets

The planets in astrology are the players who make things happen. They're the characters in the story of your life. And this story always begins with the sun, the giver of life.

Your sun sign describes your self-expression, your primal energy, the essence of who you are. It's the archetypal pattern of your self. When you know another person's sun sign, you already have a great deal of information about that person.

Let's say you're a Taurus who has just started dating a Gemini. How compatible are you? On the surface, it wouldn't seem that you have much in common. Taurus is a fixed earth sign; Gemini is a mutable air sign. Taurus is persistent, stubborn, practical, a cultivator as opposed to an initiator. Gemini is a chameleon, a communicator, social, with a mind as quick as lightning. Taurus is ruled by Venus, which governs the arts, money, beauty, love, and romance, and Gemini is ruled by Mercury, which governs communication and travel. There doesn't seem to be much common ground. But before we write off this combination, let's look a little deeper.

Suppose the Taurus has Mercury in Gemini, and suppose the Gemini has Venus in Taurus. This would mean that the Taurus and Gemini each have their rulers in the other person's sign. They probably communicate well and enjoy travel and books (Mercury) and see eye to eye on romance, art, and music (Venus). They might get along so well, in fact, that they collaborate on creative projects.

Each of us is also influenced by the other nine planets (the sun and moon are treated like planets in astrology) and the signs they were transiting when you were born. Suppose our Taurus and Gemini have the same moon sign? The moon rules our inner needs, emotions, intuition, and all that makes us feel secure within ourselves. Quite often, compatible moon signs can overcome even the most glaring difference in sun signs because the two people share similar emotions.

In the sections on monthly predictions, your sun sign always takes center stage, and every prediction is based on the movement of the transiting planets in relation to your sun sign. Let's say you're a Sagittarius. Between January 7 and February 4 this year, Venus will be transiting your sign. What does this mean for you? Well, since Venus rules—among other things—romance, you can expect your love life to pick up significantly during these weeks. Other people will find you attractive and be more open to your ideas, and you'll radiate a certain charisma. Your creative endeavors will move full steam ahead.

The planets table provides an overview of the planets and the signs that they rule. Keep in mind that the moon is the swiftest-moving planet, changing signs about every two and a half days, and that Pluto is the snail of the zodiac, taking as long as thirty years to transit a single sign. Although the faster-moving planets—the Moon, Mercury, Venus, and Mars—have an impact on our lives, the slowpokes—Uranus, Neptune, and Pluto—bring about the most profound influence and change. Jupiter and Saturn fall between the others in terms of speed. This year, Jupiter zips through Aries in under six months, but remains in Taurus from June 2011 until June 2012.

In the section on predictions, the most frequent references are to the transits of Mercury, Venus, and Mars. In the daily predictions for each sign, the predictions are based primarily on the transiting moon.

Now glance through the planets table. When a sign is in parentheses, it means the planet corules that sign. This assignation dates back to when we thought there were only seven planets in the solar system. But since there were still twelve signs, some of the planets had to do double duty!

THE PLANETS

Planet	Rules	Attributes of Planet
Sun ☉	Leo	self-expression, primal energy, creative ability, ego, individuality
Moon ☽	Cancer	emotions, intuition, mother or wife, security
Mercury ☿	Gemini, Virgo	intellect, mental acuity, communication, logic, reasoning, travel, contracts
Venus ♀	Taurus, Libra	love, romance, beauty, artistic instincts, the arts, music, material and financial resources
Mars ♂	Aries (Scorpio)	physical and sexual energy, aggression, drive
Jupiter ♃	Sagittarius (Pisces)	luck, expansion, success, prosperity, growth, creativity, spiritual interests, higher education, law
Saturn ♄	Capricorn (Aquarius)	laws of physical universe, discipline, responsibility, structure, karma, authority
Uranus ♅	Aquarius	individuality, genius, eccentricity, originality, science, revolution

Planet	Rules	Attributes of Planet
Neptune Ψ	Pisces	visionary self, illusions, what's hidden, psychic ability, dissolution of ego boundaries, spiritual insights, dreams
Pluto ♀ ♇	Scorpio	the darker side, death, sex, regeneration, rebirth, profound and permanent change, transformation

Houses and Rising Signs

In the instant you drew your first breath, one of the signs of the zodiac was just passing over the eastern horizon. Astrologers refer to this as the rising sign or ascendant. It's what makes your horoscope unique. Think of your ascendant as the front door of your horoscope, the place where you enter into this life and begin your journey.

Your ascendant is based on the exact moment of your birth and the other signs follow counterclockwise. If you have Taurus rising, for example, that is the cusp of your first house. The cusp of the second would be Gemini, of the third Cancer, and so on around the horoscope circle in a counterclockwise direction. Each house governs a particular area of life, which is outlined below.

The best way to find out your rising sign is to have your horoscope drawn up by an astrologer. For those of you with access to the Internet, there are a couple of sites that provide free birth horoscopes: www.astro.com and www.cafeastrology.com are two good ones.

In a horoscope, the ascendant (cusp of the first house), IC (cusp of the fourth house), descendant (cusp of the seventh house), and MC (cusp of the tenth house) are considered to be the most critical angles. Any planets that fall close to these angles are extremely important in the overall astrological picture of who you are. By the same token, planets that fall in the first, fourth, seventh, and tenth houses are also considered to be important.

Now here's a rundown on what the houses mean.

Ascendant or Rising: The First of Four Important Critical Angles in a Horoscope

- How other people see you
- How you present yourself to the world
- Your physical appearance

First House, Personality

- Early childhood
- Your ego
- Your body type and how you feel about your body
- General physical health
- Defense mechanisms
- Your creative thrust

Second House, Personal Values

- How you earn and spend your money
- Your personal values
- Your material resources and assets
- Your attitudes and beliefs toward money
- Your possessions and your attitude toward those possessions
- Your self-worth
- Your attitudes about creativity

Third House, Communication and Learning

- Personal expression
- Intellect and mental attitudes and perceptions
- Neighbors and relatives

- How you learn
- School until college
- Reading, writing, teaching
- Short trips (the grocery store versus Europe in seven days)
- Earthbound transportation
- Creativity as a communication device

IC or Fourth House Cusp: The Second Critical Angle in a Horoscope

- Sign on IC describes the qualities and traits of your home during early childhood
- Describes roots of your creative abilities and talents

Fourth House, Your Roots

- Personal environment
- Your home
- Your attitudes toward family
- Early childhood conditioning
- Real estate
- Your nurturing parent

Some astrologers say this house belongs to Mom or her equivalent in your life; others say it belongs to Dad or his equivalent. It makes sense to me that it's Mom because the fourth house is ruled by the moon, which rules mothers. But in this day and age, when parental roles are in flux, the only hard-and-fast rule is that the fourth belongs to the parent who nurtures you most of the time.

- The conditions at the end of your life
- Early childhood support of your creativity and interests

Fifth House, Children and Creativity

- Kids, your firstborn in particular
- Love affairs, romance
- What you enjoy
- Creative ability
- Gambling and speculation
- Pets

Traditionally, pets belong in the sixth house. But that definition stems from the days when pets were chattel. These days, we don't even refer to them as pets. They are animal companions who bring us pleasure.

Sixth House, Work and Responsibility

- Day-to-day working conditions and environment
- Competence and skills
- Your experience of employees and employers
- Duty to work, to employees
- Health and the daily maintenance of your health

Descendant/Seventh House Cusp: The Third Critical Angle in a Horoscope

- The sign on the house cusp describes the qualities sought in intimate or business relationships
- Describes qualities of creative partnerships

Seventh House, Partnerships and Marriage

- Marriage
- Marriage partner
- Significant others
- Business partnerships
- Close friends
- Open enemies
- Contracts

Eighth House, Transformation

- Sexuality as transformation
- Secrets
- Death, taxes, inheritances, insurance, mortgages, and loans
- Resources shared with others
- Your partner's finances
- The occult (astrology, reincarnation, UFOs, everything weird and strange)
- Your hidden talents
- Psychology
- Life-threatening illnesses
- Your creative depths

Ninth House, Worldview

- Philosophy and religion
- The law, courts, judicial system
- Publishing
- Foreign travels and cultures
- College, graduate school
- Spiritual beliefs
- Travel abroad

MC or Cusp of Tenth House:
The Fourth Critical Angle in a Horoscope

- Sign on cusp of MC describes qualities you seek in a profession
- Your public image
- Your creative and professional achievements

Tenth House, Profession and Career

- Public image as opposed to a job that merely pays the bills (sixth house)
- Your status and position in the world

- The authoritarian parent and authority in general
- People who hold power over you
- Your public life
- Your career and profession

Eleventh House, Ideals and Dreams

- Peer groups
- Social circles (your writers' group, your mother's bridge club)
- Your dreams and aspirations
- How you can realize your dreams

Twelfth House, Personal Unconscious

- Power you have disowned that must be claimed again
- Institutions—hospitals, prisons, nursing homes—and what is hidden
- What you must confront this time around, your karma, issues brought in from other lives
- Psychic gifts and abilities
- Healing talents
- What you give unconditionally

In the section on predictions, you'll find references to transiting planets moving into certain houses. These houses are actually solar houses created by putting your sun sign on the ascendant. This technique is how most predictions are made for the general public rather than for specific individuals.

Lunations

Every year, there are twelve new moons and twelve full moons, with some years having thirteen full moons. The extra full moon is called the blue moon. New moons are typically when we should begin new projects, set new goals, seek new opportunities. They're times for beginnings. They usher in new opportunities according to house and sign.

Two weeks after each new moon, there's a full moon. This is the time of harvest, fruition, when we reap what we've sown.

Whenever a new moon falls in your sign, take time to brainstorm what you would like to achieve during weeks and months until the full moon falls in your sign. These goals can be in any area of your life. Or you can simply take the time on each new moon to set up goals and strategies for what you would like to achieve or manifest during the next two weeks—until the full moon—or until the next new moon.

Here's a list of all the new moons and full moons during 2011. The asterisk beside any new moon entry indicates a solar eclipse; the asterisk next to a full moon entry indicates a lunar eclipse.

LUNATIONS OF 2011

New Moons

*January 4—Capricorn
February 2—Aquarius
March 4—Pisces
April 3—Aries
May 3—Taurus
*June 1—Gemini
July 1—Cancer
July 30—Leo
August 28—Virgo
September 27—Libra
October 26—Scorpio
*November 25—Sagittarius
December 24—Capricorn

Full Moons

January 19—Cancer
February 18—Leo
March 19—Virgo
April 17—Libra
May 17—Scorpio
*June 15—Sagittarius
July 15—Capricorn
August 13—Aquarius
September 12—Pisces
October 11—Aries
November 10—Taurus
*December 10—Gemini

Every year there are two lunar and two solar eclipses, separated from one another by about two weeks. Lunar eclipses tend to deal with emotional issues, our internal world, and often bring an emotional issue to the surface related to the sign and house in which the eclipse falls. Solar eclipses deal with events and often enable us to see something that has eluded us. They also symbolize beginnings and endings.

Read more about eclipses in the big picture for your sign for 2011. I also recommend Celeste Teal's excellent book *Eclipses*.

Mercury Retrograde

Every year, Mercury—the planet that symbolizes communication and travel—turns retrograde three times. During these periods, our travel plans often go awry, communication breaks down, computers go berserk, cars or appliances develop problems. You get the idea. Things in our daily lives don't work as smoothly as we would like.

Here are some guidelines to follow for Mercury retrogrades:

- Try not to travel. But if you have to, be flexible and think of it as an adventure. If you're stuck overnight in an airport in Houston or Atlanta, the adventure part of this could be a stretch.
- Don't sign contracts—unless you don't mind revisiting them when Mercury is direct again.
- Communicate as succinctly and clearly as possible.
- Back up all computer files. Use an external hard drive or a flash drive. If you've had a computer crash, you already know how frustrating it can be to reconstruct your files.
- Don't buy anything expensive.

- Don't submit manuscripts or screenplays, pitch ideas, or launch new projects.
- Revise, rewrite, rethink, and review.

In the overview for each sign, check out the dates for this year's Mercury retrogrades and how these retrogrades are likely to impact you. Do the same for eclipses.

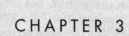

CHAPTER 3

Career Tips for the Transition

From our perspective in 2009, things look about as bleak as the dark side of the moon. The economy is in meltdown, unemployment in some states is as high as 10 percent, and every week there's a bailout announcement for a bank or insurance company. Foreclosures and homelessness are on the rise, the prices of gas and food are soaring, and health-care costs are daunting even to those fortunate people who can afford to buy health insurance.

And yet many people flourish during economically difficult times, and it may have more to do with their attitudes and beliefs than with the so-called reality of the situation. These people tend to have an unshakable belief in themselves and their own talents and abilities. They don't buy in to the consensus beliefs propagated by a 24-7 news cycle on TV and the Internet. They maintain positive, upbeat attitudes and look upon every challenge as an opportunity.

Several years ago, friends of ours—a married couple who are both writers—had pretty much hit rock bottom. The wife admitted that she was ready to start cleaning pools just to have a steady income. Then, practically overnight, everything turned around. Her husband sold a novel that became a popular cable TV show, a producer commissioned her to write a script, and suddenly, their bank account fattened, they bought a second home, a new car, and a boat, and the world opened up for them. It can open up for you too.

We create our realities from the inside out. Everything you see around you is a manifestation of a belief that you hold. Some of our beliefs have been passed down to us by well-meaning family members, mentors, teachers, and friends, and we adopt those beliefs because we respect the people who handed them to us. But what do you believe about your talents and your ability to earn your living doing what you love? How do you handle stress or change?

In 2011, we all have a chance to delve into those beliefs and get rid of the ones we have adopted out of convenience. We can either go with the flow, change with the times, or offer up resistance. The more we resist, the more pain we experience. The more we go with the flow, the greater our capacity to discover where we should be. Which path will you take?

Using Synchronicity in 2011

The Swiss psychologist Carl Jung coined the word "synchonicity." It means "the coming together of inner and outer events in a way that can't be explained by cause and effect and that is meaningful to the observer." An easy example is illustrated by something that has probably happened to most of us. You wake up thinking about a friend or ex-lover you haven't seen for a long time. Shortly afterward, this person phones you or e-mails you. Or perhaps you're in your car, thinking about an issue or concern, and the first thing you hear when you turn on the radio seems to address what you were thinking about.

Meaningful coincidence. When it happens to you, when you don't dismiss these experiences as random curiosities, your life is enriched and the guidance that's offered becomes a navigational tool for moving through life successfully. In times of stress or major transitions—marriage, divorce, birth, a move, a career change or change in employment and income—synchronicities may occur more frequently. Decipher the message if you can, and know that synchronicities indicate we're in the flow, exactly where we're supposed to be.

Your Career Path in 2011

Whether you're a student or a CEO, unemployed or employed, like your job, tolerate it, or detest it, there are things you can do during this transition to maximize your opportunities.

Aries

Because you're a cardinal fire sign, your entire life is about movement, action, doing. You're the pioneer, the entrepreneur, the one who really does march to the beat of a different drummer. Your pioneering spirit, in fact, is your most valuable tool for navigating any professional changes you encounter this year.

You refuse to recognize defeat in anything. So what would be a setback to someone else is an opportunity to you. This year, you realize you must follow your passions wherever they lead. Ignore the naysayers who insist it can't be done, that to succeed you must follow the methods that are tried and true. You know otherwise and leave your competition gasping in the dust.

Notable Aries: Marilyn Ferguson, author of *The Aquarian Conspiracy;* Vincent van Gogh, who needs no introduction

Taurus

You hear the music of the spheres, poetry flows through your dreams, you're a mystic in disguise. You're the most enduring, taciturn, and physical of the twelve signs. You always finish what you start, even if it's just a plate of food. Your resolute determination is your greatest asset for navigating any professional changes this year.

This year, particularly in the second half, the stars align in such a way that you experience an explosive expansion in your life. This expansion can affect any area upon which you place your focus and intent. You already know your own value; this year, everyone around you learns it as well.

Notable Tauruses: George Lucas, Shirley MacLaine

Gemini

Your mind is a regular beehive, constantly buzzing with information, bits of conversations, who said what and when. You're the consummate communicator of the zodiac, always willing to share what you know and eager to hear what others know, curious about everything.

Your ability to multitask and your curiosity are your greatest assets for navigating any professional changes this year. One way or another, your curiosity takes you to wherever you need to be so that you can connect with the right people at the right time, and say exactly the right things. Your versatility and your communication abilities shine this year.

Notable Geminis: author Whitley Streiber, underwater explorer Jacques Cousteau

Cancer

You're completely attuned to emotions—yours and everyone else's. It's easy for you to slip into someone else's skin and feel what they feel. You hurt as they hurt. You weep as they weep. You laugh as they laugh. Like fellow water sign Pisces, you're a psychic sponge. You have an extraordinary memory that is intimately linked to your emotions, and your intuition is remarkable. All of these traits are your strongest assets for navigating professional changes this year.

Whether you're just entering the job market or retiring, the stars line up in such a beneficial way for you that you end up exactly where you're supposed to be at this time in your life. Embrace whatever change comes your way, and trust that the universe works for your highest good.

Notable Cancers: Nobel Prize–winning authors Hermann Hesse and Ernest Hemingway; Jeff Lindsay, creator of *Dexter*

Leo

You were born to express your creativity through performance. You love the applause, the recognition, the immediate gratification and feedback. Of course, not every Leo is an actor or actress, but every Leo loves drama. So whether you're on the stage, in front of a classroom, or counseling a patient in therapy, your creative flair moves through you like a force of nature. This asset will help you navigate any professional changes that come about this year.

Most of the year looks particularly promising. There will be enough excitement, unpredictability, and drama to suit you, and it's possible that you could find yourself in a different job or career altogether before year's end.

Notable Leos: Madonna, Mick Jagger, Zelda Fitzgerald, J. K. Rowling

Virgo

Your gift is details. Whether it's your own life that you're honing, sculpting, and shining like some fine gem, or a particular project or relationship, you can see the finished product in a way that others can't. You also have a particular gift or ability that you're always willing to provide to others, without thought of compensation. These traits carry you through any professional changes you go through this year.

For all the signs, the year looks promising, but for earth and water signs in particular, the period from June 4, 2011, to June 12, 2012, is especially powerful. You, of course, will sift through all the details and withhold judgment and decisions until all the details are in.

Notable Virgos: famed editor Max Perkins, Stephen King

Libra

You can work a room like a seasoned politician, spreading peace and harmony even among people who can't agree on anything. That's your magic. And yet the very qualities that you can instill in others often elude you. Not that any of us could tell by looking at you. Libra is a master of social camouflage. It seems that nothing ruffles you. But within, you're struggling to maintain harmony without compromising your principles. Your sphere is relationships. More than any other sign, you can see the many sides of an issue and understand that your truth may not be everyone's truth. But you can live with the paradox. It's your gift.

Any professional challenges you encounter in 2011 will be overcome through the sheer force of your grace under pressure. You can tap into your vast network of friends and acquaintances for support, leads, whatever you need.

Notable Libras: F. Scott Fitzgerald, past-life researcher and writer Carol Bowman

Scorpio

You're the emotional vortex of the zodiac, a spinning whirlwind of contradictions. You aren't like the rest of us, and that's the way you prefer it. You dig deeply into everything you do, looking for the absolute bottom line, the most fundamental truth, and then you excavate everything at the discovery site just to make sure you've gotten it all.

Professional challenges that you encounter this year will be met with the same fortitude and resilience that drives you through life—head-on but in secret. No one around you will have a clue about what you're doing. Your intuition will enable you to move in the right direction at the right time.

Notable Scorpios: Jodie Foster, Picasso, poets Sylvia Plath and Anne Sexton

Sagittarius

You're the life of the party, just like your fellow fire sign Leo. But your approach is different. Where Leo seeks recognition and applause, you're after the big picture, and it doesn't matter how far you have to travel to find it, how many people you have to talk to, how many books or blogs you must read. When your passion is seized, you're as doggedly relentless as Taurus. One part of you operates from raw instinct; the other part of you is aware of how to work the system.

You don't recognize professional challenges. For you, any bump in a road simply means you take an alternate path to get to where you want to go. You may not be able to connect the dots, but you always have your eyes on the forest rather than the trees.

Notable Sagittarians: Nostradamus, author Shirley Jackson, Steven Spielberg

Capricorn

You're the achiever, the builder, the classic type-A personality whose focus is so tight that everything and everyone becomes part of your journey toward . . . well, the top of the hill, the pinnacle of whatever you're attempting to reach. You can build anything anywhere. A fictional world, a belief system, an invention, a concept, a family, a video world. Name it, and you can build it.

Any professional challenges you encounter in 2011 will be tackled the same way that you tackle any other challenge in your life—you find a way around it. Or through it. As a cardinal earth sign, you value what is tangible, practical, efficient, and your journey through any obstacle reflects it. Never fear. This year, the stars are stacked in your favor.

Notable Capricorns: Carlos Castaneda, J. R. R. Tolkien, Jack London

Aquarius

You're not easy to pigeonhole. Sometimes you seem to be the paragon of independence. And yet you enjoy the company of groups who share your passions. You're the one who thinks so far outside the box that people close to you may accuse you of communication with aliens, ghosts, goblins, elves. Even if it's true, you just laugh and continue on your journey into the strange, the unknown, the heart of the universe.

If you encounter any challenges professionally during 2011, it's not that big a deal for you. Somehow, you work your way around it and come through on the other side, smelling like the proverbial rose. And you do it the way you do everything else: by delving into the areas about which you're passionate even if your interests don't fit into consensus beliefs.

Notable Aquarians: Charles Darwin, Jules Verne

Pisces

Dreamer, healer, mystic—all these epithets fit you, Pisces. You live within a rich, inner world that is both a buffer and a conduit to deeper experiences. You don't need anyone else to tell you this. At some level, you already know it, appreciate it, embrace it. While it's true that you're a sucker for a sob story—an attribute that can turn you from hero to martyr in the space of a single breath—there's no concrete evidence that you're more of a victim than any other sun sign.

Any professional challenges that come your way during 2011 will be met with your powerful intuition, your prodigious imagination, and your unique way of dealing with adversity through faith in your role in the larger scheme of things. The tentacles of your psychic abilities are active 24-7, at your disposal, and awaiting your instructions. You're in stellar company.

Notable Pisces: Anaïs Nin, Albert Einstein

CHAPTER 4

Love and Romance in 2011

In 1950, Swiss psychologist Carl Jung undertook an astrological study about the compatibility of 180 married couples and used fifty aspects—or angles that planets make to one another. This was in the days before personal computers and astrology software that can erect a natal chart and compare several charts in just seconds. The study took several years, and the results are intriguing.

He found three aspects to be the best indicators for compatibility: a sun-moon conjunction, where one partner's sun sign is the same as the sign of the other person's moon; a moon-moon conjunction, where both individuals have their moons in the same sign; and a moon-ascendant conjunction, when one partner's moon is in the same sign as the other person's ascendant. In his book *Synchronicity: An Acausal Connecting Principle*, Jung noted that the first two aspects "have long been mentioned in the old literature as marriage characteristics, and they therefore represent the oldest tradition."

The sun-moon conjunction makes perfect sense astrologically. Your sun sign describes your overall personality; the sign of your moon describes your inner world, your emotions, what makes you feel secure. So if you're a Pisces involved with someone who has a Pisces moon, for example, there's a beautiful give-and-take between you. You understand each other. If you have different sun signs, but your moons are in the same sign, the emotional and intuitive connections are so strong, you probably finish each other's sentences.

What about that third aspect, with the moon and ascendant in the same sign? This one also makes perfect sense. The ascendant is the doorway to your chart and describes, among other things, the persona you project to the outside world. So an individual with his or her moon in the same sign as your ascendant feels emotionally secure in your presence and sees the person behind the mask you wear.

Another compatibility aspect includes Venus, the planet that symbolizes love and romance. The most common I've seen are: Venus-sun, Venus-moon, Venus-ascendant, Venus-descendant cusp (cusp of the seventh house of partnerships), and Venus-Mars in the same sign. Another interesting connection I've noted is among couples who have mirror charts, in which the sign of one partner's ascendant is the same as the other person's descendant. In other words, let's say you have Scorpio rising and your partner has Scorpio on the cusp of his or her seventh house. This aspect brings balance to the relationship.

But because one size doesn't fit all, you and your partner may have other aspects in your charts that make you compatible. For the purpose of this book, we're going to be looking only at sun-sign combinations for compatibility.

Your Best Matches

Aries

Your freedom and independence are paramount to your happiness, so you need a partner who understands and respects your space. But because you're a stranger to compromise—a vital part of any relationship—you may find intimate relationships challenging. Once you're involved, your passions are fierce and can easily topple into the dark extremes of jealousy, possessiveness, suspicion.

Your entrepreneurial and fearless spirit enjoys a partner who can compete with you on any level—on those long hikes into the wilderness, in the boardroom, in the classroom, in the garage where you're building your newest invention. You get the idea here, right, Aries? Boredom is your nemesis. So which signs are good matches for you? Let's take a closer look at some of the possibilities.

Sagittarius. This fellow fire sign will give you all the freedom you crave—and then some. She'll match you joke for joke, drink for drink. If she's the physical type, and many of them are, she'll match you on those hikes. But for a Sadge, those hikes may be in some far-flung spot like Tibet. Like you, Sadge pushes herself, but she's more adaptable than you are. And sometimes she may come off like a know-it-all. But overall, this combination holds great promise.

Gemini. This air sign's wit and versatility and ability to talk about virtually anything appeal to you. He's generally not possessive either, a major plus when you're in one of your darker moods. His mind is sharp and lightning-quick, and he probably has a vast, complicated network of friends and acquaintances. Also appealing. So what are the negatives? Gemini generally isn't as independent as you are and may spend more time with his friends than he does with you. But overall this combination is lively, fun, and never boring.

Leo. Another fire sign. On the surface, it looks like a good match. Leo possesses an infinite capacity for enjoyment, which appeals to you. But she also loves having center stage—not just sometimes, but most of the time—and that can be a major turnoff for you.

Libra, Aquarius. Libra is your opposite sign. The match could be fantastic because you balance each other. Where you're the loner, she's the social butterfly. If you're independent, she's a networker with more friends than a hive has bees. Whether this works depends on the signs of your natal moons, ascendants, and Venus. You and Aquarius could be a winning combination. His independence matches yours, he's as sharp as the proverbial tack, and he pulls no punches in expressing what he wants when he wants it. Downside? He may not be as physical or competitive, and lives much of his life in his head.

Aries. Depends on the signs of your moons. Strictly on the basis of sun signs, you're both so independent the relationship may never get off the ground!

Taurus

Stable, dependable, patient. You bring these qualities to any close relationship, and once you commit, it's usually for keeps. You aren't into drama, artifice, flamboyance—not for yourself and not in a partner either. But you enjoy a partner who is physically attractive or who has a particular artistic gift that you appreciate—music, art, a way with words, anything that appeals to your senses.

If you're a Taurus who is into sports and health, then a health-conscious partner is a major plus. But there's another side to you—an inner mystic, a quiet, observant Buddha who remains calm and centered, in tune with unseen forces. You would do well with a partner who possesses that quality as well.

Leo, Sagittarius, Aries. Unless you have a moon, rising, or Venus in one of those signs, the fire signs probably won't work for you. Too much drama, boisterous behavior, and anger to suit your tastes.

Virgo, Capricorn. Fellow earth signs. Virgo could be the ticket. She's as practical as you are and, in many instances, just as mystical. Capricorn is focused, as physical as you are, but may not be as mystically inclined.

Scorpio. Your opposite sign, so there may be a good

balance. She's secretive and can be vengeful, but she's just as mystical as you are.

Gemini

In a romantic relationship, conversation and discussion top your list. In fact, any potential partner must seduce your mind first—with ideas, information, books, and theories that connect seemingly disparate bits of whatever it is that rushes through your head 24-7. You're up front about what you feel, but those feelings could change at a moment's notice—a dichotomy that can be confusing to a partner. And to everyone else around you, for that matter. No wonder your sign is represented by the twins.

For you, everything starts with the need to know why. You then set about to find out why, and in the course of your journey, you may be distracted by a million other pieces of information that are eventually integrated into your journey. This means, of course, that your journey toward the why of the original question may not end in this lifetime! So you need a partner whose curiosity matches your own.

Sagittarius, Aries. Sadge is your opposite sign. He matches you in curiosity, but may not be up to snuff in other areas. With Aries, there's never a dull moment. She's a match for your quickness and wit, but may not have the curiosity you do about other people.

Libra and Aquarius. Usually compatible in that both signs value information and communication.

Pisces might be a good match because it's the only other sign represented by two of something. And his imagination will appeal to you.

Cancer

In romance, it's always about feelings first—not the mind, not even the body, but emotions. Your partner has to be as dedicated to her inner world as you are to yours, so that your inner worlds can merge. That's the ideal. And yet because you're a cardinal sign—like Aries, Libra, and Capricorn—there's a certain independence in you that demands emotional space. Contradictory, but not to you.

Despite your emotional depth, you tend to avoid confrontations. Like the crab that symbolizes your sign, you retreat into your shell at the first sign of trouble. Yet how can you smooth out anything in a relationship if you can't discuss disagreements? It's as if you expect disagreements to be ironed out telepathically. So if that's true, your best matches romantically are probably other water signs. Let's take a deeper look.

Pisces, Scorpio. Both signs are as psychic as you are, but in different ways. Pisces is the softer of the two signs, dreamier. Scorpio might overwhelm you, but gives you the emotional space you need.

Taurus. A good match. This earth sign helps you to ground yourself in the real world and gives you emotional space—maybe more than you need!

Capricorn, Virgo. Cappy is your opposite sign, so the possibility of balance is there. Virgo might be too picky for your tastes, but shows you how to communicate verbally.

Air signs? Fire signs? Not so good, unless you have a moon, ascendant, Venus, or Mars in one of those signs.

Leo

You've got enough passion for all the other signs in the zodiac—and then some. That passion is often linked to the attention of others, which probably explains why so many actors and actresses have a Leo sun, moon, or ascendant. Your life is about drama, and the higher the drama, the deeper your passion. But it's that passion that busts through obstacles, that burns a path toward where you want to go in both life and love.

Your compassion extends to anyone in a tough situation—or to any creature that needs love and reassurance that we humans aren't heartless. So let's be real here. Your partner—whoever he or she is—probably has to love animals the way you do. Even if there are twenty strays in your backyard, your partner must be amenable to the idea that you feed the multitudes. Not an easy request, says the universe, but there are some strong possibilities.

Sagittarius, Aries. Sadge, symbolized by a creature that is half human and half horse, usually has animal companions—not pets, but companions. There's a big difference. She's your match in the compassion area. She understands your need to connect to an audience. But she may not stick around to be a part of that audience. The energy match with Aries is great. But unless you've got the moon, ascendant or Venus in Aries, she may not shower you—or your animal companions—with enough attention.

Gemini, Libra. These two air signs could be excellent matches for you, Leo. You'll enjoy Gemini's lively intellect and Libra's artistic sensibilities.

Virgo

You're the absolute master of details. You collect massive amounts of information, sift through it all with an eye for what works and what doesn't, and toss out everything that is extraneous. Your quest for perfection is never compromised, and it's evident in the inner work you do, honing your own psyche, and in everything you take on in the external world. These qualities can make a romantic partnership somewhat challenging because your partner goes under the same microscope that everything else does.

You're a layered individual, and you benefit from a partner who understands that and knows how to peel away those layers without making you feel vulnerable or exposed. A partner who enjoys every single one of those layers. So who's your best match?

Taurus, Capricorn. Fellow earth signs. Taurus takes all the time the relationship needs to peel away the layers of your personality so she could find the gold at your core. She's patient, resolute, determined. Capricorn might consider the relationship as just one more challenge to be conquered, but could be a nice balance to your penchant for details.

Cancer, Scorpio. These two water signs complement you. Cancer grasps who you are emotionally, but may not be as willing as you are to discuss elements of the relationship. Since your sign is ruled by Mercury, the planet of communication, that could be a drawback. Scorpio's emotional intensity could be overwhelming, but he'll be delighted to peel away the layers of your personality!

Gemini. Even though air and earth aren't usually compatible, Gemini and Virgo share Mercury as a ruler. Communication in this combination is likely to be strong, fluid, with a constant exchange of ideas.

Libra

There's a certain duality in your psychological makeup that isn't mentioned very often. It's not due to a penchant for secrecy or deviousness, but to a reluctance to hurt anyone's feelings. As a result, you often find yourself paralyzed by indecision.

You have a need for harmony and balance in relationships. You dislike confrontation and dissent, so all too often you surrender to your partner's wants at your own expense. So which signs are good matches for you?

Gemini, Aquarius. Fellow air signs understand your psychological makeup. Gemini experiences some of the same duality that you do, but for different reasons. He isn't bothered by dichotomies, since his own life is predicated on it. And he appeals to that part of you who needs to communicate honestly. Aquarius may be a bit too rigid for you, insisting that you bend to his desires, but the depth and breadth of his vision attracts you at a visceral level.

Sagittarius, Leo, Aries. Any of the fire signs could be an excellent match. Sagittarius never bores you and enjoys you for who you are. Leo may want more attention than you're willing to give, but her warmth and compassion will delight you. You and Aries, your opposite sign, balance each other.

Taurus, Virgo, Capricorn. Of the three earth signs, Taurus is probably the best match because you share Venus as a ruler. That means you have similar tastes in music and art and probably share some of the same attitudes and beliefs about money.

Scorpio

As the most emotionally intense sign of the zodiac and one of the most psychic, your powerful and magnetic personality can intimidate even heads of state. Your life patterns are about breaking taboos, digging deeper, looking for the absolute bottom line in whatever you do, in any relationship in which you become involved. You feel and intuit your way through life, and your partner must understand that.

All of this brooding and mulling takes place in the privacy of your own head. The side you show others is lighter, funny, with a dry wit that can charm, seduce, or spar with the best of them. Given the complexities of your personality, which signs are most compatible with yours?

Pisces, Cancer. Of these two water signs, Pisces matches you in raw intuitive ability, but may be too indecisive to suit you long term. Cancer can be just as secretive as you, but unless you've got a moon or rising in Cancer, this sign could be too clingy.

Taurus, Virgo, Capricorn. The earth signs are compatible matches. Taurus, your opposite sign, brings sensuality to your sexuality and helps to dispel your suspicions about other people's motives. Her earthiness grounds your psychic ability. Virgo's discerning and gentle nature mitigates your emotional intensity. Capricorn's determination appeals to that same quality in you.

Leo, Scorpio. Both are fixed signs, and there seems to be something between them that is powerful. Look at Leo Bill Clinton and Scorpio Hillary Clinton.

Sagittarius

You're so multifaceted, with so many different talents, that a relationship presents certain dilemmas—namely, commitment to another person. It's so much easier to commit to, well, your own interests! Also, there's that little ol' thing called personal freedom, which you value every bit as much as Aries.

Like Libra, there's a curious duality in your makeup, best explained, perhaps, by the symbol for your sign— the mythological centaur. Half horse, half human, this figure might be defined as the wild woman (or man) versus the conformist. A part of you operates from gut instinct and the other part of you is acculturated. Which signs are your best matches?

Aries, Leo, Sagittarius. As remarked under the Aries section, a relationship with this sign may not go anywhere because you're both so independent. Aries might want to be in charge all the time, and you get fed up and hit the open road. Leo could be a terrific choice, particularly if one of you has a moon in the other's sun sign. Another Sadge would be intriguing.

Libra, Aquarius, Gemini. Of these three air signs, Libra is the best match. Even if she lacks your intuitive gifts, her focus, direction, and resolute determination equal yours. Gemini, your opposite sign, could also be a good match. You share a fascination with the paranormal, and your energies would balance each other's.

Earth signs? Water signs? Probably not, unless you have a moon, rising, or some other prominent planet in those elements.

Capricorn

You build relationships in the same careful way that you build everything else in your life—a brick at a time. A conversation here, a dinner there, a movie, a moonlit walk, an exchange of beliefs. You're methodical, consistent, disciplined. Pretty soon, the foundation is solid, the chemistry is exactly right, and you know exactly what you want.

A relationship, of course, involves the human heart—not bricks and mortar—and that's where it may get tricky. You could discover that your methodical approach doesn't work as well in a relationship as it does with your career. Your success will depend, to a certain extent, on your compatibility with your partner.

Taurus, Virgo, Capricorn. Taurus's solidity and dependability appeal to you, and he's as private as you are. But his still waters run deep, and he may not express his emotions as readily as you would like. Yet the match would be a good one. Virgo understands what drives you. Another Capricorn—i.e., a type-A personality—would wear you out!

Scorpio, Pisces. While either of these water signs is compatible with your earth-sign sun, Pisces may be too ambivalent for you, too indecisive. Scorpio is a strong match. All that intensity appeals to you at a visceral level, your sex lives would be fantastic, and you share a similar determination.

Cancer. Your opposite sign might work if the Cancer has a moon or rising in your sign.

Fire signs? Air signs? Again, it depends on the distribution of fire- and air-sign planets in your natal chart.

Aquarius

In love and romance, as in life, your mind is your haven, your sanctuary, your sacred place. It's where everything begins for you. From your visionary, cutting-edge ideas to your humanitarian causes and interests in esoterica, you're a wild card, not easily pigeonholed. It doesn't make any difference to you whether your partner shares these interests, as long as he or she recognizes your right to pursue them.

There's a rebel in you that pushes against the status quo, and that's something your partner has to understand. Your connections to people and to the world aren't easily grasped by others. Too weird, they think. Too out there. But that's fine. You understand who and what you are, and in the end, that's all you need. So, which signs are your best matches?

Gemini, Libra. Your air-sign compadres are excellent matches. Gemini suits your prodigious intellect, causes, and ideas. Good communication usually is a hallmark of this relationship, and Gemini is supportive of your causes. With Libra, the focus is on relationships—Libra's and your connection to five million others. But the right mix exists for a strong partnership. A relationship with another Aquarian could be challenging since you'll both insist you're right. But if you can move past that, you'll do fine. Another Aquarius may be like looking in the mirror 24-7. Not for the fainthearted.

Aries, Leo, Sagittarius. With these fire signs, you enjoy the freedom to be your own person. Life with Aries is never boring. The conversation and adventures are stimulating, but he may not share your humanitarian and esoteric interests. Sagittarius loves your mind and insights, your idealism and rebellion against the establishment. Great compatibility overall. Leo is your opposite sign, suggesting a good balance between your head and his heart.

Earth or water signs? Only if you have prominent planets in either of those elements.

Pisces

It's true that your inner world is often more real and genuine to you than anything in the external world. The richness of your imagination, the breadth of your intuition—these qualities create a kind of seductive atmosphere that's tough to move beyond. But because you're a physical being who has to eat and sleep, work and function, love and triumph and yearn, you have to move beyond it. And so you do.

But always there's an inner tension, a kind of bewilderment, a constant questioning. *Where am I going? What am I doing? Do I really want to do this or that?* Your head and your heart are forever at odds, so no wonder your sign is symbolized by two fish moving in opposite directions. In romance and love, this indecisiveness can be problematic. So which signs are most compatible for you?

Scorpio, Cancer. Scorpio's emotional intensity could overwhelm you, but he balances your indecisiveness with his unwavering commitment to a particular path. Intuitively, you're on the same page, a major plus. Cancer's innate gentleness appeals to you, and she appreciates you exactly as you are.

Taurus, Capricorn. These two earth signs appeal to you at a visceral level. Taurus's solid, grounded personality comforts that part of you that is so often torn between one direction or another. Her sensuality is also a major plus. Capricorn's singular vision and direction are mysterious to you, but there's much to learn from her.

Virgo. Your opposite sign can bring balance.

Fire signs probably won't work for you unless you have a moon or rising in a fire sign.

Gemini is probably the most compatible air sign for you. Since you're both symbolized by two of something—two fish, the twins—he understands your dichotomies.

CHAPTER 5

Money and Luck in 2011

On Christmas Day 2002, Jack Whitaker of West Virginia won the largest lottery amount ever—nearly $315 million. The winning numbers were 53-14-5-16-29. The Powerball was 7. So who is this lucky Jack Whitaker?

Whitaker bought that ticket for one dollar at the convenience store where he stopped mornings to buy breakfast. He checked his ticket after the drawing on Christmas night in 2002, thinking he had missed by one digit. But the next day, he heard the winning ticket had been sold at the store he frequented, and double-checked his ticket to discover he'd won the largest undivided lottery pot in American history. He chose a onetime payout—$114 million after taxes.

He formed a foundation that launched a campaign to eventually feed and clothe poor people in each of West Virginia's fifty-five counties. He also gave a total of $7 million to three preachers and began to build two churches. But it wasn't long before Whitaker's "luck" went south. In August 2003, $545,000 in cash and cashier's checks were stolen from his SUV outside a strip joint, establishing his image as a drinker, gambler, and carouser. Within two years of his win, he was arrested for assault and threatening to kill a bar manager. Then he was arrested for a DUI and accused of groping women at a racetrack. Shortly before Christmas 2004, the body of his seventeen-year-old granddaughter, his only grandchild and his pride and joy, was found wrapped in a tarp under a junked van outside her boyfriend's house.

In many ways, Whitaker's "luck" reflects the definition of that word by dictionary.com.

1. the force that seems to operate for good or ill in a person's life, as in shaping circumstances, events, or opportunities: *With my luck I'll probably get pneumonia.*
2. Good fortune, advantage or success, considered as the result of chance. *He had no luck finding work.*
3. A combination of circumstances, events, etc. operating by chance to bring good or ill to a person. *She's had nothing but bad luck all year.*
4. Some object on which good fortune is supposed to depend. *This rabbit's foot is my luck.*

Notice that three of the four examples in these definitions are blatantly negative. Why? Perhaps our consensual belief about luck is that it's usually bad! What are *your* beliefs about luck? And while we're on the topic of beliefs, what are *yours* about money? About great wealth? While astrology is helpful in determining our lucky times, it may be that our beliefs have more to do with how lucky we are. Did Jack Whitaker, for example, feel *guilty* about winning all that money? Did he, at some level, feel he didn't deserve it? If so, then that belief may have attracted the unlucky events that happened within two years of his winning the lottery.

It's a good idea to examine your own beliefs about money and luck so that you can take full advantage of astrology's timing.

Jupiter

From chapter 2, we know that Jupiter represents luck, expansion, success, prosperity, growth, creativity, spiritual interests, higher education, and the law. It also governs publishing, overseas travel, foreign countries and any of our dealings with them. But for the purpose of this chapter, we're going to focus on Jupiter's impact on our money and luck—both natally and for 2011.

In 2011, Jupiter occupies three signs—Pisces for the first three weeks, then Aries between January 22 and June 4, and Taurus between June 4, 2011, and June 11, 2012. For Pisces, Aries, and Taurus, Jupiter's transit through your signs is known as a Jupiter return and occurs about every twelve years. It's generally considered a fortunate time.

In appendix 1, find the sign for your natal Jupiter and return to this chapter for the description. In the second part of this chapter, read about how Jupiter's transits in 2011 will impact your sun sign.

Natal Jupiter in Aries

You're zealous in your beliefs and convinced you're right even if you aren't. Life for you is personal and immediate, with a certain urgency that underscores everything you do, think, tackle, believe. Your life is expanded through your own initiative and actions—i.e., you make your own luck but seize opportunities when they come your way.

In terms of your finances, Jupiter in Aries urges you to follow every synchronicity, hunch, and impulse you experience to pursue the untried, the unexplored, the unique. That dusty manuscript or screenplay sitting in a desk drawer? Pull it out, go over it, figure out where to submit it—and do so. That job you read about on the Internet? Go for it; send in your résumé. That grad school you would like to attend? Make it so by taking the first step and applying. Since your sign creates its own luck, that makes you the entrepreneur, the explorer, the one who ventures where no one else has dared to go. You have to wonder about that, right?

Natal Jupiter in Taurus

Your approach to everything in life is practical. You try to integrate your spiritual and philosophical beliefs into your daily life. You're persistent and resolute in everything you do, so when you're lucky, it's because your hard work has brought you to the right place at the right time. You enjoy exploring everything the earth has to offer, so foreign travel appeals to you. But your travels may have a higher purpose—to study archaeology in Egypt, to explore Incan ruins in Peru, to attend culinary classes in France, or to do something else about which you're passionate.

Jupiter in Taurus urges you to be practical about your finances. Pay yourself a certain set percentage from every paycheck, and invest only in what you feel is safe. Your intuition is strong, so if a particular investment resonates for you, if you feel it in your gut, then it's probably fine. But Jupiter here also urges you to enjoy yourself and to be generous with your time and energy.

Natal Jupiter in Gemini

Your hunger for knowledge and the acquisition of information and facts expand your world—not just sometimes but always. Your deep need to communicate what you learn could prompt you to teach, write, or get into film, photography, or any other venue of self-expression. Your travels are often related to your quest for knowledge so that even if you're traveling for pleasure, there's a deeper agenda, something else you're after.

Your concept of "luck" may possess a duality that others find curious. Sometimes, you believe you make your own luck, that you create the circumstances in which it can flourish. Other times, it seems to you that luck comes out of the blue. Regardless, you tend to be luckiest when you're doing what you love—and that's also when you do the best financially.

Natal Jupiter in Cancer

You may hold on to the spiritual and moral ideals of your parents or other influential people from your childhood, and pass those teachings down to your own children. Home and family are important to you, and there may be periods when you're nostalgic for the good ol' days. Benefits come to you through parents, family, home-related activities, real estate, and land. Your travels abroad may be connected to nurturing—in third-world communities, in animal-rescue centers, in areas where children are in desperate need of help and care.

You tend to be luckiest when you listen to your hunches. Your intuition also works magic with money. You may have a feeling, for instance, about a certain investment or whether to deposit your money in a particular bank or CD. Or you focus on a financial manifestation with such intense desire that it unfolds pretty much as you imagined it. Check your gut feeling against the facts, if you feel compelled to do so, but it's likely that your feelings will match up with the facts every time.

Natal Jupiter in Leo

Your beliefs are like live theater. You act on them, promote them, discuss them all over Facebook, MySpace, and every other social network. In doing so, you attract others who help to expand your world and opportunities. Your exuberance is infectious. Even if others sometimes interpret it as pride, you go on your merry way, making other people smile and feel better about themselves. You benefit from the attention of others and through overseas trips involving education, sports, even diplomatic issues.

As long as you live with compassion rather than pride, your luck comes to you through others—friends, family, acquaintances, coworkers, employees. You love spending money, especially on items that bolster your self-esteem.

Your best earnings come to you when you're passionate about what you're doing.

Natal Jupiter in Virgo

Your legendary work ethic and the services you perform for others, without thought of compensation, are the ways you expand your spiritual and philosophical horizons. Your work always has to be purposeful, though. You aren't interested in working just to work. You may be quite adept at creating a niche for yourself in the marketplace—you see a gap and fill it. Thank your critical and analytical mind for that! Your travel may be connected primarily to business and professional pursuits, but even then you're absorbing information, noting details. You're always observant.

You bring this same gift for observation and analysis to your finances. You aren't a penny pincher, but you aren't a lavish spender, either. Moderation seems to be your litany. With luck, you, like individuals with Jupiter in Taurus, create the circumstances for it through your hard work.

Natal Jupiter in Libra

Your realm, and the way your life undergoes its greatest expansion, is in relationships, your associations with friends and acquaintances generally, and through marriage and partnership specifically. You benefit from the opposite sex. Your travels—particularly those abroad—may be connected to working with groups in some capacity. Perhaps you're spreading a specific belief system or technique. Maybe you're a teacher traveling with a select group of students to an ancient site or an attorney in search of information on ancient legal texts. You get the idea, right? You're an individual who connects people with information.

Thanks to your vast network of friends and acquaintances, you have abundant input about money and investments. Your spouse or partner is savvy about handling finances, but so are your friends. As far as luck is concerned, well, you must already know the answer to that one. Your luck is found in your relationships. All of them.

Natal Jupiter in Scorpio

Your greatest assets are your willpower, determination, and need to understand how everything you experience fits into the nature of reality. Heady stuff, for sure. But business as usual for you, who apparently was born with your spiritual beliefs already intact. Well, maybe you weren't born with the entire belief system intact, but you certainly brought its DNA into this life, and will investigate and test it throughout the course of your life. You gain through inheritances, research, psychic exploration.

Your finances, like other areas of your life, seem to be black-and-white, either very good or very bad. There are always exceptions to this rule, of course, since we all have free will. But generally, that's the pattern. As for luck, yours comes from doing what you're doing, Scorpio. Move in the direction that your instincts and hunches take you.

Natal Jupiter in Sagittarius

Jupiter rules this sign, so it's very happy here, functioning at optimum levels. Your deep need to understand spiritual and philosophical issues broadens your life. Education, publishing, the law, and foreign travel all prove beneficial. You're capable of grasping the larger picture on anything you're involved in—from a job or specific project to a relationship. This placement for Jupiter is considered lucky, so when the planet returns to this sign every twelve years, it should be a very fortunate time!

You spend money as quickly as you earn it, and you

should strive to pay yourself first from every paycheck. If you feel you can't save, tell yourself you're saving for a trip you would like to take or for a car you would like to buy. You're naturally lucky, and by being true to your vision, whatever it is, you create an environment for more luck!

Natal Jupiter in Capricorn

You gain through your dad, employers, and business dealings. Your philosophical and spiritual expansion occurs primarily through your own efforts—i.e., you study, learn, and integrate parts of what you've learned into your own belief system. You have a great appreciation for money and may strive to accumulate wealth, but not because you're greedy. For you, money spells freedom.

Since your luck comes to you the same way that everything else does—through hard work and persistence—you may wonder how it can be considered luck. It goes something like this: After years of putting in time and effort, you happen to be in the right place at the right time when the big payoff finally comes.

Natal Jupiter in Aquarius

Your progressive views on everything from politics to religion expand who and what you are. You're an intellectual explorer who delves into many different kinds of belief systems, perhaps in search of a common thread or theme. Your tolerance for other people's beliefs, no matter how different they are from yours, deepens your understanding of how the universe works. You benefit through your professional endeavors, quests, and group associations.

Your finances are a wild card. The better educated you are, the more you insist on calling your own shots, doing what you love. Ultimately, that may bring you greater wealth, luck, and happiness than pursuing the status quo.

Natal Jupiter in Pisces

Jupiter corules Pisces, so it's content in this sign and functions well here. Your compassion and emotional sensitivity, imagination and intuition expand your spiritual foundations. You benefit through psychic investigation and research and anything connected to behind-the-scenes activities.

Your luck comes through anything connected to intuition and psychic development or the use of your prodigious imagination. Money often slips through your fingers like water, but when you learn to save and invest, you can easily increase your net worth by using your intuition. Since your heart is big, one of your challenges is to avoid becoming a sucker for a sob story—particularly when the sob story involves you lending (or giving) money to someone else.

Jupiter in 2011 and Its Impact on Your Sun Sign

Since Jupiter symbolizes expansion, luck, and everything that we would like to experience 24-7, it's only fitting to find out how its transits in 2011 will affect each of us. Find your sun sign and read all about Jupiter's impact on you this year. The dates: January 22 to June 4, Jupiter transits Aries; from June 4, 2011, to June 11, 2012, Jupiter transits Taurus.

Aries

When Jupiter moves through your sign, your life undergoes an explosive expansion. From March 11 forward, Uranus will also be in your sign. The combination attracts people who are quirky in some way or who are experts in their fields. These individuals may appear in your life suddenly and disappear just as abruptly. Even so, they act as agents of change, and some facet of your life could veer in a new direction.

For clues about some of the events that could transpire during this period, look back twelve years. What was going on in your life then?

For the year that Jupiter transits Taurus and your solar second house, your income increases. New financial opportunities come along. Even if you're spending more money, you're earning more. Your personal values may undergo some sort of change, and it could become important to you to earn your living in a way that is in line with your deepest beliefs.

Taurus

While Jupiter transits Aries between January 22 and June 4, your personal unconscious is far more accessible to you. Through dreams, meditation, and daydreaming, you're able to gain insights into your own psyche, any issues you've buried, and even into your past lives. In a sense, this transit prepares you for Jupiter entering your sign.

While Jupiter is in your sign, you'll experience a period of greater prosperity and growth, when the world really is your playground. Events, relationships, everything unfolds with greater smoothness and ease. Your finances may increase, career opportunities seem to come out of nowhere, you get married, you start a family, you land a great job, you travel abroad, you build a home—in other words, before this huge opportunity arrives, focus on what you would like to manifest in your life. Create your wish list. Be prepared!

Look back twelve years for clues about how this transit may unfold for you. What was going on in your life in 1999?

Gemini

While Jupiter is in Aries, a fire sign compatible with your air-sign sun, your social life is a whirlwind. So from January 22 to June 4, buckle up and enjoy the ride, Gemini. Jupiter will be expanding your circles of friends and acquaintances and your wishes and dreams. Overseas travel is a strong possibility. You might head off to college or graduate school, or you could take a seminar or workshop in a topic that interests you. It's also possible that you venture into unexplored territory related to your work or profession, perhaps in your search for new ideas or new solutions to old problems.

During Jupiter's transit of Taurus, your unconscious will be easier for you to delve into, just like it was for Taurus during Jupiter's transit through Aries. Dream work, meditation, yoga, or some other kind of .mind-body activity may benefit you. Consider a past-life regression with a qualified therapist. Everything you learn during this yearlong transit is creative fodder, Gemini, and is preparing the way for Jupiter's transit into your sign in 2012.

Cancer

Think of the Big Bang, of how rapidly the universe expanded after it happened. Now think about your career. That big bang is what you'll experience professionally when Jupiter transits Aries and your career sector. Every action you take and every professional decision you make will expand your career in some way. You may be offered a better-paying job or one that better suits your goals. You could change careers altogether or suddenly be promoted and land a substantial raise.

Between June 4, 2011, and June 11, 2012, Jupiter will be moving through Taurus and your solar eleventh house. Expect expansion with your social contacts, your wishes, and your dreams, even with opportunities to promote and publicize your work or product or that of your company. Since this transit forms a beautiful angle to your sun sign, other areas of your life will benefit as well.

Leo

With Jupiter in fellow fire sign Aries for nearly five months—January 22 to June 4—you're in for a treat! Your opportunities for overseas travel, higher education, and publishing soar off the charts. Suddenly, you're quite the entrepreneur—the lone explorer of uncharted worlds, the one with so many irons in the fire that you may have to hire help to see everything through to completion. You could move to another country, work in another country, or even marry someone who lives abroad. It all seems to be moving you toward the next Jupiter transit, through Taurus.

This one impacts your career. Between June 4, 2011, and June 11, 2012, your career will go through incredible growth. You could experience anything from a new job to a new career path to a promotion and a significant raise. Even if it seems you're spending money quickly, you've got plenty more coming in.

Virgo

While Jupiter transits Aries and your solar eighth house, you may be delving into the weird and the strange more than usual. You're reading books about ghosts and hauntings, past lives, and communication with the dead, or you're attending seminars or workshops on any of these topics. It's possible you'll have experiences in these areas. You also may get significant breaks with taxes, insurance, mortgages, loans.

Once Jupiter enters fellow earth sign Taurus, you're in very comfortable territory. If you're a writer, this transit expands your publishing opportunities, could bring about significant foreign sales, and makes it easier to sell what you write. Regardless of what profession you're in, your business could expand to overseas markets. You head off to college or graduate school, go to law school, or even move overseas.

Libra

During Jupiter's transit of Aries, your opposite sign, your business and personal partnerships expand. If you're involved in a relationship when the transit starts, then things may enter a deeper level of commitment before the transit ends in early June. If you're married or in a committed relationship, then Jupiter in Aries could prompt you and your partner to do business together or to get involved in some sort of joint project.

Once Jupiter enters Taurus, you and your partner may be accruing items like art and jewelry for investments, you could delve more deeply into esoteric subjects like ghosts, past lives, and communication with the dead, and you may combine your resources in some way. An example? If you and your partner have separate homes, during this transit, you may decide to sell one place and move in together. This transit should bring breaks with mortgages, loans, taxes, and insurance.

Scorpio

During Jupiter's transit through Aries, your daily work starts expanding. You might get promoted, land a new job, launch your own business, or write a novel or screenplay. You may quit work altogether and go on to graduate school or head out on the trip of a lifetime. This transit could have any number of ramifications. Events that unfold always depend on where you are in your life at the beginning of the transit and on what changes you desire.

When Jupiter transits Taurus, your opposite sign, you experience some of the same events that Libra does when

Jupiter transits Aries. However, because the Scorpio-Taurus axis is a different sort of energy altogether, your experiences are apt to be more intense, sexual, passionate. If you're not involved when the transit starts, there's a possibility you meet that special someone and the relationship quickly escalates into the love of your life.

Sagittarius

Jupiter's transit through fellow fire sign Aries should be magnificent for you, Sadge. It expands your creativity, your love life, and everything you do for fun and pleasure. This transit feeds all your Sadge attributes—your hunger for travel, for action and movement, for exploring your various interests and passions. From March 11 on, Uranus is also in Aries, so it's a double whammy of fire energy that attracts interesting and exciting people and experiences. These transits also suggest the possibility of a sudden, unexpected pregnancy.

When Jupiter transits Taurus, the expansion shifts to your daily work. You're promoted, you land a new job, you work out of your home, and you have greater responsibilities. If you own your own business, then you may add more employees or expand your product or services to overseas markets.

Capricorn

When Jupiter moves through Aries, you may refurbish your home in some way. Or your family may grow—a child is born, a relative or friend moves in, or you rent out a room. One way or another, your domestic environment undergoes expansion.

The time to anticipate is when Jupiter transits fellow earth sign Taurus, a yearlong window of opportunity. Your love life and creativity expand, and more opportunities surface to enjoy yourself. What a concept for a type-A personality, right? Use this transit to launch new projects, to meet people, to network, and to do what pleases you.

Aquarius

You'll enjoy Jupiter's transit through Aries. Suddenly, your daily life, your conscious mind, and your relationships with relatives and friends will expand, broaden, deepen. You may find yourself involved in community and neighborhood activities, or you may sign up for classes or workshops, or you could be traveling more. If you're a writer in the travel business, or if you do any public speaking, this transit will attract new opportunities.

During the year that Jupiter transits Taurus, your daily work routine will change considerably. You may assume more responsibility, be promoted, be hired for a new job that suits you better, or start your own business. Travel related to your work may be more frequent. You might obtain additional training of some kind or head to college, grad school, or even law school. Your novel could get published.

Pisces

Wow. You're in for a treat, Pisces. With Jupiter's transit through Aries and your solar second house, your earnings should increase significantly. Your expenses may go up, but don't fret. You'll be earning more. Your values may broaden and become more inclusive.

But you really reap the benefits of Jupiter's transit through Taurus, an earth sign compatible with your water-sign sun. During the period from June 4, 2011, to June 11, 2012, your daily life broadens. You may meet new people, travel more frequently, or take courses and workshops in topics that interest you. Your conscious mind absorbs everything you see, hear, taste, touch, and smell. It's as if a whole new world opens to you.

CHAPTER 6

Family Dynamics

Take a look at your own family. Does everyone get along? Are there certain issues that surface time and again? If you have siblings, do they each seem to have different roles in the family? One might be the rebel, for instance, and another might be the intellectual. And what about your parents, partner, and kids?

Families often have commonalities in their respective charts that illustrate the deep connections among them. The parents might have opposing signs, like Taurus/Scorpio, Gemini/Sagittarius, so there's a kind of balance. Then one child might have a moon in Sadge, and the other child has a Gemini sun. There's an infinite number of combinations, and some aren't as obvious as sun or moon signs. But for the purpose of this chapter, let's keep things simple.

Your Parenting Style

Aries

Your parenting style isn't like anyone else's—that's for sure. Man or woman, you encourage independence in your children from a very young age. You may be one of those parents who keeps close tabs on your child's growth progress: *7 months, crawling; 9 months, utters first word; age 2, a puzzle prodigy!* Any rules you lay down are in the name of safety rather than an attempt to control your child's every move and decision.

You may fine-tune your parenting style at each stage of your child's growth, but there are certain constants that probably won't change. In addition to the emphasis on independence, you have a finely honed sense of privacy and probably won't violate your child's unless you have a reasonable suspicion that you should. That's more likely to happen during the turbulent teen years. You give your child plenty of freedom to make his own choices. However, when you do offer guidance or advice, you may blurt it out, which could create some major tension if your child is an adult.

An Aries mom can be brash, funny, exciting, unpredictable. Kids enjoy her company because everything with her is an adventure. But she can be fiercely protective—that's the ram who symbolizes her sign— ready to defend her child's turf at the slightest provocation. She isn't nurturing in the traditional sense of the word—i.e., you won't find her slaving over a hot stove preparing the evening meals. She's more likely to have a pizza delivered. But when her child's in need, she's there in a flash.

When an Aries dad hangs out with the kids, there's an air of impatience, brashness, restlessness. If he encourages his child to take risks—in sports, love, life—it's because he himself is so fearless. He's terrific at organizing activities, but they happen on the fly. He usually has great pride in and passion for his kids.

Taurus

Your parenting style reflects your stability, determination, and patience. You enjoy your children immensely and strive to nurture their talents, strengths, and gifts. You try to create a beautiful home environment, a place in which everyone delights, where your kids feel comfortable bringing their friends.

You probably enjoy music, art, books, movies, and politics, and these interests are reflected in your environment—and are passed on to your kids through a kind of osmosis. So don't be surprised when your son or daughter cranks up the music so loud it threatens to shatter crystal or when the weekly allowance is blown at the local bookstore!

Since you're the most stubborn sign in the zodiac, that stubbornness certainly surfaces in your parenting. Your child says yes. You shake your head no. The child keeps saying yes, yes, his voice growing louder and louder until your patience snaps, and the legendary bull's rush seizes you. No, you shout, and slam your door. End of story, end of argument, end of struggle.

Since Venus rules your sign, your bull's rush usually passes quickly, and peace and tranquillity are restored. But you still refuse to change your mind!

A Taurus mom is loyal and dedicated to her role as a mother. It won't be her only role, but she's likely to consider it her most important role. She's in the line for school drop-offs in the morning, in that same line for pickup in the afternoon. And in between, she's in court, defending someone like you or me, or she's writing the great American novel, or teaching English to recalcitrant seventh graders. Or she's selling real estate or jewelry, or scooping the next big political story.

The Taurus dad works hard and patiently at whatever he does. He finishes everything he starts—and that includes the projects his kids begin for their science classes! He, like his female counterpart, is usually health-conscious and watches his diet, exercises regularly, and takes good care of himself. Part of this could be vanity, but whatever it is, his kids pick up on it and sometimes take up the same sports in which dad indulges.

Gemini

Ideas. That's what you're about, and it's evident in your parenting style. From the time your child is very young, you read to her, talk to her, encourage her to express herself verbally. You buy her puzzles, coloring books, picture books, anything that expands her knowledge and creativity. Your fascination with information and relationships is found in the way you encourage her to reach out to other people, to make friends, to invite them to her house. Don't be surprised if by the time your child is a teen, she has several thousand friends on Facebook!

You're a voracious reader, and it's likely that your home has hundreds—if not thousands—of books. This love of reading is something you pass on to your child, and by the time she's preparing for college, her facility with language and ideas is a major plus. It's said that a typical Gemini is actually two people—the twins are the symbol for your sign—so you're comfortable with duality. This can be confusing to a young child, particularly if you vacillate between what's allowed and what isn't.

With Mercury ruling your sign, any connections between the Mercury in your chart and the sun, moon, rising, or Mercury in your child's chart portend strong communication.

A Gemini mom is the supreme multitasker. She can simultaneously pack school lunches, talk on the phone, and write a novel in her head. At times, she may appear scattered to her kids, but then she suddenly comes out with a zinger of logic or insight that stops them in their tracks. Glances are exchanged; eyebrows shoot up. She's a fount of information and eagerly passes on what she knows to her kids—and their friends and the friends of their friends. If anything, when her kids are with their friends, she must learn to back off and give them space.

A Gemini dad is quick, witty, enigmatic. Just when his kids think they've got him figured out, he does or says something that makes him impossible to peg. His intellect is as finely honed as a Gemini woman's, but takes him in different directions. He might be an avid sports fan, a master at chess, a general aviation pilot, or an animal lover. His interests and passions are passed on to his kids.

One thing is certain: A home with at least one Gemini parent in it is never boring!

Cancer

You're the nurturer of the zodiac—the one who needs roots, a home, a place or state of mind and spirit that you can call your own. You're a gentle, kind person who takes everything to heart—and this is certainly reflected in your parenting style. Through your example, your kids learn to respect all forms of life, to never hurt others, to treat them as they would like to be treated.

You can be overprotective, for sure, and before your child hits his teens, you'll have to come to grips with how to handle those feelings. Emotionally, you rarely reveal yourself. Like the crab that represents your sign, you tend to move sideways, skirting unpleasant issues, anxious to avoid confrontation, reluctant to discuss the heart of the matter. Your exceptional intuition keeps you in tune with your children, alerting you when they're in danger or unhappy. You forgive easily but rarely forget. So if one of your kids hurts your feelings, you'll remember it thirty years from now.

A Cancer mom is the prototypical nurturer—always there for her kids, supportive of their wishes and dreams. And yes, if she cooks, you'll find her whipping up delectable dishes that include everyone's favorite foods, whatever they are. Her home is her palace, but it could be the cabin of a boat, a tent in the wilderness, an RV. No matter where she is, she tends to the creature comforts of her family. As a parent, she has rules, but they're emotionally based, just like everything else in her life, so they won't change unless the emotions behind them change first.

A Cancer dad, like his female counterpart, is kind, affectionate, and nurturing, but only to a point. When he feels his personal space is being violated in any way, he backs off, scurries into his crab's shell, and retreats quickly. For a child, he's hard to figure out. Sometimes he's the hero of the child's latest adventure story; other times he's the wet blanket at the party. If he's into metaphysics and alternative healing, then chances are he's in deep, and his kids will pick up on this interest and explore on their own.

Leo

You love being the center of attention and often surround yourself with admirers. The world is your stage. But that's just the beginning of your story! You strive to succeed—to shine—at everything you do and to make an impact in every situation. Your personal magnetism draws admirers who are willing to help your cause, whatever it is. You prefer to hang with people whose beliefs are similar to your own, but you can get along with just about everyone—as long as no one steals your thunder. Your kindness, generosity, and compassion are nearly legendary.

As a parent, you love unconditionally and fiercely. You tend to instill certain qualities into your children—optimism, loyalty, integrity, honor. When they're young, you enjoy their company and watching them progress to each stage—from crib to crawling to kindergarten. Once they're off to school, particularly by the time they reach middle school and then high school, you may feel marginalized in some way. You really shouldn't. You've got enough interests and passions to fill your next five lives, and your ambitions keep propelling you forward. Generally, you delight in seeing your children fly off into the world, doing what they love.

The Leo mom is usually up front about everything—what she feels, why, and for how long. She's definitely disappointed when her kids aren't as forthright, but she gets over it! She likes being at the helm—at home, at work, while traveling—and can be a bit bossy at times. Her kids quickly learn to either fall in line or stand up to her. Mom enjoys nice clothes and probably dresses with a flair and style all her own. She's clever at creating impressions and moods through the way she looks and acts—it's the actress in her—but her kids undoubtedly learn to see through it to the gem beneath.

The Leo dad is easy to get along with as long as you keep a couple of rules in mind. Never tell him what to do, and let him have center stage. If both of your parents are Leos, the one thing you can count on in your household is plenty of drama! The Leo dad is fun, outgoing, and full of magic. He snaps his fingers, and things happen. He has great leadership ability—and not just as a dad—and his energy and frankness endear him to children of any age.

Virgo

Your mind is lightning-quick, just like Gemini's, and you're so mentally dexterous and agile that the competition can't keep pace with you. Due to your attention to detail, to the discerning turn of your intellect, you tend to delve more deeply into subjects than Gemini, and when you gather information, it usually has a purpose. You pass this ability on to your children, and it serves you well as a parent—i.e., not much escapes your notice. Your kids will never be able to put anything over on you! Since you're Mercury-ruled, like Gemini, you need sufficient outlets for all your mental energy.

You're an attentive parent who does all the expected things—for school, health, your child's happiness—but who may not play by the book. In other words, you probably won't raise your children the way you were raised. If you were brought up in a religious household, your child won't be. If your parents stressed school over fun, you may do the opposite. If your parents were inordinately strict, you won't be. It's not that you have the heart of a rebel (although you might!), but that your finely honed intellect connects all the dots, and you grasp what's needed for your children to evolve and to achieve their full potential.

The Virgo mom is vibrant, upbeat, conscientious, loving. Even though she never tries to project a particular image, others sense something different about her, perhaps her softness, her caring. Deep down, she can be a worrywart, fretting about the smallest details, the inconsistencies in life, her kids, her family. It's part of her insecurity. When she's in that mode, she can be critical—of her kids, her husband, herself. But she can be cajoled out of that mood by lively discussions about ideas, books, travel, any kind of information that seizes her passions. She's generous with her kids and strives to enrich their world through her own wisdom.

The Virgo dad is as intellectually curious as his female counterpart. He's a hard worker, detail-oriented, with a biting humor that is rarely malicious. He may take his role as dad a bit too seriously at times, but his kids quickly learn how to loosen him up. He's an attentive father—the kind who reads to his kids at night, who listens to their dramas and woes as teens, who applauds loudly when they graduate from college. Always with him—and with the Virgo mom—there is tremendous pride in his children, as if he can't quite believe his extreme good fortune.

Libra

Ah, take a deep breath and exhale slowly. Can you taste the air? The wind? The fragrance of autumn or winter, summer or spring? You love beauty in every shape and form, and when there's no obvious beauty, you find it in what you can imagine. You're an excellent strategist, a natural diplomat, and you often mitigate chaos and drama, dissent and disagreement. And sometimes you assume these roles to your own detriment, just to keep the peace.

As a parent, this tendency to keep the peace at your own expense could be thankless. So strive not to be a martyr, okay? Strive not to bend over backward to please everyone. Once you can do that, your natural artistic tendencies take over in your parenting. You nurture your children's passions and interests, their gifts and talents as they emerge. You're tuned in to who they are on a soul level and understand how to help them bring that soul into their conscious awareness. Your love of art, music, literature, and every other creative talent is passed on to your kids. Your grasp of the complexities of relationships is translated into language they speak. Facebook, MySpace, and every other social networking group become their community. In short, you usher your children into the finer beauties of the twenty-first century.

The Libra mom creates a domestic environment in which her children flourish. But she also has her career, friends, passions, and interests that get mixed up in this collective soup called life and that, in turn, affect her kids. She brings in music, art, gardens, books, and people. Lots of interesting people. She creates moods and atmospheres and invites her children to participate. The lessons they learn, the insights they carry away from these encounters influence them for life. There's no pinning down the Libra mom. Just when you think you've got her figured out, she surprises you. Boring? Never. Not a chance.

The Libra dad loves having a team—wife, kids, friends of kids, neighbors, even stray animals, it doesn't matter. Everyone and everything is part of this team. Membership is open. He's an excellent organizer, supportive of his children's endeavors and dreams. But his high ideals can be problematic once his kids are adults, making choices that don't measure up—in his mind—to those ideals. Like the Libra mom, he rarely loses his temper. He would rather work around a problem in a tactful, diplomatic way. But when he blows up, nothing is left unsaid.

Scorpio

You're intense, passionate, and strong-willed. You often try to impose your will on others—a trait that may serve your children when they're young, but can prove to be problematic as they get older. Like Aries, you're fearless, but you possess an endurance that Aries lacks, and you can plow your way through virtually any obstacle or challenge. This trait serves as an example to your children to never give up in their pursuit of what they want.

Your passions are such that you're never indifferent. You live in a world of either/or, approval or disapproval, agreement or disagreement, right or wrong. While this trait drives home the importance of values and purpose, it can be challenging for children, whose lives are more nuanced. Your ability to dig deeply for bottom-line answers indicates that you will usually know what's going on in your children's lives.

The Scorpio mom places a high value on honesty. It's the foundation of who she is. So it's no surprise that she expects honesty from her children. Even though she herself is secretive, she won't tolerate secrets from her child. She respects their privacy, but if she suspects something is going on that needs parental intervention, she investigates until she uncovers the truth. She's a loving, devoted mother who is very protective of her kids. At times, she may be too protective and strive to shield them from the outside world.

The Scorpio dad is as intense as the Scorpio mom. And unless he has a moon or rising in an air or fire sign, he may be just as much of a control freak too. He often has a magnificent talent or interest that he pursues because he's passionate about it and not because he expects to make money at it. He's a nurturing parent, particularly when it comes to his children's talents and abilities and the educational training that helps them navigate life successfully.

Sagittarius

You're a wild card. There's a part of you always looking for the larger picture, the broader perspective, and another part that believes you're always right, and yet another part that focuses on the future and the larger family of humanity. You can be very logical, but there's also a mystical element in your psyche that enables you to glimpse the future.

You dislike having your freedom restricted in any way, so you probably don't have a roll call of rules and regulations for your children. You're a loving parent, but you expect your kids to find their own way. And yet, when they make mistakes, you may offer advice that makes you sound like a know-it-all. Your versatility and natural optimism are hallmarks of your parenting style.

The Sagittarius mom thinks big. When she suggests a family outing, it isn't just a trip to the next town for a picnic. It's a trip across country or to some far-flung corner of the world, and who cares if it's beyond the family budget? She wears many hats and excels in everything she does as long as she doesn't feel confined. Her independent spirit radiates from her every pore, and her kids quickly learn to honor it. She offers her children broad guidelines and her own wisdom, but doesn't force her opinions on them.

The Sagittarius dad has a broad, sweeping vision about life, love, and the universe. He talks about it freely with his kids, never holding back. He is loving and devoted to his children, but because he expects big things from them, he may not be satisfied with what they achieve. He enjoys foreign travel and, given his financial situation, exposes his children to foreign places whenever he can. This man is always moving and has dozens of projects going on simultaneously, and his children learn early on that goals are attained through action.

Capricorn

You're the worker bee of the zodiac: industrious, disciplined, efficient, focused. You dislike inertia in others, so it's likely that your children aren't couch potatoes! You probably get them involved in sports when they're young and nurture whatever athletic abilities they have. They learn their work ethic from you and develop common sense, a trait they witness constantly in you.

Even when you were a kid, you had a mature air about you, and as you get older, that maturity is a kind of calm presence, a rock-solid dependability that your children come to expect. Never mind that you're a worrier, that even when you've prepared long and hard and have all the bases covered, you're certain you've forgotten something. Your kids rarely see that side of you. You love them unconditionally—that's what they see.

The Capricorn mom always seems to know what she's doing. She appears to be self-confident, certain about who she is, tough as nails. But when her children come to know her as a person separate from her role as mother, they discover she's not tough at all. She simply runs her home and family life as though it's a business, and she's the CEO. Even if she has a career—and many Capricorn women do—she's totally devoted to her kids. She might be a little rigid with rules and regulations, but if so, she learns that such excessive control results in outright rebellion.

The Capricorn dad is as diligent a worker as the Capricorn mom. He's got work ethic written all over him. He prides himself on being well-prepared for just about anything—including being a parent. He either has the answers or will find them—for himself, for his children, or their friends. He excels at problem solving. He can be dictatorial and bossy, but if his kids call him on it, he backs off. He's as completely devoted to his kids as he is to his career goals. In fact, one mirrors the other.

Aquarius

You're such an original thinker, a visionary, that of course you apply these talents to parenting. Your household is really atypical. You might live on a boat, in a commune, in an RV, or hey, maybe even on the space station. Your family structure isn't business as usual, either. But you aren't interested in typical. Everything you do is different from the status quo. You think in unique ways, way outside the box, and you rarely, if ever, trust what authority tells you to believe. This ability to think and perceive in new ways is passed on to your children.

Your interests are vastly varied, and any causes in which you get involved are discussed and communicated with your children. They learn early in life that mom's or dad's interests and causes don't have to become theirs but deserve respect. There probably aren't many rules in your family. Individuality is honored and encouraged.

The Aquarius mom is a complete paradox. She's a peace-loving rebel who moves against the tide of the status quo, yet conforms when it suits her. She has the patience of a saint—until she doesn't—and she can be more stubborn than Taurus, unless it suits her purpose to bend with the wind. If her children are as eccentric as she is, they have learned the value of individuality and probably share mom's love of freedom as well. Mom allows her kids the freedom to make their own decisions, revels in their achievements, and never lets them down.

The Aquarius dad considers his family—partner, kids, animals, and orphans of all sizes and shapes—to be his sanctuary. Even if he seems undemonstrative and emotionally remote at times, his love for his kids runs deep. He takes every opportunity to expose them to everything that interests him—from ancient sites like Stonehenge to books on what the future may look like. If he's a movie buff, his children are exposed to movies at a young age. If he's a traveler, his kids will be well traveled. He's terrific at sharing his knowledge, expertise, and curiosity.

Pisces

Your wonderful imagination and remarkable intuition prove valuable in your parenting style. Your imagination enables you to enter the world of your children with ease and playful joy. Your intuition enables you to stay attuned to their emotions even if they don't discuss what they're feeling. Pisces individuals with highly developed gifts—psychics—may have to take a break now and then from parenting just to find their own centers. It's too easy for this type to be overwhelmed with what their kids are feeling.

At times, you fluctuate between rigid left-brain logic and that softer intuitive certainty that you're doing the right thing. Try not to set down rules and restrictions when you're feeling like this. Moodiness and ambivalence can cause you to backtrack from your own rules. Guard against being a sucker for a sob story.

The Pisces mom often has a strong psychic connection to her children. If they have been together in past lives, chances are she has a grasp on which lives and how everyone's respective roles played out then. She's able to understand what they're feeling even when they're clueless. She is rarely dogmatic with her children and any household rules she lays down are probably for the sake of safety—and her own peace of mind. Her love for her kids is bottomless. They're her greatest joy, and she just keeps on giving and giving.

The Pisces dad is a great listener. His self-containment, gentleness, quiet strength, and attention are enviable qualities that enable him to forge tight bonds with his offspring. He encourages and supports his children's artistic interests, and he may have artistic or musical talent himself. Like his female counterpart, he must learn to balance the demands of his inner life with his responsibilities in the outer world.

Kids of the Zodiac

Now that we've looked at adults and their parenting styles, let's explore the kids of the zodiac.

Aries

She's the kid who is off by herself, exploring fields and meadows for unusual bugs. Or she's the fearless teen who leaps into a rushing river to rescue a kitten stranded on a rock. Or on the family camping trip where the matches and lighter fluid have been left behind, she's the one who makes a fire by rubbing sticks together or by using a magnifying glass to amplify the sunlight. Inventive, independent, entrepreneurial. Welcome to the world of the Aries child. And whether she's a toddler or an adult, high drama and action swirl around her.

Taurus

He's the loner. Or he has a small group of friends with whom he hangs out. But whether it's his friends or his family, no one really knows him. He's like an iceberg: Nine-tenths of his personality is hidden. He only shows what he wants you to know. And yes, these still waters run deep. So much goes on inside his head as he figures out where he belongs in the scheme of things that he wouldn't have a clue where to begin verbalizing any of it. So he nurtures his creative gifts, enjoys the sensual pleasures of physical existence, and moves forward at his own pace, patient, certain that the answers will come to him when he needs them.

Gemini

If Taurus is the loner, she's the social butterfly, flitting from one person to another, one event to the next, and along the way she's passing on what she has learned, what she suspects, what she believes. She's impatient, quick, dexterous. Her life is propelled by a single burning question: *Why?* Everything she does, every connection she makes, and everyone she knows and loves serve to answer that question. Somehow. In some way. Forget trying to pigeonhole your Gemini child. It just won't happen. When she's young, provide her with an environment where she can learn and explore at her own pace. Nurture her self-confidence and her belief in herself. With those tools, she's well-equipped for her journey out into the larger world.

Cancer

She's a tough one to figure out. She feels her way through life, but you may never know about it. She'll talk if she's in the mood, but otherwise nothing and no one will prod her into an explanation about what she feels. As a parent, you sort of have to divine your way through this kid's childhood and beyond. She needs roots. She needs to feel she's an integral part of the family and is appreciated. Much of her life as an adult is based on her childhood memories—the smells and sights and emotions she was feeling at a particular time. If her childhood is happy and secure, she grows into a happy, secure adult.

Leo

The Leo child is like his own tribe. From the time he's very young, he has dozens of friends, and they all hang out at his place. Even as he gets older, his friends are eager to spend time with him; some of them are orphans and strays attracted by his innate generosity and compassion. Like fellow fire sign Aries, the Leo child is basically fearless. He accepts every dare and takes risks that would leave other kids gasping in awe. Most Leo kids enjoy the company of animals and their homes tend to have a lot of pets.

Virgo

She's impatient, she wants everything yesterday, and she's graced with abundant energy. She has questions about everything, and she is so eager to learn that in the right environment, she explores until she drops from exhaustion. Like Cancer, she can be moody, but these swings usually occur when she doesn't understand something. Her restless mind gnaws away at the puzzle, dissecting it, scrutinizing the minutiae, until she gets it. She has enormous compassion—a quality that is evident at a very young age—and her ability to connect people is as easy for her as connecting disparate bits of information is for a Gemini. Even when young, Virgo kids show discernment. They may be picky about what they eat, read, or watch on TV.

Libra

The Libra child can be found listening to music in the comfort of his own room, connecting with friends on Facebook and MySpace, or hanging out with friends in some familiar and pretty spot. He isn't the type to play touch football (unless he's got a lot of fire or earth in his chart) or hunt for bugs under rocks or dissect frogs in a lab. As a youngster, the Libra child may have an imaginary playmate or one special friend to whom he confides. He's loyal to his friends, sometimes to a fault, so any friends he has as a youngster are probably going to be friends for life.

Scorpio

She's distinctive in some way—physically, mentally, intuitively. She has fixed opinions even as a youngster, as if she came into life with a particular agenda or belief system. She feels deeply—one of the trademarks of this sign—and the intensity of her emotions may lead to sudden outbursts if her feelings are hurt or she doesn't get what she wants. She flourishes in an environment that is varied and rich, where she can explore her creative abilities. She won't always be forthright about what's going on inside of her, but if you simply come out and ask her, her response may surprise you. She's wiser than her years.

Sagittarius

This kid is Mr. Popularity, and that is evident from the time he's old enough to crawl and interact. He's vivacious and optimistic; he makes other people feel good about themselves. It makes him a people magnet. He can be opinionated and blunt. He doesn't think about what he's going to say before he says it—a tendency that can be disconcerting to people who aren't accustomed to him. But he needs the freedom to express himself and to know it's okay to defend what he believes. Rules and structure are a good idea as he's growing up. He probably has a fondness for animals, which isn't surprising for a sign symbolized by a figure that is half human, half horse!

Capricorn

From the time she utters her first word, she's as comfortable being and conversing with adults as she is with her peers. Sometimes, she has a seriousness about her that is usually evident in her eyes, in the way she watches and appraises you, sizing you up for who knows what reason.

Other times, she can be as wild and playful as any other child. Even then, her organizational skills are evident, and she can be bossy. She is infinitely patient and intent on achieving her goals.

Aquarius

To this kid, all people truly are equal, so his friends span the racial and socioeconomic spectrum. He's an extrovert, eager to know what makes other people tick, but he's also perfectly happy when he's by himself. His mind is as busy as a Gemini's, but in a much different way. Where a Gemini child collects trivia and information, the Aquarian child is immersed in the stuff of the universe. Although he enjoys people and gets involved in all sorts of groups, he's not a follower, and he will always defend not only his opinions, but his right to have those opinions.

Pisces

She doesn't need many rules. She's so sensitive to her environment and to the people who inhabit it that a cross look from her mom or dad keeps her in line. She's a dreamer whose imagination soars through time and space with the ease of a bird through the sky. If her intuitive gifts are allowed to develop, this child can become a genuine medium, clairvoyant, mystic, or healer. Her strong creative drive manifests itself early.

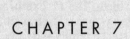

CHAPTER 7

Saturn and Karma

Saturn governs the rules and parameters of physical life. It represents responsibility, structure, discipline, limitations, delays, obedience, authority, and the building of foundations. It also symbolizes karma—the issues and concerns we bring in from past lives. In other words, there are no free rides with this planet. Wherever it appears in your birth chart indicates an area where you will learn lessons this time around.

Saturn's lessons can be harsh, but it teaches us through experience what we need in order to grow and what our souls intend to accomplish in this life. It shows us our limitations and teaches us the rules of the game. Without it, our lives would be chaos. Individuals with well-aspected Saturns in their birth charts—the angles other planets make to it—have a practical outlook. With a poorly aspected Saturn, growth may be restricted or limited in some way, and the person's outlook could be rigid.

The sign that Saturn occupies shows how we handle obstacles in our lives, how we deal with authority, and how we cope with serious issues. The house placement in your natal chart indicates the area of your life that's affected. If you have Saturn in your tenth house, your career ambition is one of the driving forces in your life, and you'll work tirelessly to succeed. If your Saturn is in Leo, you may need to learn that it isn't all about just you and your career.

Every twenty-eight to thirty years, we experience a Saturn return, when transiting Saturn returns to the place it occupied at our birth. The first return, around the age of twenty-nine, brings major life transitions—we get married or divorced, start a family, move, begin a career. The second return, between the ages of fifty-eight and sixty, is considered the harvest. We experience major events—retire, our kids have left home, we downsize, we move, we inherit money.

Whenever a Saturn transit hits a natal planet, that period should be navigated carefully, with understanding of what's required of you. Saturn stays in a sign for roughly two and a half years, and takes about twenty-nine years to circle the zodiac. It entered Libra in late October 2009, retrograded from January 13 to May 29, 2010, and then entered Libra again on July 22, 2010, and will be there until early October 2012. In appendix 2, locate where your birth date falls, find out what sign your natal Saturn is in, and then read the description below.

Natal Saturn in Aries

Your impetuosity and rashness need to be tempered somewhat so that you think before you act. You consistently encounter circumstances that force you to develop patience and initiative. If you push against these circumstances, setbacks occur. With Saturn, you can't take shortcuts. This position of Saturn urges you to develop resourcefulness and discipline and to complete what you start. Once you learn these lessons, you're capable of innovative and unique creations.

The downside with this placement is that you're prone to defensiveness and a kind of self-centered attitude that puts people off. Tact and diplomacy will take you further and, in the end, may be one of the lessons you're here to learn.

Natal Saturn in Taurus

One of your lessons this time around is to develop persistence and resoluteness, an unshakable belief in yourself and your talents. This belief helps you to win material security and comfort through hard work, discipline, and perseverance. You may not be the fastest-moving person in the world, but you hang in there long after the competition has bitten the dust.

You must learn how to handle money and your finances. You tend to be frugal even when you don't have to be, but this frugality may become one of your hobbies. You might hit garage sales, flea markets, or any spot where secondhand goods are sold, and you could develop a business around this practice. On the other hand, if this frugality turns to miserliness, you may want to rethink your attitudes and beliefs about money. The downside is a preoccupation with materialism.

Natal Saturn in Gemini

Since Saturn corules air sign Aquarius and is exalted in air sign Libra, it's pretty comfortable in air sign Gemini. It brings discipline and structure to your mental process, and suggests that you must learn how to think through problems logically, working them out in detail so that your solutions are practical. Saturn here may restrict a free-flowing expression of ideas, but once you've learned to channel your ideas in a pragmatic way, perhaps through writing or some sort of group activity, you reap the benefits. In other words, it's not enough to have a great idea. How can the idea be put into practice to benefit not only you but others?

Communication is important to you, but it has to be organized, structured in some way, honest, and dependable. That may be one of the lessons you're here to learn. Downside? If you don't do the grunt work this placement demands, your obstacles multiply.

Natal Saturn in Cancer

This placement may restrict your intuitive gifts and your emotions. Or it could provide the proper structure for expressing both. It depends on how you use your conscious desires and intent to create your life. It depends too on your deepest beliefs. Do you believe we have free will or that life is somehow scripted, destined? Are events random, or do they rise from some hidden quantum order? While your crablike tenacity helps you to navigate successfully through obstacles, Saturn here urges you to confront obstacles head-on, to reveal what's in your heart, and to channel your intuitive talents in a practical, focused way.

Your home and family are important to you, but strive not to impose so many restrictions in this area that the people who are closest to you—and you yourself—feel suffocated.

Natal Saturn in Leo

This placement is all about power and recognition. The desire for both, however, takes many forms. At one extreme, it results in a need to control your environment and everyone inside of it and a hungry ambition that blinds you to everything else. At the other extreme, this placement results in structures that help you to channel your ambition in a constructive, directed way. This placement also suggests that your ego and need for recognition can be your worst enemies, so be aware of that tendency and do whatever you can to mitigate it.

For boomers born with this configuration, there can be multiple setbacks that prompt you to work harder, put in longer hours, meet all your obligations—and then some. Eventually, if you learn patience and resilience, you succeed. You achieve your goals. Cooperative endeavors are beneficial with this placement—i.e., anything in the professional arena in which you have partners, where you're a team player, where your voice is just one among many.

Natal Saturn in Virgo

The tendency with this placement is that you're such a perfectionist you get bogged down in details. You walk into someone else's house and immediately notice dust that screams to be cleaned. Or you enter your son's apartment and are overwhelmed by the disorder and chaos. But if you can direct this tendency toward your work and career, you can handle anything, manifest anything, and perform a service that helps many people understand their roles in this lifetime. It's simply a matter of separating the essential from the inconsequential.

Your intuition is highly developed, just waiting for you to pay attention, to connect all the dots. Find humor in everything you do. Take breaks from work. Treat yourself to a trip to Paris or some far-flung corner of the globe. Learn to revel in your experiences.

Natal Saturn in Libra

Your lesson this time around is to learn the value of cooperation. The success of any partnership, personal or business, involves the ability to compromise. What can you live with to keep the peace? How much can you surrender without giving away your personal power? Your values? Karma is part and parcel of your most intimate relationships, and the sooner you recognize that, the better off you are. The question is how you recognize which relationships are karmic and which are just the luck (or misfortune) of the draw. Well, it's about what you feel when in the presence of another person. It comes down to resonance.

The dark side of this placement is a tendency to surrender too much in the hope that you can keep the peace. The real key here is the ability to forgive and forget and move on.

Natal Saturn in Scorpio

In your work, you're as much of a perfectionist as Saturn in Virgo. But in everything else, you're pure Scorpio—after the bottom line, the absolute truth, the real deal. You're secretive in the way you handle stress and difficulties of any kind, and must learn how to deal with this stuff in a calm, centered manner. Allow your intuition to guide you. It's an infallible tool. Your persistence, resilience, and determination are among your greatest assets.

That said, there's a proclivity here for incredible discipline in achieving your goals, but you may need help and help won't be forthcoming unless you ask for it. *Can* you ask for it? Is a request for help even in your lexicon? Check out the sign of your moon. If it's in a water or earth sign, chances are good that you realize you are part of a collective of like-minded individuals. Start there. You won't be disappointed.

Natal Saturn in Sagittarius

Your pursuit of philosophy and religious and spiritual beliefs is one of the primary driving forces in your life. You may have a desire to be recognized as an authority in one of the above areas or in higher education, publishing, politics, or the law. You probably have a strict moral code that guides you, but which could stifle creative thinking. Any kind of rigid approach to problem solving complicates your challenges and problems. It's best to loosen up, to allow yourself the freedom to explore your ideals free of political or religious restraints.

You're happiest if you can structure your life by incorporating your ideals into your daily life in a practical way. Your professional reputation is vitally important to you, but try not to obsess about every little detail. You're after the big picture. The darker side of this placement is self-righteousness.

Natal Saturn in Capricorn

Saturn rules this sign, so it's very happy here and functions at optimum capacity. Your ambitions are powerful, and from the time you're old enough to understand what a career is, you are pursuing your own. Your talents are varied, and you may be able to integrate all of them in some unique way to achieve what you desire. Your goals are specific; your discipline is astounding.

The usual description about this placement is that the person may appear cold, detached, remote. But I've found this isn't necessarily true. My daughter and her friends—all of them born in 1989 when Saturn was in the early degrees of Capricorn—are among the most joyful group of people I've ever known. But they're also incredibly focused in their pursuit of educational goals, which certainly fits this placement.

Natal Saturn in Aquarius

Saturn, as the coruler of Aquarius, is pretty comfortable here. Your visionary qualities are channeled and expressed in practical ways that benefit others. Your intellect is organized, focused, objective, and capable of innovative discoveries and solutions. With this placement, there's usually mathematical and scientific ability and the ability to conceptualize. The challenge is to integrate your abilities into your daily life and to ground them. You benefit from regular physical exercise, which serves to remind you there's more to life than the mind! Yoga, tai chi, or any other mind-body discipline would be a good place to start.

The downside of this placement can be a lack of feeling, intellectual pride, and impersonal relationships.

Natal Saturn in Pisces

The consensus about this placement is that it's difficult. But any challenges can be overcome by channeling your intuitive ability through a structure that Saturn provides. Instead of letting your memories of the past trap you, use memories of past triumphs as a springboard to achieve what you desire. Your psychic ability is the doorway to spiritual and creative development and to higher spiritual truths.

There can be an inordinate amount of worrying that accompanies this placement, so be sure you always allow yourself a refuge where you can kick back and relax. It helps to practice yoga, to meditate, to nurture yourself first.

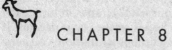

CHAPTER 8

Freedom and Individuality

One night in March 1781, a man stood in the back garden of his home in Bath, England, peering through a six-inch telescope he had made. He was surveying stars ten times dimmer than can be seen by the naked eye, and he noticed that one "star" seemed different. And so Sir William Herschel discovered Uranus, the first discovery of a planet using a telescope and the first time in modern history that the known boundaries of the solar system were expanded.

It was the peak of the Enlightenment. The first glimmers of the Industrial Revolution and the Romantic movement in literature and art were just around the corner. The Articles of Confederation—the first constitution of the thirteen American colonies—had been ratified less than two weeks before Herschel's discovery. The American Revolutionary War had been in full swing for several years and the colonial army finally won in October 1781. In other words, it was a time of revolt, rebellion, liberation.

Uranus's discovery, like those of the other outer planets, happened just as a radical shift was occurring in mankind's collective psyche. It's as if the planet itself was the expression of man's emerging realizations. In mythology, Uranus is linked to Prometheus, the son of a titan who stole fire and gave it to mortals. Sounds like a rebel, right?

No coincidence, then, that Uranus symbolizes freedom, individuality, revolution, the bright fire of genius. In astrology, the sign of your natal Uranus indicates the motivations behind your hopes, wishes, and dreams. It can describe the people and groups with whom you hang out. But it's the house it occupies in your natal chart that is most telling. It helps to explain the work that you do and your soul's purpose this time around.

Uranus rules electronics, lightning, astrology, earthquakes, tornadoes, the Internet, radio, TV, phones, upheavals. You get the idea, right? And in case you want to check this out in more detail, pick up a copy of Rex E. Bill's *The Rulership Book,* the definitive tome on which planets rule what. Uranus takes eighty-four years to circle the zodiac. You would be surprised at how many people die as they approach their Uranus return at that age. Those who survive and live well beyond it are people whose wisdom and insights benefit the rest of us.

Carol Bowman

Let's take an example. Carol Bowman, a reincarnation researcher and therapist and author of two groundbreaking books on children's past lives, is a Libra with Uranus in Cancer on her midheaven—the cusp of her tenth house of career. It's just one degree from an exact conjunction, so the planet is technically in her ninth house—worldview. Since Uranus rules Aquarius, her natal Uranus rules her fifth house—children, creativity, romance, and enjoyment. Here's how this placement has played out in her life so far.

On a July 4th weekend when Carol's son, Chase, was four years old, he exhibited an abnormal terror of firecrackers. The fear continued beyond the firecrackers and the long weekend, and Carol realized that something weird was happening. Rather than taking Chase to a doctor, Carol sought an alternative route. She consulted a friend, a professional hypnotist, and the moment Chase climbed onto Norman's lap, he spontaneously recalled a life in which he was a black Civil War soldier who had been shot in the wrist. He described the bayonet rifle that he held, the smells and sights on the battlefield. Not long afterward, a chronic rash on Chase's wrist, in the same spot where he had been shot in that Civil War life, cleared up. Carol knew she was onto something.

Over the course of the next year, Carol talked to other parents—on playgrounds, at school functions—and gradually began to formulate a theory. A friend wrote to Oprah about Carol's research and theories, and a year later, Oprah called and invited Carol onto her show. This story is recounted in *Children's Past Lives*, her first book, and aptly illustrates how her son (fifth house and children) launched her search for unconventional truths (Uranus). From Oprah, Carol went on to write her book, which has since been published in dozens of languages. A few years later, she wrote *Return from Heaven*, about reincarnation within the same family.

In the years since then, she has been featured on dozens of TV shows and hundreds of radio shows (Uranus and electronics). She was instrumental in bringing the best-documented case of reincarnation in the Western world to a larger audience—the story of James Leininger (*Soul Survivor*), which was featured on *20/20*.

She now has a thriving regression practice (the Cancer part of the equation), and is considered one of the foremost experts on children's past lives. She has not only honored Uranus at her midheaven, but has surpassed it.

A curious footnote to Chase's story: Shortly after he turned eighteen and registered for the draft, he came home and told Carol a weird thing had happened. "Look at this," he said, and showed her the underside of his wrist. The rash had returned.

Once you have located the sign for your natal Uranus in appendix 3, read the description below.

Natal Uranus in Aries

Your mission, should you choose to accept it, is to forge new paths, to break ground in new belief systems, inventions, innovations. The house that holds your natal Uranus is vitally important in that it shows you where you're most likely to think and act outside the box.

You're blunt, outspoken, and often outrageous. You rebel against the status quo in just about every area of your life. Look at the era between 1928 and 1934. The U.S. was in the throes of the great depression, yet it was the era of flappers, F. Scott Fitzgerald, bootlegging, rebellion against the status quo. Individuals born during this period tended to be adventurers who pushed forward into the unknown, seeking new ways to live, love, and evolve. And that's what we're looking at in 2011, when Uranus enters Aries again. In a year of transition, we need people who see where we would like to be tomorrow or a fifty years from now. We need fearless leaders. And that's what you are.

Natal Uranus in Taurus

This generation knows how to handle money and finances, but their methods won't be those of their parents and grandparents. They're looking for reform and practicality instead of excess, efficiency where there has been waste. Uranus is in its fall in Taurus, which means that there may be too great an attachment to materialism to bring about significant change. Then again, change begins in your head, with your thoughts and beliefs, so how this plays out for you depends on your intent and desires.

With Uranus here, you're capable of making the most innovative idea or far-out invention absolutely practical. You have tremendous drive, determination, and purpose. Your stubbornness can be a detriment to your goals if it's carried to extremes. This placement for Uranus can indicate unusual artistic and musical abilities.

Natal Uranus in Gemini

This generation of individuals brings new ways of thinking and communicating. You'll find them Twittering, communicating on Facebook and MySpace, using iPhones, and taking their electronics with them wherever they go. They're always connected.

Your ingenuity and intuitive smarts propel you to explore areas about which you're passionate, and here you gather information and then disseminate it. You seek freedom from the status quo, insisting on your right to define your own beliefs. Your frequent travels expose you to new people and ideas, and it all becomes fodder for your creative endeavors. You're mentally and intellectually restless, and you may have a hundred different things going on at once. But this restlessness enables you to think outside the proverbial box and to break through habitual living patterns.

Natal Uranus in Cancer

This generation pursues freedom through emotional expression and intuitive explorations. They won't live the way their parents have and, as soon as possible, break free from parental authority.

You may pursue an unusual career that encompasses your interests and passions and enables you to integrate your psychic sensitivity into your work. In fact, psychic or spiritual work may be an integral part of your atypical family life. Your home is unique in some way, completely different from your childhood home. Electronic gadgets and contraptions may be common at your place.

Because you insist on emotional freedom, you can sometimes be moody. When you feel that way, reach for a thought that lifts your spirits!

Natal Uranus in Leo

This generation is after freedom in love and romance. Their attitudes toward sex are definitely not like those of their parents. They insist on their right to pursue these areas on their own terms, the way they see fit.

You feel restricted by the status quo in the areas mentioned above, in the arts, in ideas about leadership. So you create your own standards. In terms of the arts, you dislike critics and reviewers telling you what's good and what isn't. They represent the status quo, after all, and you insist on your right to make up your own mind. So your tastes in art, music, and theater are apt to be unconventional.

Since there's an inherent tendency with this placement toward egotism, strive to work with issues that affect the larger family of humanity rather than personal concerns.

Natal Uranus in Virgo

This generation has original ideas about science, technology, health, computers, and communication devices and equipment. They are innovators in these fields, and they are able to bring the most outrageous ideas down to earth and make them practical.

You're a meticulous researcher and communicator. You insist on your right to express yourself in whatever way you want rather than through some set standard. You apply this right across the board in your life. When you don't feel well, you seek alternatives to traditional medicine. When you feel slighted or hurt, you correct your mood through inner work. You have an unusual business sense, but you may go through a lot of abrupt changes in your employment. When you do, you see it as opportunity rather than defeat.

Natal Uranus in Libra

This generation's ideas about marriage and relationships are radical, totally different from those of the status quo. Whether it's communal living or open marriage or something else entirely, they insist on their right to define relationships and social conduct according to their rules.

You have unconventional ideas about laws, specifically about laws as they apply to marriage and partnerships. Your feelings could prompt you to work toward reform of existing laws and paradigms. You seek freedom through your closest partnerships, and if your partner isn't in agreement, the relationship may be fraught with problems. So be up front with your partners about your beliefs. You'll save yourself a world of heartache.

This placement suggests deep insight into relationships—motives, needs, issues. Creatively, it can produce gifted musicians.

Natal Uranus in Scorpio

This generation will see intense and profound change in their lifetimes and will have to learn to adjust to whatever rises from the ashes—a different world, new paradigms, new ways of being and interacting.

Your intense and powerful emotions require decisive action, so it's no wonder that you have zero tolerance for people you perceive as lazy or indecisive. You have great psychic ability, which enables you to discern other people's motives, issues, and agendas, but your insights may be erratic and charged both emotionally and sexually. You may have scientific ability, strong occult talents, and a profound grasp of metaphysical ideas—reincarnation, life after death, communication with the dead. You're not the superficial type by any stretch of the imagination!

The darker side of this placement can be a fierce

temper and an inability to tolerate views different from your own.

Natal Uranus in Sagittarius

This generation ushers in new ideas about religion, spirituality, philosophy, education, publishing, astrology, and the occult. They are truth seekers who insist on their right to look for that truth in their own way, at their own pace.

You're one of those people to whom weird things happen. Your spiritual beliefs may range from the truly bizarre to the more conventional—but not entirely conventional. You're attracted to the spiritual beliefs of foreign cultures and to foreign countries generally. You look for the unusual or the eccentric in foreign countries that you visit. Your travel is usually involved with a quest of some sort—as opposed to travel that's strictly for business or pleasure. You may travel suddenly, on the spur of the moment, with nothing more than a change of clothes, your iPod, and your ATM card.

The downside of this placement is a rigidity about your spiritual and political beliefs.

Natal Uranus in Capricorn

This generation will bring about major changes in government, business, banking, insurance, health care, and probably every other institution we take for granted. They will build new structures and paradigms from the ruins of everything that has been collapsing under Pluto in Capricorn. The oldest of the Uranus in Capricorn people were born in 1989 and those among them who were eighteen at the time of the 2008 election voted overwhelmingly for Barack Obama.

You're ambitious, but your drive to succeed and achieve is not of the same patterns as that of your parents. While you don't rid yourself entirely of these old, tired patterns, you strive to restructure old ideas in new ways, to find new solutions to old problems.

In your natal chart, find which house Uranus is in. This will tell you where you can expect sudden change, reform, innovation. If Uranus in Capricorn is in your tenth house, your career will be the area where you're building new structures and finding new solutions.

Natal Uranus in Aquarius

Uranus rules Aquarius, so it's quite comfortable—and powerful—in this position. This generation of individuals has strong intuitive and scientific talents and grasps metaphysical truths. They don't hesitate to get rid of old paradigms and to search for new belief systems that serve not only themselves, but the family of man.

You insist on your right to make your own decisions about your life and your own value judgments about everything you experience. You don't think like other people do. The consensus reality is foreign to you. Intellectually, you're independent, innovative, and able to spot future trends. Use this ability to serve that which is larger than yourself, and you'll do just fine!

The darker side of this placement is a stubbornness as rigid as that of Uranus in Taurus or Leo. It works against you.

Natal Uranus in Pisces

In this generation, there are psychics and martyrs, two sides of the same coin. The psychics see what might be, and the martyrs are chained to the past. Somehow, this generation must bridge the two.

You seek freedom through your intuitive gifts, your imagination, your dreams. You possess the ability to dive into the unconscious and receive inspiration from your dreams, images that come to you through meditation, and any of your psychic impressions. Your challenge is to accept these truths on faith—rather than spending time trying to confirm their validity in the external world. In a sense, you're like a character on the TV show *Lost*, plunged into a strange world but urged to accept certain things on faith alone.

Hopefully, you'll do better than the *Lost* characters by dealing with thorny situations as they arise. Good luck with that!

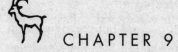

CHAPTER 9

Health and Fitness Secrets for the Sun Signs

If you were an alien watching the evening news and the drug commercials that sponsor it, you might get the impression that Americans are a sickly lot in search of the quickest fix. While drugs certainly have their place, more and more Americans are seeking alternative treatments for whatever ails them. From acupuncture to yoga and homeopathy, from vitamin regimens to nutritional programs, we want control over our own health and bodies.

Health and fitness are more than just eating right and getting sufficient exercise. They also involve our emotions, our inner worlds, our belief systems. How happy are you in your job? Your closest partnerships? Your friendships? Are you generally happy with the money you earn? What would you change about your life? Do you believe that you have free will or that everything is destined? Is your mood generally upbeat? Do you feel you have choices? Do you feel empowered? By asking yourself these kinds of questions, you can glean a sense of your emotional state at any given time. And the state of your emotions may tell you a great deal about the state of your health.

Louise Hay, author of *You Can Heal Your Life* and founder of Hay House publishing, is a living testament to the impact of emotions on health. As a young woman, she was diagnosed with vaginal cancer. The doctors wanted to operate, but Hay bought herself time—three months—by telling them she didn't have the money. She then took control of her treatment.

Because Hay had been a battered child who was raped at the age of five, it wasn't surprising to her that the cancer had shown up where it had. She knew that cancer was "a disease of deep resentment that has been held for a long period of time until it literally eats away at the body." She felt that if she could change the mental pattern that had created the cancer, if she could release the patterns of resentment, she could cure herself.

She set out a program for her treatment—and forgiveness was the top of her list. She also knew she had to love and approve of herself more. In addition, she found a good therapist, a nutritionist, and a foot reflexologist. She had colonics three times a week and exercised. Her treatment is spelled out in her book. The end result? Within six months, the doctors pronounced her free of cancer.

In her book, there's an invaluable list: next to every ailment and disease is the probable emotional cause. And the new thought pattern that will lead to healing. Her techniques may not be for everyone, but when dealing with health and fitness issues, remember that medical science doesn't have all the answers, and you, in fact, may be your own best healer.

The Physical You

These descriptions fit both sun and rising signs. For a more complete look at the physical you, your entire natal chart should be taken into account, with a particularly close look at the sign of your moon—the root of your emotions, the cradle of your inner world.

Aries

Rules: head and face

Appearance

Physically, these people tend to have ruddy complexions, narrow chins, and arched eyebrows. Sometimes, they have scars or moles on the head or face. Aries men often have profuse body hair, and in both men and women, the hair is sometimes tinged with red.

Health and Fitness

Aries rules the head and face, so these areas are often the most vulnerable physically. Headaches, dizziness, and skin eruptions can be common. If you're athletic, do more of whatever it is that you enjoy. Competitive sports? Great, go for it. Long-distance runner? Run farther. Gym? Double your time and your workout. Yoga once a week? Do it three times a week. One way or another, you need to burn off your excessive energy so that it doesn't turn inward and short-circuit your body!

As a cardinal fire sign, you're an active person who gravitates toward daring, risky sports—mountain climbing, rappelling, bungee jumping, trekking through high mountainous regions, leaping out of airplanes. It's probably a great idea to have good health insurance or to have a Louise Hay attitude toward your health: *I'm attracting only magnificent experiences into my life.*

For maximum benefit, you probably should try to eliminate red meat from your diet. Chicken and fish are fine, but a vegan diet would be best. Herbs like mustard, eyebright, and bay are beneficial for you. Any antioxidant is helpful—particularly vitamins C, E, A, or lutein for your eyes, zinc, CoQ10, black cohosh if you're a female in menopause, or saw palmetto if you're a man older than fifty. If you pull a muscle or throw your back out of whack, look for a good acupuncturist and avoid painkillers.

Taurus

Rules: neck, throat, cervical vertebrae

Appearance

Their necks betray them. For a Taurus, the neck is usually thick and sturdy, and it rises from broad, often muscular shoulders that seem to bear the weight of the world. They tend to be attractive individuals with broad foreheads and expressive faces. Yet their faces can be as inscrutable as fortune cookies when they are hiding something or feel threatened in some way. They usually look more youthful than other people their age, the result of good genes and a daily regimen of exercise.

Health and Fitness

Thanks to the sensuality of your sign, you may be a gourmet cook and enjoy rich foods. But because your metabolism may be somewhat slow, you benefit from daily exercise and moderation in your diet. In fact, moderation in all things is probably a good rule to follow.

As a fixed earth sign, you benefit from any outdoor activity, and the more physical it is, the better it is for you. Hiking, skiing, windsurfing, and biking are all excellent pursuits. You also benefit from any mind-body discipline like tai chi or yoga. The latter is especially good since it keeps you flexible, and that flexibility spills over into your attitudes and beliefs and the way you deal with situations and people. You probably enjoy puttering in a garden, but because you have such an artistic side, you don't just putter. You remake the garden into a work of art—fountains, bold colors, mysterious paths that twist through greenery and flowers. Once you add wind chimes and bird feeders, nature's music adds the finishing touches.

If your job entails long hours of sitting in front of a computer, your neck and shoulders may be more tense than usual. You would benefit through regular massages and hot-tub soaks.

If you're the silent type of Taurus, then chances are you don't discuss your emotions. This tendency can cause health challenges if you keep anger or resentment bottled up inside you. Best to have an outlet—through exercise or some sort of creative endeavor. Art, music, photography, writing—any of those would help. Better yet, learn to open up with at least one or two people!

Gemini

Rules: hands, arms, lungs, nervous system

Appearance

Geminis generally radiate a lot of nervous energy. It keeps them slender and wiry, and they're always on the move—if not physically, then mentally. They often have twinkling eyes, clear-cut features, noses that turn up slightly at the end. Some of them have thick hair. They talk and move fast, many are ambidextrous, and they usually have excellent coordination.

Health and Fitness

You benefit from periodic breaks in your established routine. Whether it's a trip to some exotic port or a trip to the grocery, it's a breath of fresh air, a way to hit the pause button on your busy mind. Regular physical exercise helps to bleed off some of your energy and keeps your youthful body supple and in shape.

As a mutable air sign, you need intellectual stimulation and a constant array of experiences and information that keep your curiosity piqued. Otherwise, it's too easy for all that nervous energy to turn inward and affect your health. The kind of work you do is important in the overall scheme of your health. You do best in a nonroutine kind of work with flexible hours or in a profession in which you make your own hours! Any job in communication, travel, or public relations would suit you. When you're passionate about what you do, you're happier. If you're happy, your immune system remains healthy.

With your natural dexterity and coordination, you would do well at yoga. If you don't take classes yet, sign up for some. Not only will they keep you flexible, but you'll benefit mentally. Meditation would also be an excellent practice for you. Anything to calm your busy head!

Since your respiratory and nervous systems are your most vulnerable areas, your diet should include plenty of fish and fresh fruits and vegetables. If you live in a place where you can garden, plant some of these items in a garden for optimum freshness. Vitamin C, zinc, the B vitamins, and vitamins E and A are also beneficial for you. With your energy always in fast-forward, it's smart to get at least seven and preferably eight hours of sleep a night. If you're the type of Gemini with high metabolism, you benefit from eating several small meals throughout the day rather than just the usual three.

Cancer

Rules: breasts, stomach, digestive system

Appearance

Cancers are recognizable because of their round faces. Their bodies are sometimes round, though not necessarily overweight. Those who don't have round-ness as part of their physical appearance may have some other distinguishing trait—liquid, soulful eyes, a lovely shaped mouth, or generally expressive features. They're moody individuals, and their moods are often reflected on their faces, in the way they walk and carry themselves.

Health and Fitness

As a cardinal water sign, you benefit from proximity to water. If you can live or work close to a body of water, you'll notice a marked difference in your energy and intuition and how you feel and think. Even a vacation close to the water is healing. And this seems to hold true not only for Cancer sun signs, but for moon and rising signs in Cancer. The body of water can be anything—a lake, river, ocean, salt marsh, or pond.

Not surprisingly, you benefit from any kind of water sport, even a day at the beach or a picnic by the river. The point is that water speaks to you. It feels like your natural element. You might want to read *The Secret of Water* or any of the other books by Masaru Emoto. You will never think of water in the same way again, and you will be more conscious of how human emotions affect water—and thus our bodies, since we consist of nearly 70 percent water.

Emotionally, you may cling to past injuries and hurts more than other signs, or you may still be dragging around issues from childhood or even from a past life. Unresolved emotional stuff can lodge in your body and create problems. So it's important that you rid yourself of past resentments and anger. Use hypnosis to dislodge these feelings. Forgive and forget. Have a past-life regression. Read Louise Hay's book *You Can Heal Your Life.*

If you have a moon, rising, or another planet in an earth sign, consider regular workouts at a gym.

Leo

Rules: heart, back, spinal cord

Appearance

From Jacqueline Kennedy to Madonna to Presidents Obama and Clinton, the typical Leo looks regal. Hair that is thick or in some way distinguished, compelling eyes, a smile that can light up the dark side of the moon—these are the Leo hallmarks. Male or female, Leos project dignity and intelligence, and they move with a certain elegance. In a crowded room, the Leo is usually the one surrounded by people!

Health and Fitness

Leo rules the heart. So you benefit from a low-fat diet, exercise, work that you love, and relationships in which you are recognized as the unique person that you are. Yes, those last two things count in the overall picture of your health!

Let's talk about your work. Acting, of course, is what you're known for. And performance. And politics. And, well, anything in which you can show off your abundant talents. So if right now you're locked into a humdrum job and you don't receive the attention you feel you deserve, then your pride and ambition are suffering. That, in turn, creates resentment that could be eating you alive. Turn the situation around by finding a career or an outlet in which your talents shine and you're appreciated and recognized. You're a natural leader whose flamboyant style and magnetism attract the supporters who can help you.

You have a temper, but once you blow, that's it. Unlike Cancer, you don't hold grudges or harbor resentments or anger from childhood. You tend to be forward-looking, and your natural optimism is healthy for your heart and immune system. Anything you can do to maintain your cheerful disposition is a plus. When you feel yourself getting down, rent comedies, find books that make you laugh out loud, and blog about your feelings.

Virgo

Rules: intestines, abdomen, female reproductive system

Appearance

Their physiques are usually slender and distinctive in some way—beautifully sculpted fingers and hands, nice legs, gorgeous teeth. They're physically attractive as a rule, which they enhance through their fastidious attention to detail. Their eyes may be unusual in some way, and their features tend to be sharp, clearly defined. They're fastidious about personal hygiene.

Health and Fitness

If you're the type of Virgo who worries and frets a lot, the first place it's likely to show up is in your digestive tract. You might have colic as an infant, stomach upsets as a teenager, ulcers as an adult. The best way to mitigate this tendency is to learn how not to worry and to simply go with the flow.

You do best on a diet that includes plenty of fresh fruits and vegetables, fish, and chicken. Try to stay away from fried or heavily spiced foods. Red meat might be difficult to digest. If you live in a place where fresh fruits and vegetables are difficult to find during the winter, supplement your diet with the appropriate vitamins and minerals. If you're a fussy eater—and some Virgos are—then the vitamin and mineral supplements are even more important.

You benefit from hot baths, massages, anything that allows you to relax into the moment. Yoga, running, swimming, gym workouts—any of these exercise regimens benefit you. Some Virgos, particularly double Virgos—with a moon or rising in that sign—have an acute sense of smell. If you're one of those, be sure to treat yourself to scented soaps and lotions, fragrant candles and incense, and any other scent that soothes your soul.

Virgo is typically associated with service, and you may find that whenever you do a good deed for someone, when you volunteer your time or expertise, you feel better about yourself and life in general. The more you can do to trigger these feelings, the healthier you'll be. You have a tendency toward self-criticism that's part and parcel of your need for perfection, and whenever you find yourself shifting into that critical frame of mind, stop it in its tracks. Reach for a more uplifting thought. This will help you to maintain your health.

Libra

Rules: lower back, kidney, diaphragm

Appearance

Even in a crowd of beautiful people, they stand out in some way. As a Venus-ruled sign, they have distinctive features—beautiful eyes, gorgeous skin, well-formed bodies, expressive mouths. They're often slender, good-looking. They enjoy beauty—in their partners, their surroundings, in their aesthetic tastes. So it isn't surprising that they often dress beautifully and have homes that are boldly colored and uniquely decorated.

Health and Fitness

If your love life is terrific, your health probably is too. You're happiest when you're in a relationship, preferably a committed, lifetime relationship. When things between you and your partner are on an even keel, your energy is greater, your immune system works without a hitch, you sleep more soundly, and you're more apt to have a healthier lifestyle.

You prefer working in an environment that's aesthetically pleasing, where there are congenial people and a minimum of drama. If your work situation doesn't fit that description, it could affect your health—and for the same reasons as a love life that is lacking. Your lower back, kidneys, and diaphragm are vulnerable areas for you, and unvented emotions could manifest in those areas first. If it isn't possible to change jobs or careers right now, find an artistic outlet for your creative expression. Music, photography, art, writing, dance, or any area that allows you to flex your creativity.

You benefit from yoga, walking, swimming, and any kind of exercise that strengthens your lower back muscles. Meditation is also beneficial, particularly when it's combined with an awareness of breathing.

The healthiest diet for you should consist of foods with varied tastes, plenty of fresh fruits and vegetables, organic if possible, and a minimum of meats. Anything that benefits your kidneys is good. Drink at least eight glasses of water a day so that your kidneys are continually flushed out.

Scorpio

Rules: sexual organs, elimination

Appearance

The body types vary, but the eyes are nearly always compelling, intense, piercing. They rarely reveal what they're feeling, and they are masters at disguising their expressions. Their masks are carefully honed through years of hiding their emotions. Many Scorpios have thick eyebrows, sharp noses, seductive mouths. Their voices are often husky and low.

Health and Fitness

As a fixed water sign, you probably benefit from a proximity to water every bit as much as Cancer does. Lake, ocean, river, ocean, pond, salt marsh—take your pick. If none of these is available, put a fountain in your backyard or somewhere in your house and create a meditation area.

It's important that you have a quiet center where you can decompress at the end of the day, particularly if you have a busy family life and a lot of demands on your time.

You tend to keep a lot of emotion locked inside, and if the emotions are negative—resentment, anger—they fester and affect your health. So try to find someone you can talk to freely about your emotions—a partner, friend, family member. Or pour these feelings into a creative outlet. One way or another, get them out.

Scorpio rules the sexual and elimination organs, so these areas could be where ill health hits first. Be sure that you eat plenty of roughage in your diet, and enjoy what you eat while you're eating it. Stay away from the usual culprits—fried or heavily processed foods. You do best with plenty of fresh food, but may want to consider eliminating red meats. Consider colonics treatments for cleaning out the bowels.

For your overall health, it's important to enjoy sex with a partner whom you trust. Avoid using sex as a leverage for power in a relationship.

Sagittarius

Rules: hips, thighs, liver

Appearance

They tend to come in two types: tall and broad through the shoulders, or shorter and heavier. The second description comes from Jupiter, which rules the sign, and causes them to indulge their appetites. They look athletic, have high foreheads that get higher in men as they age and their hair recedes. They move quickly, but not necessarily gracefully.

Health and Fitness

As a mutable fire sign, you can't tolerate any kind of restriction or limitation on your freedom. You must be able to get up and go whenever you want. If you work in a job that demands you punch a time clock, where your hours are strictly regulated, or you are in a relationship where you feel constricted, you probably aren't happy. And for a naturally buoyant and happy person like you, that could spell health challenges. Sadge rules the hips, the sacral region of the spine, the coccygeal vertebrae, the femur, the ileum, the iliac arteries, and the sciatic nerves, so any of these areas could be impacted healthwise.

You benefit from any kind of athletic activity. From competitive sports to an exercise regimen you create, your body craves regular activity. You also benefit from yoga, which keeps your spine and hips flexible.

If you're prone to putting on weight—and even if you're not—strive to minimize sweets and carbs in your diet. The usual recommendations—abundant fresh vegetables and fruits—also apply. If you're the type who eats on the run, you may be eating fast food or heavily processed foods, and you should try to keep that at a minimum or eliminate it altogether. Even though your digestive system is hardy enough to tolerate just about anything, the fast foods and processed foods add carbs and calories.

Antioxidants are beneficial, of course, and these include vitamins C, A, and E. Minerals like zinc and a glucosamine supplement for joints should be included in your diet.

Capricorn

Rules: knees, skin, bones

Appearance

As a cardinal earth sign, these individuals understand the benefits of exercise, and their bodies show it. While they generally aren't muscular—some are, but not as a rule—they look to be in shape. Their bodies are often angular and slender, and their faces, regardless of their age, have a maturity about them.

Health and Fitness

Since you seem to have been born with an innate sense of where you're going—or want to go—it's likely that you take care of yourself. You know the routine as well as anyone—eat right, stay fit, exercise, get enough rest. But there are other components to living long and prospering (to paraphrase Spock). And those are your emotions.

You, like Scorpio, are secretive, although your motives are different. For you, it's a privacy factor more than anything else. You keep your emotions to yourself and may not express what you feel when you feel it. This can create blockages in your body—notably in your joints or knees. It's vital that you learn to vent your emotions, to rid yourself of anger before it has a chance to move inward.

You're focused, ambitious, and patient in the attainment of your goals. But your work—your satisfaction with it—is a primary component in your health. If you feel you've reached a dead end in your career, if you're frustrated more often than you're happy with what you do, it's time to revamp and get out of Dodge. By taking clear, definite steps toward something else, you feel you're more in control of your destiny, and you mitigate the possibility of health challenges.

Since your knees are vulnerable, running is probably not the best form of exercise for you—unless you do it only once or twice a week and engage in some other form of exercise the rest of the time. For a cardio workout that isn't as tough on your knees, try a rowing machine. For general flexibility, there's nothing like yoga!

Aquarius

Rules: ankles, shins, circulatory system

Appearance

Tall and slender or short and round, their body types are as different and varied as they are. But many have deep-set eyes and classic profiles. Many of them move as quickly as Geminis; others move like molasses. Most aren't particularly coordinated, but some are. So it's tough to spot these individuals in a crowd. But as soon as you listen to them for five minutes, they're easier to peg. They talk eloquently about their ideas and ideals, and you'll recognize them by their discussions of alternative foods, alternative fuels, alternative lifestyles, alternative everything.

Health and Fitness

Let's start with the effect of Uranus ruling your sign. It sometimes can set your nerves on edge—too many sounds, too much chaos around you, loud noises deep into the night, the backfiring of cars, the incessant drone of traffic, even a crowd at the local mall. You're sensitive to all of that. It's part of what makes it important for you to have a private space to which you can withdraw—a quiet backyard filled with plants, a room inside your house with an altar for your Wiccan practice filled with scents from candles or incense that soothe your frazzled nerves. Or perhaps a book on tape can shut it all out. But shut it out you must to protect your health.

Because you live so much inside your own head, exercise is definitely beneficial for you. It doesn't have to be anything complicated—yoga done in the privacy of your own home, long walks, regular bike rides. But do something to ground your body, to get your blood moving, to silence the buzz inside your head. It will all benefit your health.

Nutrition? Well, for an Aquarian, this can go any number of different ways. You enjoy different types of food, so that's a place to start—with what you enjoy. The foods are likely to be unusual—organically grown, for instance, prepared in unusual ways, or purchased from a local co-op. If you live in the city, then perhaps you purchase food from a grocery store you've been frequenting for years. The idea here is that you know what's best for your body, what you can tolerate, what you need. Even though Aquarians aren't generally as in touch with their bodies as earth signs, they have an intuitive sense about what works for them. In the end, that's all that matters.

Pisces

Rules: the feet, associated with the lymphatic system

Appearance

Common wisdom in astrology says there are two types of Pisces: the whale and the dolphin. And this goes for the sun, moon, or rising in Pisces. The whale is large, but also tuned in to everything and everyone on the planet. The dolphin is slender, sleek, quick, joyful, graceful. But both body types usually have extraordinary eyes that are not only soulful, but seem to be able to peer through time.

Health and Fitness

Let's start with emotions. Let's start with the fact that you're a psychic sponge, able to absorb other people's moods and thoughts with the ease of a magnet attracting every other piece of metal around it. It's why you should associate only with optimistic, upbeat people. The negative types steal your energy, wreck your immune system, and leave you in a tearful mess at the end of the rainbow with nothing to show for your journey.

Like your fellow water signs Cancer and Scorpio, you

probably benefit from proximity to water. Whether you live near water, work near it, or vacation near it, water refreshes your soul, spirit, intuition, and immune system. Read Masaru Emoto's books on how water responds to emotions and intent. You'll never think about water or your sun sign in the same way again.

You benefit from any kind of exercise, but try something that speaks to your soul. Swimming. Rowing, but in an actual boat, on an actual river instead of in a gym. Even kicking your legs in a hot tub is beneficial. Pay attention to the water you drink. Is your tap water filled with fluorides? Then avoid it, and look for distilled water. Drink at least eight glasses a day. Indulge yourself in massages, foot reflexology, and periodic dips in the ocean.

Meditate. Find the calm center of your storm.

CHAPTER 10

Neptune: Your Visionary Self

Neptune symbolizes all that is veiled, hidden—our personal unconscious, the realm of dreams and psychic visions, spiritual insights and artistic inspiration, flashes of insight, mystical tendencies, imaginations, compassion. On the downside, it represents all forms of escapism—alcoholism, addiction, delusion, deception, illusions, our blind spots. The natural ruler of Pisces, it takes about fourteen years to move through a sign, and roughly 168 years to cross the zodiac.

The sign of your natal Neptune describes your visionary attributes and those of your generation and how these characteristics are most likely to manifest themselves. Anyone born between late November 1984 and late January 1998, for example, has Neptune in Capricorn. This placement suggests that spiritual ideals, artistic achievement, psychic abilities, and everything else ruled by Neptune are expressed in grounded, practical ways. It's not enough for someone with Neptune in Capricorn, who has psychic ability, to just read for others. These people would feel compelled to share their abilities with others, perhaps through writing or public speaking or some other venue.

The house placement describes how Neptune's attributes affect you personally. So if this same individual has Neptune in the tenth house of career, it indicates the person is capable of achieving recognition for a unique achievement. The knowledge or ability that allows the person to do this comes through his or her higher self, as if the information is channeled. Challenges can be overcome by remaining true to his or her dream.

Now turn to appendix 4, locate where your birthday falls, and find your natal Neptune. Then read the description below.

Natal Neptune in Aries

The last time Neptune was in Aries, during the middle of the nineteenth century, the Civil War was raging. The next time it will be in Aries will be from 2025 to 2039. It's unlikely that anyone born during the Civil War is still alive—but if you are, you might want to get in touch with the *Guinness Book of World Records*! So we'll keep these descriptions short and to the point.

This placement for natal Neptune fires up the imagination and enables you to act on psychic impulses. If your psychic ability is highly developed, it's possible for you to explore uncharted territory, perhaps by creating new methods for nurturing and using intuition.

Natal Neptune in Taurus

Neptune was last in Taurus in 1871, and it will transit that sign again from 2039 to 2053. So, again, we'll keep this one short!

With Neptune in fixed earth sign Taurus, imagination, artistic inspiration, and intuitive abilities are given concrete expression. No pie in the sky for you! You bring the most outrageous and creative ideas down to earth. There may be inspirational qualities in how you deal with money.

Natal Neptune in Gemini

Neptune was last in this sign in 1883 and will be there again in 2052. This position brings heightened intuition and an imagination that are channeled through logic and reason—right brain to left brain, in other words. If you maintain a solid center within yourself, you're capable of great focus.

Natal Neptune in Cancer

Between July and December 1901 and from 1902 to 1915, Neptune was in Cancer. It won't be there again until the latter part of the twenty-first century. This placement brings enhanced psychic ability, particularly where family is concerned. You have high ideals about family and home life.

Natal Neptune in Leo

The roaring twenties, the last time Neptune was in Leo, characterize the flamboyance and idealism that accompany this placement. You fight for your ideals and your imagination finds expression in artistic performance. This placement won't happen again until very late in the twenty-first century.

Natal Neptune in Virgo

In September 1928, about a year before the stock market crash that triggered the great depression, Neptune entered Virgo. You carefully analyze spiritual issues and use your imagination to bring difficult concepts and abstract ideas into concrete form. You're after what's practical and useful to others.

Natal Neptune in Libra

Neptune was in Libra between August 1943 and October 1956, so the baby boomers born between 1946 and 1956 all have this placement. It's an idealistic placement—witness the antiwar movement of the 1960s and the rise of alternative living styles. Your imagination and spirituality find expression through beauty and harmony. Just ask any flower child of the sixties!

Natal Neptune in Scorpio

Baby boomers born after October 19, 1956, have this placement, which lasted until early January 1970. Your powerful imagination allows you to explore the depths of esoteric subjects—everything from reincarnation to communication with the dead. You may have unusual ideas about sexual relationships. This placement can suggest drug or alcohol abuse.

Natal Neptune in Sagittarius

Your intuition may be highly developed and allow you to grasp a broad spectrum of spiritual issues. When you travel, you're on a quest for something indefinable—something that will answer your most burning questions. Generationally, this placement can give rise to religious cults.

Natal Neptune in Capricorn

You're part of a generation of individuals who will be rebuilding the society that Pluto in Capricorn has knocked down. You'll be bringing spiritual concepts and ideals into a practical form that benefits all of humanity, not just one segment of the population. On a personal level, try not to be so practical that your imagination is stifled.

Natal Neptune in Aquarius

Spiritual enlightenment is the ideal. You're part of a generation of individuals who can bring about tremendous change and innovation through discoveries and a visionary way of conducting their lives. You have to learn to do this in your own life as well.

Natal Neptune in Pisces

Vivid imaginations, highly developed intuition, tremendous capacity for compassion. You're part of a generation of seers, innovators, and visionaries who will connect to deeper spiritual truths. The risk is to avoid becoming separated from reality and losing yourself in illusion.

CHAPTER 11

The Astrological Community

In recent years, there's been an explosion of astrological sites on the Internet. In fact, if you Google "astrology," more than thirty-six million links show up. Perhaps in uncertain times, people are looking for information and insights through nontraditional sources. Or maybe astrology has gone mainstream.

Astrology sites offer a vast spectrum of services, from free natal charts, daily transits, and monthly horoscopes to political and world predictions. Here are some of the best sites:

www.astro.com: Enter your birth data and obtain a free natal chart. This site is also chock-full of information about astrology. Great for the beginner, the intermediary, and the advanced astrologer. Something for everyone here. There are also some terrific articles by well-known astrologers.

www.astrologyzone.com: Susan Miller's site is a favorite for neophytes and pros alike. Every month, she writes around three thousand words per sign about what you can expect in the upcoming month. Her predictions are eerily accurate!

www.moonvalleyastrologer.com: Celeste Teal is the expert on eclipses, a specialized area of astrology that few have researched the way she has. Her two books on eclipses are seminal works.

www.astrocollege.com: Lois Rodden's site is extraordinary. This woman spent most of her life collecting birth data and then created a piece of software that is invaluable in research. This site also rates and sells astrology software. Lois has passed on, but her work survives.

http://astrofuturetrends.com: Author and astrologer Anthony Louis does just what the site says: predicts future trends, covers political stuff, and provides an overall view of astrology.

www.starlightnews.com: Click on Nancy's blog. Here, you'll find the latest predictions and insights about world affairs. Nancy's predictions about politics have been right on. Before the 2004 election, she made some predictions about tight senatorial races that were totally accurate. She also called the presidential race in 2008. We've been following her closely ever since.

www.astro-yoga.com: This site combines astrology and yoga. We created it and this system of yoga.

www.tjmacgregor.com: Here, you'll find monthly astrological predictions for writers.

www.ofscarabs.blogspot.com: About synchronicities—what they are, how they show up in our lives, what they might mean, and hundreds of stories.

Software

Computers have transformed everything about astrology. In the days before, you had to figure all this stuff by hand, through complicated mathematical formulas that left you gasping.

Our first piece of software was a really simple program we found at some computer store for ten bucks. It erected a chart in about sixty seconds. There it was: rising, moon, sun, planets, the houses, everything set up on the computer screen as if by magic. In the late 1990s, we bought our first really terrific astrology software from Matrix for about three hundred dollars. In the years since, http://www.astrologysoftware.com has supplied us with endless data and information, and revolutionized the study of astrology.

But it's not just enough to have a great piece of software. When your computer crashes, when you receive updates that screw up, when Windows updates to a new system, you call the Matrix help line, and their people walk you through it until everything works. And the employees on their help lines aren't outsourced. You won't reach India. You'll talk to someone in Michigan who is not only an astrologer, but a computer geek who knows how to fix your problem. And if by some fluke they can't fix your problem, they'll credit you for one of their other terrific programs.

The only complaint we have about Matrix is that to activate the software, you have to call or contact them through the Internet to receive a special code. If your computer crashes, if you buy a new PC or laptop—well, it's annoying. When you pay this much for software, you shouldn't have to obtain a special access code.

Another great piece of software is SolarFire. Astrologers are as dedicated to this program as they are to Matrix's software. Check out http://www.alabe.com for current prices. While the two programs offer similar features and capabilities, preferences seem to be individual. Both Matrix's Winstar and astrolabe's SolarFire offer many alternative features—like reports for natal, transit, and progressed interpretations

Kepler's astrology program—http://www.astrosoft ware.com—is beautiful in its rendition of charts, interpretations, and just about anything any astrologer could use or need. We like it for its ease, its beauty. But it's not a Winstar or SolarFire.

If your exploration of astrology takes you deeper, there are other software programs that take you there. Bernadette Brady is the undisputed mistress of fixed stars. Her software program, Starlight, is remarkable not only for its accuracy, but for its presentation. You will never think of fixed stars in the same way once you play with this program. What won't make sense in a natal chart interpretation suddenly snaps into clarity when you use Brady's software. Be sure to download a print to file version for the software—through a pdf—so that you can maximize usage. Their Web site: http://www.zyntara.com.

Lois Rodden's AstroDatabank is the software that Lois Rodden developed. It contains more than thirty thousand birth records, "carefully documented and coded for accuracy with the popular Rodden Rating system. AstroDatabank includes intriguing biographies, revealing personality traits, important life events, and significant relationships." For the curious, the researcher, the neophyte, and the pro alike.

Both Winstar and SolarFire produce computerized report software. These reports are handy for when a friend of a friend is in a fix, and you don't have the time to interpret transits and progressions for the person's birth chart. Winstar also produces software on the tarot and numerology.

Day Watch, another Winstar program, is forecasting software that is invaluable for astrologers. From their site: "Certainly it creates personalized astrological calendars, a great tool for professional astrologers and those who have an understanding of astrological terms, symbols, and technique. But Day Watch also contains a full range of onscreen and printable interpretations of events that even someone with absolutely no astrological training can read, understand, and immediately put to use in their daily lives."

At the beginning of every month, we bring up our personalized calendars, which tell us what is happening daily in our natal charts and also list which planets are changing signs in that month, on what date, and which planets are turning retrograde or direct. Each month includes an ephemeris and lunar charts for the new and full moon. The program also offers various types of reports.

Getting a Reading

So now you're ready for an astrological reading. But where do you start? Which astrologer should you use?

The best way to find an astrologer is through someone who has gotten a reading and recommends the individual. If you don't know anyone who has had an astrological reading, then the next best course is to head over to the nearest bookstore and look through the astrology books. Browse through titles that interest you. Note the author's style. If the author uses a lot of astro jargon or seems to write in a depressing or heavy-handed way, move on. Once you find an author whose book you like, check to see if he or she has a Web site and get in touch with the person.

Rates for a reading vary from one astrologer to another and usually depend on what you want. Would you like just an interpretation of your natal chart? Would you like a forecast for the next six months or a year? Do you want a compatibility chart for you and your partner? Some astrologers prefer to do phone readings, and record the reading. Others prefer to work through e-mail. If the astrologer you've chosen lives close to you, all the better. Have the reading done in person.

What to Expect During a Reading

Every astrological reading begins with your natal chart, so an accurate birth time is essential. It should come from your birth certificate or a parent's memory. An approximate time means the entire reading won't be as accurate.

This reading differs from a daily horoscope you find in a newspaper or on a Web site because it's tailored to your specific chart—rather than just to your sun sign. If you're getting a reading only on your birth chart, the astrologer interprets the entire chart, not just pieces of it. The astrologer looks at the signs and house placements of the various planets and the angles the planets make to one another.

Take a look at the sample chart at the end of this chapter. It's the natal chart for a young woman whose sun and moon are in Virgo in the sixth house—08⊙♍33 and ☽17♍09. Her rising sign is Pisces at 19 degrees and 39 minutes—19 ♓39. You'll find it to the left of the horizontal line between houses one and twelve. Also in her sixth house are Mars in Virgo—18♂♍03—and the south node of the moon in Leo—25☋♌50.

As astrologers, we would pay close attention to this woman's sixth house because it holds three planets and her south node and would talk about her Pisces rising. We would also go to the opposite house, the twelfth, and talk about this woman's north node in Aquarius and the part of fortune in Pisces, both in the twelfth house. Then our focus would go to the other clusters on planets in her seventh and tenth houses. Our interpretation would also include an interpretation of Jupiter, the ruler of the chart because it rules Pisces and she has that sign rising. Jupiter 05♃♋52 is the lone planet in the young woman's fourth house. And what about Pluto 12♀♏48—in her eighth house? That certainly has to be taken into account.

The next thing we might discuss would be the phase of the moon under which she was born—a new-moon baby, born within twenty-four hours of a solar eclipse. Then we would move on to the aspects—the angles the planets in her chart make to one another. Notice the boxes to the lower left of the chart. It's called an aspect grid, and it's where you can see the aspects at a glance. Let's talk a little about these.

Aspects

Think of aspects as a symbolic network of arteries and veins that transport the blood of the chart. They connect our inner and outer worlds, accentuate certain traits and play down others. Each aspect represents a certain type of energy, so there really aren't any good or bad aspects because energy is neutral. It's what we do with the energy that counts. It comes back to free will.

Look at the young woman's chart again. In the tenth house, Saturn in Capricorn 07♄♑23 and Neptune in Capricorn 09♆♑43 are considered to be conjunct, within about two degrees. A conjunction is 00 degrees of separation, but can be as wide as 5 or 10 degrees, depending on the chart and which astrologer is doing the interpretation. The degree of separation is called an orb. Some astrologers use small orbs, but others assign larger orbs for the sun and moon and smaller orbs for other planets. The closer the orb, the more powerful the combination.

So we might say that Uranus 01♅♑22 in Capricorn is conjunct with both Saturn and Neptune. In a moment, we'll get to what a conjunction and the other aspects mean.

The traditional aspects have been used since the second century A.D. They are the conjunction, sextile, square, trine, and opposition. These aspects are considered to be the major or hard angles, and are also the most powerful. There are other minor aspects that astrologers use, but for the purpose of this chapter, we'll only talk about the traditional aspects.

Conjunction, Major Hard Aspect, 0 Degrees

This aspect is easy to identify—clusters of planets within a few degrees of each other, usually but not always in the same sign and house. But it's a complex aspect because energies combine, fuse, merge. Think of it as power, intensity. So if you have conjunctions in your natal chart, the astrologer who reads for you should address what it means, how you can use it to maximize your potential.

Let's go back to the young woman's chart. With her Saturn and Neptune conjunct in her tenth house of career, there's already a tension and power in her chart. Saturn builds structures and boundaries and seeks to hold back, restrict. It's about rules and responsibilities. Neptune urges us to allow boundaries to dissolve, to release the ego, to reach for higher ideals. So this woman will confront these dualities in her career—her tenth house.

With Uranus thrown into the mix, these experiences and dualities will come at her out of the blue, suddenly and without warning. Her career will be unusual, strange, filled with idiosyncratic people and defined by strange experiences—the Uranus influence. Uranus shakes up the status quo, and when it's conjunct Saturn—even widely, by 7 degrees in this case—she will feel conflicted at times about which path to follow, which choices to make.

In this same chart, notice the close conjunction between the moon and Mars in the sixth house. One degree of separation. One possible repercussion is that her emotions are especially intense, even volatile at times, when it comes to her work routine and the maintenance of her health. Her health stuff may occur in fits and starts—one week she'll run two miles a day, the next week she's a couch potato, and the next week, she meditates and practices yoga. It's the same way with her work. Erratic, moved by the spirit and passion of the moment. But because Mars is in Virgo, she's diligent, a hard worker at whatever she takes on.

Since Mars is within a degree of the seventh-house cusp, this passion she has spills over into her personal and business partnerships.

Sextile, Major Soft Aspect, 60 Degrees

Again, look at the young woman's chart. An example of a sextile occurs between her sun at 8 degrees Virgo in her sixth house and her Jupiter at 5 degrees Cancer in her fourth house. The orb, according to the aspect grid, is 2 degrees and 41 minutes. Close enough to have significant impact.

A sextile is a point of ease. It represents a free-flowing energy between the planets involved. No tension. The sextile is a kind of buffer, a shield against turmoil, indecision, instability. But if there are too many sextiles, the person may be too passive!

In the young woman's chart, her Pluto in Scorpio in the eighth house—12♀♏49—is closely sextile her Neptune in the tenth, within 5 degrees of her Saturn in the tenth, within a 6-degree orb of her Virgo Mars in the sixth, and with 5 degrees of her Virgo Moon in the sixth. That's a whole lot of energy stacked in her favor, which suggests that whatever she does on a daily basis with her work somehow feeds into the larger picture of her career. During her college years, she was able to manifest jobs out of thin air—while in school and during the summers.

When she was in high school, for instance, she and her parents vacationed in the Caribbean and South America so they could enjoy windsurfing spots because her dad is a windsurfer. So she learned to windsurf and became so proficient at it that she was able to teach windsurfing at her college, through the sailing club, to any students who were interested. The college paid her ten bucks an hour. Gas money! Food money!

From the time she was old enough to walk, she enjoyed horseback riding and loved working with horses, being around them. She lived near an equestrian community, so becoming a barn rat was not a tough thing to do. During the summer of her freshman year, with her parents breathing down her back about getting a job, she manifested a job teaching riding at an equestrian summer camp.

These examples are precisely the kinds of experiences that accompany the sextiles in her chart. That Pluto in Scorpio—a sign that planet rules—gives her enormous power and ability to home in on what she needs and wants and make it happen.

Square, Major Hard Aspect, 90 Degrees

Friction, angst—that's how squares feel in a natal chart. The sky, of course, is never falling, but the friction and angst are quite real and act as triggers for action, forward thrust. They force us to develop, evolve, and reach aggressively for our desires.

How does this play out in real life? Look at the young woman's chart. She has three squares to her natal Mercury in Libra, in her seventh house of partnerships, all of them from that cluster of planets in her tenth house of career. Her natal Mercury—05♀♎33—is square to those tenth house planets from between 2 to 4 degrees. Ouch. The need to achieve something professionally is very strong. But it's not just about achieving. She wants to make her mark on the world, to leave something behind, some sort of legacy, something unique that bears her stamp. And because Mercury rules communication and this young woman enjoys writing and is good at it, that could be one of her signatures.

Mercury is also square her Jupiter in Cancer in the fourth house, suggesting that she may try to take on too much—in her writing, her life, her partnerships. Hit the pause button, breathe, ask for guidance through imagination, visualization, your family (fourth house), and your dreams.

Squares spur us to action.

Trines, Major Soft Aspect, 120 Degrees

This aspect works like a sextile, linking energies in a harmonious way. It's associated with general ease and good fortune. Again, though, if there are too many in the chart, passivity may result.

Look at the chart again. The young woman's 8 degree Virgo sun in her sixth house is closely trine to both Neptune and Saturn in Capricorn. The Saturn-Sun trine enables the young woman to set realistic goals and to attain them. The Neptune-Sun trine gives her deep compassion, psychic and artistic ability. She's able to attract the right opportunities for her career. The trine to Uranus is a bit wider—7 degrees—but is still significant. It suggests that her profession is or will be unusual and that her freedom is important to her. It's doubtful this young woman will be found in an office, confined to a nine-to-five job. Whatever she does is likely to be unique.

Opposition, Major Hard Aspect, 180 Degrees

This aspect feels like a persistent itch that you can't reach and usually involves polarities—Taurus-Scorpio, for example, or Aries-Libra. It brings about change through conflict and sometimes represents traits we project onto others because we haven't fully integrated them into ourselves.

In the woman's chart, her natal Jupiter in Cancer is opposed to all three planets in her tenth house. Jupiter expands everything it touches, so with Saturn, the woman's professional success comes about through persistence and dedication and by working with her beliefs in a constructive, positive way. With her Jupiter opposed to Uranus, the freedom to call her own shots, make her own schedule, to do her own thing, is paramount. In a chart that lacks direction and focus, this aspect can lead to involvement with revolutionary groups or religious cults. In a strong chart like this one, however, the Uranus-Jupiter opposition can indicate involvement in humanitarian efforts. The Neptune-Jupiter opposition can indicate utopian ideals, getting suckered by a sob story or trusting smooth talkers with a devious agenda. But it can also lead to great spiritual awareness and enhanced psychic ability.

Some other minor aspects that astrologers use are:

- the semisquare, 45 degrees. It creates irritation and friction between the planets involved.
- the septile, 51 degrees. Indicative of harmony and union in a nontraditional way. Can suggest spiritual power.
- the quincunx or inconjunct, 150 degrees separation. Indicates a need for adjustment in attitude and beliefs.

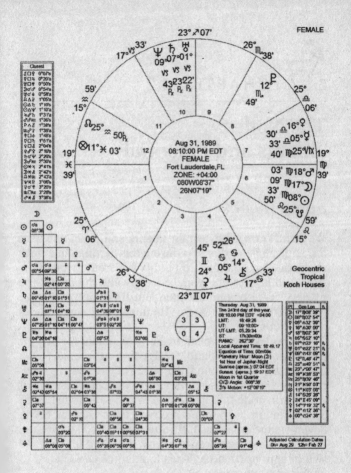

FEMALE

Aug 31, 1989
08:10:00 PM EDT
FEMALE
Fort Lauderdale, FL
ZONE: +04:00
080W08'37"
26N07'19"

Geocentric
Tropical
Koch Houses

Thursday Aug 31, 1989
The 243rd day of the year.
08:10:00 PM EDT +04:00
LMT: 18:49:26
UT: 00:10:00>
UT-LMT: 05:20:34
ST: 17h30m00s
RAMC: 262°30'
Local Apparent Time: 18:49.17
Equation of Time: 00m06s
Planetary Hour: Moon (☽)
1st Hour of Jupiter-Night
Sunrise (approx.): 07:04 EDT
Sunset (approx.): 19:37 EDT
Moon in 1st Quarter
☉/☽ Angle: 008°38'
☽'s Motion: +12°06'19"

Adjusted Calculation Dates
Dir= Aug 29 12h= Feb 27

139

CHAPTER 12

The Nodes: Talents and Potential

Some Basics

We're all born with certain talents and potentials that our souls hope to develop during this lifetime. In a birth chart, these potentials are readily apparent through the signs and houses the planets occupy and the angles the planets make to one another. But there are two other points astrologers look for: the north and south nodes of the moon.

The nodes aren't planets. They're points formed by the moon's orbit around the Earth that intersect with the Earth's path around the sun. They're always separated by 180 degrees, so they form an axis of energy. If your north node falls in Gemini, your south node falls in Sagittarius, the sign that is six away from Gemini. If you haven't done so already, turn to appendix 5, locate the time span that includes your birth date, and find out the sign of your north node. Then look at the table below to find your south node.

The south node represents our comfort zone, the accumulation of characteristics, attitudes, and talents that we bring into this life from other lives or—if you don't believe in reincarnation—that are laid down early in childhood. We retreat to our south node when we're hurt, feel sick or threatened, or perhaps in a new relationship and aren't sure yet where things are going. The south node is the psychological equivalent of comfort food.

The north node symbolizes the direction we should move in this life to fulfill our talents and potential and to evolve spiritually. It represents the soul's agenda this time around.

LUNAR NODES

If your north node is in	*your south node is in*
Aries	Libra
Taurus	Scorpio
Gemini	Sagittarius
Cancer	Capricorn
Leo	Aquarius
Virgo	Pisces

The sign of your north node describes the types of experiences you should strive for in this life. It can also describe the psychological bent, potential, and talents that you should try to develop, to reach for, in order to achieve your potential. The sign of the south node describes all of the above—but from previous lives.

The house placement of your south node describes the area that is your comfort zone. The house placement of your north node describes the area where your greatest potential and talent can be achieved.

Turn back to the chart in chapter 11. Notice that the woman's south node in Leo ☋25♌50 falls in her sixth house of daily work and health. Her north node in Aquarius ☊25♒50 falls in her twelfth house. These signs suggest that to achieve her potential, it's necessary to detach from her emotions and understand why she feels she must be on center stage all the time. She might do this through humanitarian work of some kind, working with groups to achieve a common goal, spreading her ideas to the masses.

She feels most comfortable when she's in the spotlight,

and she's such a warm, caring person that she's a people magnet (south node in Leo). The house placement of her south node suggests that she feels most comfortable in her daily life when others are recognizing her for her achievements. But the path to achievement for her lies in inner exploration, where she's required to dive into her unconscious and make sense of it, perhaps through some creative endeavor or through humanitarian work.

Nodes Through the Signs

Aries North Node

Your comfort zone lies in the embrace of others. You're at ease in most relationships, and you seek balance in everything you do. Sometimes, your need for balance is so great that you bend over backward to accommodate others and end up compromising your own values. That's your comfort zone—Libra south node—speaking.

It's your south node that constantly sends you off in search of the perfect partner, the elusive soul mate. But you probably won't find the ideal partner until you know who you are and what you believe separate from your parents, family, authority figures, and anyone else who seeks to define you. That's where your Aries north node comes in.

This node is about you—your independence rather than your codependence, about following your impulses, passions, and hunches rather than pressing the pause button on all that and doing something to please someone else. You're here this time to develop independence in thought, action, words, deeds. You're here to define your values according to who you are rather than through group consensus. Don't hesitate to take risks. Live like the *Star Trek* motto: boldly going where no man (or woman) has gone before.

Easier said than done because it begins with solitude, a state of being that is foreign to you. In fact, as you begin to carve time for yourself, your Libra south node may throw a major tantrum and urge you to get out and about, to hurry to that party, that get-together, that crowd of friends and strangers so that you can work the room. Resist those temptations, regardless of the comfort they promise. Ignore the criticisms of others—a difficult challenge because Libra south node can't abide disapproval. The moment it detects disapproval, it causes you to run around apologizing to everyone.

While your Libra south node seeks to smooth things over with family, friends, coworkers, and everyone else who disapproves, your Aries north node coaxes you to continue following impulses and forging your own path. It urges you to take off at a moment's notice with just a backpack and your ATM card and head for parts unknown. It demands that you become an individual separate from the collectives called family, relationships, the community. It pushes you beyond consensus reality to test the limits of your soul. Once you're able to do that, you can successfully draw on your Libra south node for harmony and balance.

Examples: Ram Dass, Jay Leno, Neil Armstrong

Taurus North Node

With this fixed earth-sign node, your mission this time around is to define your values and realize your potential through everything the physical universe has to offer. It's a magnificent banquet of sensual delights, glittering beauty, unimagined riches. Your playground is physical reality, and you're supposed to build something meaningful and lasting while you're here. You're supposed to do it patiently, with resilience to any obstacles in your way.

But your Scorpio south node resists. It demands that you merge with whatever you're doing, that you become the project, the relationship, the ideal, and that you control it. It urges you to work privately, in secrecy, never letting on what your real agenda is. Your south node investigates, researches, digs for answers and truth, and does it with a kind of terrible impatience and intensity. Your north node asks that you take some things on faith and trust and allow events to unfold naturally, organically.

The Scorpio south node suggests that in past lives, you've dealt with crises, calamities, excessive sexuality, suspicion, deceit, profound transformation. This time around, one of your callings is to find the calm center of the storm. While everything is collapsing around you, while people you care for are losing their minds and swept up in high drama, you are as still and centered as Buddha.

To achieve this, of course, requires practice. Start meditating. Have an exercise routine that grounds you completely in physical reality. Yoga, running, swimming, tai chi, biking, the gym—do anything that heightens your awareness of your physical body. And be selfish. Yes, that last part sounds strange because we're taught from a young age to practice the opposite. But for the Taurus north node, selfishness is self-empowerment. It means you put your own needs and desires first. You're a survivor. Once you do that, you won't feel the need to manipulate and control others.

The sensuality part of the Taurus north node can be troublesome because all too often, you're working from the raw sexuality of your Scorpio south node. Try to balance your sensuality. Instead of leaping into sexual relationships, ease yourself into sensual relationships. Experiment. Follow your passions in areas other than sex. Otherwise, the seductiveness of the Scorpio south node takes you into the really dark places—excessive sex, drugs, eating, spending, booze. Kurt Cobain, heroin addict and suicide, is the dark example of this nodal axis. Jacques Cousteau, underwater explorer, and J. R. R. Tolkien, author and creator of the Hobbit world, are more evolved examples. They built legacies, and touched the lives of millions.

Other examples: Greg Allman, Lucille Ball, Pearl Buck, Harry Houdini

Gemini North Node

It is as if you're searching for a unified theory of the universe. Why, why, why? Your insatiable curiosity urges you to gather information to answer these burning questions and then to disseminate what you learn in any way you can, through many venues simultaneously. That's why you're here this time around. And as one of the two signs symbolized by two of something, you multitask with ease.

Your Sagittarius south node practically guarantees that you have a worldview or belief system that serves as a solid foundation in your life. It enables you to take in other people's belief systems and to compare and contrast them with your own. But when you're deep inside this comfort zone, you may think your belief system is the only truth. You may grow intolerant of other people's spiritual and political beliefs and become a self-righteous stick-in-the-mud.

It's likely that someone in your immediate circle of family and friends holds a belief system radically opposed to yours—friend, partner, relative, neighbor, coworker. This opposition probably leads to heated discussions and arguments. You're intent on convincing the other person that you're right, but this only creates further dissent. Instead, look at this person as your teacher. What can you learn from him or her? Listen with an open mind and really listen. All too often, you're so intent on what you're going to say next that you're deaf to what the other person is saying.

Once you're aware of this pattern within yourself, you can catch yourself before it happens. Maintain your curiosity. It's one of your most valuable resources. When someone says something that pushes your buttons, ask yourself why you feel the way you do. Resistance is usually a clue to something within yourself that you should explore and strive to understand.

Always believe in yourself. Yes, this can be challenging for a Gemini north node person. The twins that symbolize Gemini indicate duality in your personality. One twin urges you to reach for the seemingly impossible and the other twin is laughing into her hands, snickering. The best way to reconcile this duality is to develop a firm certainty about your talents that gets you through both good times and bad.

Examples: Susan Sarandon, Deepak Chopra, Bill Clinton

Cancer North Node

You're here to navigate the world of your emotions and intuition, to learn to nurture others as you have nurtured yourself in past lives. You need to discover what makes you feel emotionally secure and to establish that security in your life in order to achieve your potential.

Your Capricorn south node brings clear goals and ambitions. But because work, goals, and ambition are your comfort zone, you may feel you have to control everything and everyone within your environment. You have a heightened sense of responsibility and believe that you must assume all the responsibility—at work, at home, with your family. Your desire to achieve and be recognized for those achievements suggests that you work extremely hard. But since these traits come from your south node, you may not make significant progress until you're living from a centered, emotionally secure place.

If you can stay in tune with your emotions, they will act as an infallible guide. When a negative emotion surfaces, don't just shove it aside, but don't obsess about it either. Take note of it and then release it and let it flow on out of you. In the same way, you should release your need for control. Control of others is an illusion fostered by your south node. The only person you can control is yourself—your own thoughts, actions, and choices, and your home and personal environments. You can't control what others think and do or believe.

The Cancer-Capricorn axis is about how we live our private and public lives. Home and family versus career and profession, right brain versus left brain, the inner world versus the outer world. The Cancer north node urges you to open your heart, to listen to the whispers of your intuition, to lower your defenses. As a cardinal water sign, this node also urges you to explore the unknown.

Examples: Elisabeth Kübler-Ross, Erma Bombeck, Daphne du Maurier

Leo North Node

Baby, let the good times roll! You're here this time around to explore all forms of creative expression. You're supposed to learn what you love, what you truly desire, to have fun and be happy, and how to manifest all of it. Along the way, you're also supposed to learn how to give and receive unconditional love. Sounds like a Disney movie, right?

Thanks to your Aquarius south node, you're tolerant of people who are different from you, understand group dynamics, believe that we're all created equal. Your comfort zone is the world of ideas, the mind, the intellect. In fact, you may be more comfortable with ideas than you are with people or more comfortable putting the group before the individual, friends before partner and family. But your Leo north node urges you to reach beyond ideas, beyond the group, to plumb the depths of your creativity and express yourself as an individual.

To navigate your Leo north node successfully, here are some essentials:

- Nurture your creativity on a daily basis—not just whenever the spirit moves you. Once you learn to do this out of sheer enjoyment, your heart opens wide, and you start to realize that it's okay to be recognized for your achievements. It's okay to stand out from the group, to step into the limelight and announce who you are.
- Ignore peer pressure. Whether this is difficult or easy depends on your age and the type of work you do.
- Create your life consciously. This requires awareness of your internal patterns. If you dislike some of the patterns you find, reshape them or break them altogether.
- Don't depend on others to make you happy. Whenever you find yourself doing this, break the habit by making a conscious decision to create your own joy. Then go do exactly that.

The beauty of the Leo north node is that it is about you—as an individual separate from any collective, any tribe. Love yourself first so that you're whole enough to love others.

Virgo North Node

You're the Swiss watchmaker immersed in the details of creating the best watch in the world. All those intricate levers, the beveled glass face, the tiny little hands. Somehow, you bring all these parts together and do it with utter perfection. Now apply the watchmaker analogy to your life. Somehow, you're supposed to bring all these disparate bits and pieces together, analyze your experiences, and then manifest your beliefs and ideals in a practical way. The heart of your journey is self-perfection.

Your Pisces south node offers some of the tools you need—a deep compassion, magnificent imagination, and excellent intuition and healing ability. But when your inner critic is screaming and you retreat into your Pisces south node out of fear, it's easy to become trapped in a victim consciousness. You know the routine—you're not good enough, not quite up to the task, there are others more qualified, and so on. First, silence the inner critic and resolve not to quit. Once you do that, the rest becomes easier.

When you feel that coiled serpent of fear in the pit of your stomach, tackle it. When you feel unable to make a decision, take a few deep breaths, and try to explore your resistance. Don't obsess about the fear or tear it apart, scrutinizing every bit of it. Just acknowledge it and try to move through it.

Share your knowledge and skills with others, without thought of compensation, but do so only because you want to, not because you feel obligated. By performing a service out of compassion rather than obligation, you mitigate the risk of victim consciousness.

Remain in the moment. Or, as Ram Dass said, "Be here now." If you are fully rooted in the moment, fear can't choke you. Read Eckhart Tolle's *The Power of Now*. By doing this, you also mitigate self-criticism. Anytime you find yourself falling into this frame of mind, tell yourself that you're perfect as you are.

Your Virgo north node urges you to navigate your daily life with reason, logic, and attention to detail. Once you're able to do this, you can draw on the south node's power of imagination and intuition and manifest virtually anything you desire.

Examples: Harrison Ford, Michael J. Fox, Kurt Vonnegut Jr.

Libra North Node

Relationships. Cooperation. Balance. That's what this lifetime is about. Specifically, you're here to learn how to balance your needs with those of your partner, kids, friends, parents, and just about everyone else. And you do it by walking in the other person's shoes.

Your comfort zone, of course, is the exact opposite of everything in the first paragraph. When you're afraid or uncertain, hurt or not feeling well, you retreat into an independent, "I can do it myself" frame of mind. You become selfish, intolerant of people who are different from you, and you aren't open to any kind of compromise.

This me-first attitude can be tough to overcome. But a good first step is to put others first. Yes, balk all you want, but it's the perfect place to start. Try it in small increments at first. Perhaps your partner needs the car at the same time that you're scheduled to have lunch with someone. Instead of insisting that you should get the car, make other arrangements. Or, once a week or once a month, put someone else before yourself—let someone else go before you in the grocery line, at the theater, the gas station. When you start doing this on a regular basis, you're moving along the path of your north node.

The Aries south node prompts you to act decisively, impulsively, rashly because you assume that you know what's going on, that you've got the right information, the right answers, and it advertently hurts someone. Better to pace yourself, to ask questions, to interact with people around you, and to gather the information you need. Use tact and diplomacy rather than the blunt force of words and actions.

Once you're able to embrace the art of relating to others, you can successfully draw on the independence and fearlessness of your Aries south node.

Examples: Madonna, Frédéric Chopin, Anaïs Nin

Scorpio North Node

You're here to learn about using personal power and magnetism in a positive, constructive way. Through intense experiences, you learn to purge your life of the nonessential or of whatever is stagnant in any area—relationships, jobs, careers, belief systems, habits. Then you can draw on your Taurus south node to build what is durable, lasting.

You've got plenty of help on this journey. Your south node gives you ample physical energy, practicality, and a stubborn determination that can see you through anything. Your Taurus south node urges you to collect things—old books, stamps, art, or jewelry, and it whispers, "I want to be surrounded by comfort and beauty." But when you become obsessively attached to these possessions, to comfort and beauty for their own sake, you may attract a situation that teaches you possessions are just stuff we own.

Your work ethic is stellar. But you make some things harder than they need to be. That's when you know you're being resistant to change. And yet change is part of what you're here to learn.

When change knocks at your door, invite it in for coffee and a chat. If you can't learn to do that, circumstances will force change, and it will be something profoundly transformative and probably not pleasant. Again, take small steps. Once a week, do something you've never done before. If you're terrified of heights, try something as dramatic as skydiving or as small as walking to the end of a high diving board.

Empower others by supporting their creative endeavors, spiritual values, raises and promotions, or anything else that is important to them. Use your exceptional intuition to gain insight into others. Who are they in the privacy of their own hearts? What are their dreams, motives, and hopes? Use your intuition as often as you can. It's like a muscle. The more you use it, the stronger it becomes.

When you feel fear that threatens to send you scampering back to your comfort zone—to the nearest mall to shop or to the comfort of rich foods, booze, drugs, the entire physical spectrum of sensual delights—stop. Breathe. And then investigate. What are you afraid of? Has it happened yet? Or are you afraid of something that may happen? Once you become aware of the pattern, you can break it, and when you break it, you're truly advancing along the path of your Scorpio north node.

Examples: Tiger Woods, Edgar Allan Poe, Francis Ford Coppola

Sagittarius North Node

Well, you're here for one thing: to find and define your own truth. Sounds like a mighty big ticket. But you do this by using your intuitive ability to grasp the big picture rather than collecting endless disconnected facts. The emphasis for you in this lifetime is on right brain, intuition, and imagination rather than on logic and reason.

Your comfort zone—the Gemini south node—is about information, facts, and figures. You can talk to anyone about anything. You have terrific communication skills, and you are one of the most social creatures in the zodiac. But when you feel threatened and afraid, you retreat into the darker aspects of your south node— you talk when you should be listening, second-guess what people are thinking and feeling, make up facts, and change rules in the middle of the game.

To use your north-node energy successfully, learn to trust yourself. Trust that inner voice of your intuition rather than the voices of everyone you consult before you make a decision. And strive to be more spontaneous. By allowing yourself freedom to take off at a moment's notice for an exotic port, to call in sick to work so you can attend your kid's play at school, to run off and get married in Vegas—well, it's part and parcel of the Sadge north node. Honor it! Spontaneity is the manifestation of your intuition.

Strive to be more patient. Your Gemini south node won't want to hear about it, but patience leads you to realize there are no quick fixes, and what's the big rush, anyway?

Your north node urges you to explore the unknown, to delve into spiritual, political, and metaphysical issues that people around you may not want to discuss. Just resist the temptation for self-righteousness and go about your business. This journey doesn't belong to anyone else. It's yours.

Examples: Drew Barrymore, Colin Powell, Zelda Fitzgerald, Angelina Jolie

Capricorn North Node

Setting goals, achieving them, taking charge, controlling your own destiny. That's it in a nutshell. That's why you're here this time around. Already, your Cancer south node is sobbing in a corner for that orphan on the news tonight, for the starving animals roaming the ruins of the latest disaster, for the latest genocide somewhere. She doesn't want to hear about your ambitions, about you taking charge, about you controlling your destiny. So she pouts, she plunges you into a depression, and here you sit, worrying yourself into a frenzy about stuff that hasn't even happened yet.

Let's back up. Your Cancer south node offers plenty of tools for your journey—intuition and compassion, a sense of personal history, deep emotions that are your gauge to what's really going on in your life. Your south node knows how to comfort anyone and anything in need. This includes strays—cats, dogs, birds, whatever finds its way to your doorstep. The problem arises when you nurture and heal at the expense of your own needs or when you nurture others without first nurturing yourself. That's when your south node becomes an impediment to achieving your potential.

Your Capricorn north node urges you to reach for everything you want and to achieve your potential through careful planning, strategizing, and hard work. But your Cancer south node keeps hurling up images of your past mistakes, the issues you dealt with in childhood, how your family might object to what you're doing. And you stop in your tracks, suddenly paralyzed and filled with doubt.

So your first order of business is to release the past. The present is your point of power. The present is the place from which you write the script of your life. Honor the past, certainly, but recognize that your childhood, your parents, and the bully in the sixth grade have no say over your life now.

Your second order of business—and imagine this as a PowerPoint presentation—is to stay tuned in to your feelings. Yet don't use your emotions to manipulate or control others. When you feel negative, don't dwell on it. Let the negativity wash through you, put one foot in front of the other, and move forward again. Third point? Always express what you feel when you feel it. Don't keep it all bottled up inside, as your south node would like. Let it all out. Not only will you feel better—you'll be advancing on the path of your north node.

And, by the way, you are in illustrious company! Examples: Indira Gandhi, Robert Redford, Oprah Winfrey

Aquarius North Node

Your whole thing now, in this lifetime, is to learn about the importance of groups. Whether it's your family group, your community, a social circle, a political or spiritual movement, or some massive humanitarian effort that impacts the family of man, you're supposed to learn you can't always be the center of attention.

Your Leo south node won't be happy about this development. It basks in applause and recognition. Yet your south node also confers a terrific personality, great warmth and magnetism, and such radiant joy for life that if you can direct those qualities toward something larger than yourself, you will succeed at everything you do.

Your ego is well developed, thanks in large part to your Leo south node. But ego alone won't do the job this time around. You're called upon to reach beyond the self, to extend yourself into the larger world, into the family of man, where you can make a tremendous difference, an integral component in a paradigm shift. You may do this through any number of creative venues, through your career, through volunteering, through your family life or the way you earn your living. But there are some definite steps you can take toward embracing your north node and foremost among them is to minimize drama.

Your south node is all about drama—in temperament, relationships, activities, in every single phase and area of your life, there may be drama that your south node stirs up. So strip away the drama, and what do you have? Someone with great talents and potential who can achieve that potential through shifting focus from self to the group.

Use your Leo south node to cultivate and nurture your creative passions. If you can pour your emotions into a creative outlet, especially one that brings insights and pleasures to a larger group, you're well on your journey into your north node.

Examples: Leonard Cohen, F. Scott Fitzgerald

Pisces North Node

Ignore everything that is said about you. That's directive number one. Second directive? Your agenda in this lifetime is about discovering the larger spiritual and creative picture that governs your life. It's about unearthing everything that is hidden in your life—power you have disowned, secrets that are kept in family vaults, in genealogy books, in the deepest reservoirs of your DNA. Your life is about bringing all this stuff into the light of day.

Your Virgo south node brings a lot to the table for this journey—a discriminating intellect, a penchant for details, a remarkable ability to connect the dots in any situation, event, crisis, relationship. You name it, and the Virgo south node grasps how all the connections are made. Your south node is terrific in any situation where rapid solutions are needed, where connections must be made at the speed of light, and where everything—all the information and details—is correct.

But, correct aside, this is the life where you go with the flow, avoid self-criticism, trust the universe to deliver what you need and desire, and develop your spiritual beliefs. All of this can be done through your work, but in terms of the big picture, the larger canvas of possibilities, the forest as opposed to the trees. Maybe you blog about your experiences. Maybe you set up a Web site that sells a particular product or service that helps others to reach their highest potential. The bottom line about the Pisces north node is, ultimately, unknown and unknowable, too mystical to penetrate unless it's your conscious path, and too complex to decipher unless your intuitive skills are remarkably developed.

But remember this: When your Virgo south node slaps its ruler across your desk in ninth grade and demands that you memorize how to conjugate the infinitive "to be" in Latin, Spanish, French, and German, it's your Pisces north node that hurls your arm upward, knocking that ruler away, and says, "Chill. I'm on my own path to enlightenment."

Examples: Matt Damon, Naomi Campbell, Isadora Duncan

CHAPTER 13

The Meaning of Numbers

Even though this is an astrology book, we use numbers in some of the daily predictions because we're attempting to remain true to what Sydney Omarr did. The legendary astrologer was also a numerologist who combined the two forms in his work. So let's take a closer look at how the numbers work.

If you're familiar with numerology, you probably know your life-path number, which is derived from your birth date. That number represents who you were at birth and the traits that you'll carry throughout your life. There are numerous books and Web sites that provide details on what the numbers regarding your life path mean.

But in the daily predictions, what does it mean when it's a number 9 day, and how did it get to be that number? In the dailies, you'll usually find these numbers on the days when the moon is transiting from one sign to another. The system is simple: Add the numbers related to the astrological sign (1 for Aries, 2 for Taurus, etc.), the year, the month, and the day.

For example, to find what number June 14, 2011, is for a Libra, you would start with 7, the number for Libra, add 4 (the number you get when you add 2011 together), plus 6 for June, plus 5 (1+4) for the day. That would be 7+4+6+5 (sign+year+month+day)=22=4. So June 14, 2011, is a number 4 day for a Libra. It would be a number 5 day for a Scorpio, the sign following Libra. So on that number 4 day, Libra might be advised that her organizational skills are highlighted, that she should stay focused, get organized, be methodical and thorough. She's building a creative future. Tear down the old in order to rebuild. Keep your goals in mind, and follow your ideas.

Briefly, here are the meanings of the numbers, which are included in more detail in the dailies themselves.

1. Taking the lead, getting a fresh start, a new beginning
2. Cooperation, partnership, a new relationship, sensitivity
3. Harmony, beauty, pleasures of life, warm, receptive
4. Getting organized, hard work, being methodical, rebuilding, fulfilling your obligations
5. Freedom of thought and action, change, variety, thinking outside the box
6. A service day, being diplomatic, generous, tolerant, sympathetic
7. Mystery, secrets, investigations, research, detecting deception, exploration of the unknown, of the spiritual realms
8. Your power day, financial success, unexpected money, a windfall
9. Finishing a project, looking beyond the immediate, setting your goals, reflection, expansion

Simple, right?

CHAPTER 14

Best Times for Love and Romance for Capricorn in 2011

Moons to Watch

If the positive events in our lives are a combination of luck, beliefs, and timing, then it's to your advantage to initiate action when the astrological timing favors it. So let's take a closer look at the timing for love and romance in 2011.

Whether you're involved or single, Capricorn, the solar eclipse in your sign on January 4 may usher in a whole new chapter in your life. Four out of ten planets are in your sign, and Venus in Scorpio forms a harmonious angle to Mars in Capricorn, suggesting that a relationship heats up big-time. If you're not involved at this time, you may be shortly. Another interesting aspect to this eclipse is that both Jupiter and Uranus form beneficial angles to it and to that passionate Venus in Scorpio. So, you can expect events to happen quickly, out of the blue, and the best thing you can do is to be ready for it all! What a terrific way to start the New Year. But it gets even better.

On May 3, the new moon in Taurus and the romance area of your chart should be incredibly enjoyable. This new moon ushers in opportunities for new romantic relationships and should be one of the best periods for you all year. Pluto forms a beneficial angle to this new moon, suggesting that power issues may be part of the equation, but you're in the driver's seat, calling the shots. Go for it! Whether you're interested in romance with all the bells and whistles, a sexual affair, or commitment, it's yours to direct.

In an existing relationship, this new moon should bring you and your partner closer together. You may decide to embark on some sort of joint creative venture, which would be a perfect expression of where you are now in the relationship.

The full moon in your sign on July 15 brings personal news that could throw you somewhat off balance but not for long. You're able to compartmentalize your emotions quite adeptly, which enables you to function well even when your mood is dark!

August 28 features a new moon in fellow earth sign Virgo, another date to circle. New opportunities in romance with people whose belief systems or spirituality is different from yours. If you're traveling overseas at this time, it's possible that you meet someone in the most unlikely place—at Stonehenge, at Machu Picchu, on a train bound for Holland. No telling. Keep your options open.

This year, you have two new moons to celebrate— the first one is the solar eclipse on January 4, and the second falls on December 24, Christmas Eve. Jupiter forms a beneficial angle to this new moon and to Pluto, suggesting that any relationships that begin around this time expand your idea of what is possible between two people. Again, with Pluto's presence power issues may surface, but since Pluto is in your sign, you're in control of the situation.

With two new moons in your sign in 2011, it's definitely to your advantage to plan for them. Make a wish list. Put up a wish board. Get to work figuring out what you would like to manifest in your life.

Great backup dates fall between May 11 and June 20, when Mars transits Taurus and the romance area of your chart. This transit may have more to do with your sexuality than with romance, but it certainly promises to be a social time, so don't turn down any invitations! Get out and be seen.

Other Dates to Circle

Between June 4, 2011, and June 12, 2012, expansive Jupiter will be moving through Taurus and the romance section of your chart. Lucky you! Buckle up for this one! Your love life is about to whip along the wild side.

If you're not involved when this transit begins, you probably will be by the time the transit ends. Any relationship that develops under this transit is likely to be one that broadens your worldview and your ideas about what is possible between two people. If you're involved already, then this transit may take the relationship to a deeper level of commitment. You and your partner may get engaged, married, move in together, start a family, or buy a home.

Look back twelve years, to when Jupiter was last in Taurus, for clues about how this transit may unfold for you. What was going on in your love life? In your life generally? In another twelve years—2023—this transit will come around again. You might want to turn to appendix 1 and locate your natal Jupiter, and then read the description in chapter 5. If your natal Jupiter is in Taurus, it means you're experiencing a Jupiter return, part of a twelve-year cycle of personal growth and expansion!

Venus

Venus is the planet that represents love and romance. Its transits through your sign or any of the other earth or water signs favor matters of the heart. These transits are discussed in the big-picture section for your sign before the daily predictions, but let's take a closer look.

When Venus transits your sign, people find you irresistibly appealing, attractive, charming, witty, seductive. Your self-confidence is buoyed, and your love life should be very nice indeed. Those dates happen twice this year—February 4 to March 1 and November 26 to December 20.

When Venus transits the other two earth signs—Taurus and Virgo—similar energies operate. From May 15 to June 9, Venus moves through Taurus and your solar fifth house. It's the sort of transit that appeals to the sensual side of your nature, Capricorn, and stirs your deepest fantasies. No question that you're the magnetic one in any crowd. Whether you're involved or not, life generally runs more smoothly, and you feel great about where you are right now.

Venus transits Virgo between August 21 and September 14, in your solar ninth house. This would be an ideal time for you and your partner to take off for a romantic getaway to some overseas location. Do whatever it is you enjoy doing together—delve into your joint creative endeavors, explore the hidden back streets of some far-flung corner of the world, or stay in bed all day!

Those dates are the romance-love highlights for the year. But what about commitment? Marriage?

Deeper Commitment Anyone?

Anytime Venus—or Jupiter—moves through your seventh house of partnership, a more deeply committed relationship is possible. There are also new moons to be considered, but that's discussed earlier in the chapter. Reread it. Then take note of the dates below. Remember, though, that these descriptions are based on solar charts—not your individual natal chart. It's to your benefit to find the cusp of your seventh house on your natal chart and then look up when Venus will be transiting that sign. Google: Venus transits 2011 or Venus ephemeris 2011.

July 4 to July 28. Whether you're involved in a committed relationship or not, this transit favors a deeper commitment between you and your partner. It's not as if you have to push to make things happen. Events and emotions unfold on their own, growing out of your deep feelings for each other.

CHAPTER 15

Career Tips for the Transition for Capricorn

In a year of transition, how can you maximize your career potential? Do you want to change jobs or careers? Do you hope to be promoted, earn more, become self-employed? Whatever your professional desires, timing may be everything.

The main transit to look for this year is Saturn's through Libra, and the career area of your chart. Saturn restricts, delays, and governs the rules of physical existence, but can also bring harvest and culmination. That last word is what this transit should be for you, Capricorn. Until October 2012, Saturn will be transiting the highest point in your chart—your tenth house. You should reap the benefits of what you've been doing professionally for the last two decades or so. If you've been diligent and hard-working—and most Capricorns are—then this period should be exceptionally good for your career.

You may assume additional responsibilities, land a plump raise, and be recognized by bosses and peers for your achievements. Since Saturn rules your sign and the tenth house, its position here complements you, and it functions well here. Your self-confidence is solid, and you feel you can achieve anything you focus on. And you can, if you follow some simple guidelines:

- Don't assume you have all the answers.
- Delegate responsibilities to others to free up time for yourself.
- Maintain your usual work ethic and sense of responsibility. Now isn't the time to start using your sick days.
- Don't ignore your inner life, your family and friends.

If what you have built in the last fourteen years or so has negativity attached to it, as it did for Richard Nixon, then this Saturn could be calamitous. Nixon, for example, resigned while Saturn transited his tenth house. The thing to remember about Saturn is that it makes sure we reap what we sow.

While this transit is going on in your tenth house, Jupiter makes two transits this year that hold importance for your career stuff. Its transit through Aries and your solar fourth house from January 22 to June 4 tests your legendary self-discipline. It will be opposed to your career area, an aspect that isn't necessarily negative, but you may be encouraged to tackle way too much at once and scatter your energies. Aries constantly pushes forward, eager and restless to move, move, move, so it's possible that you launch projects—then walk away from them before they're completed. Or you might waste a resource that's always been at your disposal—a particular employee, for instance, or your boss's goodwill! Throughout this transit, your self-confidence will remain rock-solid, but you may be too cocky, figuring that your luck simply can't fail. Know when to stop. Know when you've had enough.

Jupiter's second transit, through Taurus and your solar fifth house, runs from June 4, 2011, to June 11, 2012, and will be far more comfortable for you. It's in a fellow earth sign, and you have an innate understanding of Taurean energy—it grounds you, compels you to complete what you start, is deliciously sensual, and helps you to make the abstract practical. Since it's in your house of creativity, you are better able to find creative solutions to challenges and to delve into any artistic and musical talents you have.

Creatively, you're on a roll. A major roll. A dramatic and life-changing roll. So if you've ever thought about dusting off an old manuscript, portfolio, musical recording, dance routine, or anything else that falls in the traditional creative fields, now is the time to do it. But creativity is more than just the arts. It's an approach to life that can be found in any profession. It's about finding innovative solutions to challenges, about using resources in new and different ways. It's about thinking outside the box and you're able to do that with total ease.

Your creative endeavors help to expand your worldview, your personal beliefs, and this expansion is beneficial to your career.

The urge to travel will be strong for at least eighteen months, during these two Jupiter transits. Indulge the urge, but be sure you can afford it! You're not just after pleasure and enjoyment, but you are actually seeking something deeper: an understanding of how people in other countries go about their lives.

If you've ever considered self-employment, this could be the period in which it happens. Your goals are ambitious, your ability to work hard is tremendous, and the stars are stacked in your favor. If you would like to have a business partner, trust that someone will appear in your life who has the knowledge, expertise, or financial resources that you need.

Between now and 2024, powerful Pluto, the planet of profound and permanent transformation, will be in your sign. This transit heightens your ambition and, combined with Jupiter's transit through earth sign Taurus, should help to ground your goals, bolster your self-confidence, and generally put you in the driver's seat in your professional endeavors. Your income may plunge—or soar.

There won't be anything in between. So make sure it's the latter!

Daily Work

Your work routine consists of many connecting dots that form the larger picture of your career. It's the e-mails you write and answer, the calls you return, the office parties you attend, the conferences and seminars—in short, all the minutiae. Whenever Mercury and Venus transit your sixth house of daily work, they also form beneficial angles to your career area. Here are some dates to watch for in terms of your daily work:

May 15 to June 9. Venus's transit of Taurus should bring passion and enthusiasm to all your creative work.

The above transit overlaps by a few days with Mercury's transit through Gemini between June 2 and June 16, when you'll be doing most of the grunt communication work—answering phones, e-mails, traveling for business.

June 9 to July 4. Venus transits Gemini and your solar sixth house, bringing ease and a social tone to your daily work. You may hang out more frequently with coworkers and employees.

May 11 to June 20 and *June 20 to August 3.* Energetic Mars will be transiting Taurus and then Gemini, the creativity and daily work sections of your chart. Expect lots of forward thrust, travel, and a general relentlessness on your part to get things done.

September 14 to October 9. It's an ideal time to push your agenda forward.

September 25 to October 13. Mercury transits your career area. Great for communication, writing, blogging, and building Web sites.

CHAPTER 16

Saturn in 2011 and Its Impact on Capricorn

Saturn in Libra. Let's explore what it means for your sign. You've been experiencing this transit off and on (due to retrogrades) since late October 2009, so you undoubtedly are aware of some of its impact on your life. But since 2011 is the year of transition, there are certain steps you can take to make this transit work *for* you.

In chapter 7, we talked about Saturn's transit in Libra and its ramifications for your career. Now let's talk about it in general and how it might relate to your natal chart. Turn to the chart at the end of this chapter. This woman is a Capricorn with Aries rising and a Leo moon. Her ninth house Capricorn sun is the most elevated planet in her chart—⊙13♑03. In her seventh house, she has both Neptune Ψ23♎45 and Saturn 26♄♎23 in Libra. So Saturn's transit through Libra is going to be hitting her seventh house, affecting all her business and romantic partnerships. It will be forming a beneficial angle to her Leo moon ☽21♌48 and her Pluto ♀22♌54 in the fifth house. She has three sons, so the beneficial angle to these two planets will be important. Saturn will also be forming a challenging angle to her ninth house Capricorn sun ⊙13♑03 and a beneficial angle to her Mercury in Sagittarius ☿25♐50.

Let's start with the seventh house stuff. Even though Saturn won't begin hitting this house until November, she'll be feeling the effects before then. She's currently divorced, so Saturn's transit may bring a romantic interest who is older than she is, established. But this person may have a lot of rules and regulations that annoy her and she'll have to confront these irritations if the relationship is to last. She has spent the last fourteen years or so defining herself and won't be eager to leap into a relationship just to be involved with someone.

By December, she'll be experiencing a Saturn return—when Saturn returns to the place and degree it occupied at her birth. If we live into our nineties, we experience this cycle three times. The first occurs at the age of twenty-nine or so; the second one occurs between the ages of fifty-eight to sixty. It represents a peak, a culmination, a harvest. Something will be gained during her Saturn return, and yet she may feel that if she doesn't hurry up and do whatever she has always wanted to do, she may not have a chance to do it at all. In other words, she'll be feeling her own mortality.

With her sons now out on their own, she may be clearing away things she no longer needs—belongings, people, relationships. She may move to a smaller home or into a town house. She may take her retirement and head off into the sunset to follow her bliss. One way or another, she will have to make dramatic changes in her life.

As Saturn approaches her natal Neptune, feelings of confusion may rush in—confusion about what she really is seeking in both business and romantic partnerships, confusion about what is real and of value in her life. Fortunately, Saturn is forming a beneficial angle to both her natal moon and Pluto, which means she'll have the inner resources to deal with any challenges that come her way. She will be able to detach from her emotions and be cool-headed about her decisions. She'll be able to build on past achievements. It's important that she doesn't remain passive during this transit. She must work on old emotional patterns so that they no longer repeat themselves.

The beneficial angle to Pluto makes her aware of just what kind of personal power and magnetism she possesses, so she's capable of enormous achievements now. So even though she has some challenges with this transit, other planets compensate.

Even though one of her sons may get married or move during this transit, her relationship with them remains strong. In late December, as Saturn forms a trine with her natal Venus in Aquarius ♀28≈00 in her eleventh house, she may realize some wish or dream that she has and could find a strong romantic relationship with an equal—i.e., someone without a bunch of rules!

Saturn rules bones, skin, and teeth and Libra rules the lower back. So if she experiences any health problems, they could show up first in these areas.

Even during challenging transits, there are planets that help us draw on inner resources, provide insights, and strengthen us. Nothing in a chart is ever all bad!

Here are some guidelines for navigating this transit successfully.

- Work within the rules in every area of your life. Don't take shortcuts.
- Meet your obligations.
- Go beyond whatever is required of you—in relationships, at work, with your finances, family, with everything. Saturn likes it when you go the extra mile.
- Even if you're not the social type, make an extra effort to get out and about and socialize. Forge new relationships; cement existing ones.
- Find a calm center within yourself where you can retreat when you feel stressed. In addition to meditation, you would benefit from any kind of consciousness raising workshop or practice.
- Create or maintain a regular exercise program.
- Learn to manifest your desires.

Entire books have been written on manifestation. You might start with a DVD of *The Secret*, and then move on to the Esther and Jerry Hicks books—*The Law of Attraction*, *The Astonishing Power of Emotions*, *Ask and It Is Given*. There's also a series of "attraction books"—how to attract money, health and so on.

Once you've read the books (think of it as doing your homework), experiment with a wish board. This tool can take any number of forms. Usually, it's a posterboard that you put someplace where you'll see it often. On it go pictures, slogans, photos, anything, and everything that's a visual depiction of something you want.

Let's say that you would like to take a trip abroad—to Fiji, New Zealand, Chile. Let's say that the cost is a challenge, that you just don't have the spare money right now. So use visualization to attract the money. Create a wish board, and fill it with pictures of the places you would like to visit. Figure out what the trip will cost, then bump it up a thousand dollars and post that figure on the wish board. See yourself walking the streets of that city, that country. Smell the air; take in the colors and the spectacular sights. *Make it real*. Do this daily.

Saturn begins the year at 16 degrees Libra, retrogrades back to 10 degrees Libra, and ends the year at 28 degrees. So if you have natal planets in those degrees, you'll feel impact of Saturn most strongly.

Recommended Books and Movies for the Transition

The Law of Attraction by Esther and Jerry Hicks. Any of their books are excellent, but start with this one. Esther channels a group of souls who call themselves Abraham. The material is empowering.

The Power of Now by Eckhart Tolle. He makes a strong case for living in the moment.

Be Here Now by Ram Dass. This sixties classic is another treatise on being fully present.

The Nature of Personal Reality. Author Jane Roberts channeled a "nonphysical entity," Seth, and together they wrote more than twenty books on the nature of reality.

You Can Heal Your Life. Louise Hay's magnificent book is a must on any bookshelf!

Raising Arizona. Laughter is always the best remedy, and this early film starring Nicolas Cage will keep you in stitches.

Memories, Dreams, and Reflections. Carl Jung's autobiography is fascinating and be sure to find his take on astrology.

Marley & Me. For dog lovers everywhere.

Eat, Pray, Love. Elizabeth Gilbert's engaging memoir beautifully illustrates how one woman navigated a transitional period in her own life.

The Simpsons. Any episode and the movie. Because they make us laugh.

This list is just for starters. Add to it as you make your way through 2011. Share your experiences with others by blogging. You'll discover that you aren't alone!

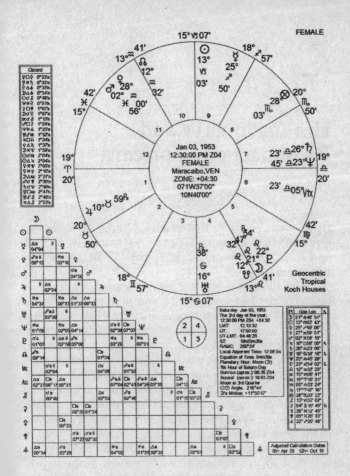

FEMALE

Jan 03, 1953
12:30:00 PM Z04
FEMALE
Maracaibo,VEN
ZONE: +04:30
071W37'00
10N40'00"

Geocentric
Tropical
Koch Houses

Saturday Jan 03, 1953
The 3rd day of the year.
12:30:00 PM Z04 +04:30
LMT: 12:13:32
UT: 17:00:00
UT-LMT: 04:46:28
ST: 19h05m36s
RAMC: 286°24'
Local Apparent Time: 12:08:54
Equation of Time: 04m38s
Planetary Hour: Moon (☽)
7th Hour of Saturn-Day
Sunrise (aprox.) 06:36 Z04
Sunset (aprox.) 18:03 Z04
Moon in 3rd Quarter
☉☉ Angle. 216°44'
☽'s Motion: +11°50'47"

Pl	Geo Lon	&
☽	21° ♌ 46' 34"	
☉	13° ♑ 02' 43"	
☿	25° ♐ 50' 06"	
♀	27° ♒ 59' 51"	
♂	02° ♒ 56' 10"	
♃	10° ♉ 58' 50"	R
♄	26° ♎ 23' 06"	R
♅	16° ♋ 03' 18"	R
♆	23° ♎ 45' 28"	R
♇	22° ♌ 54' 02"	R
☊	12° ♋ 32' 23"	
⚷	15° ♏ 08' 41"	R
As	19° ♈ 19' 31"	
Mc	00° ♑ 23' 24"	
⊗	17° ♏ 47' 16"	
2	04° ♉ 19' 49"	R
9	26° ♉ 14' 45"	R
3	13° ♍ 52' 02"	
♀	04° ♉ 19' 49"	
⚴	26° ♉ 28' 33"	
⚵	22° ♉ 20' 48"	

Adjusted Calculation Dates
0h: Apr 20   12h: Oct 19

©1994 Matrix Software Big Rapids, MI

Chart Service a Wheel

173

CHAPTER 17

Uranus in 2011 and
Its Impact on Capricorn

By now you're aware that in 2011, Uranus occupies two signs—Pisces, where it has been since the spring of 2003, and Aries, which it enters on March 11, 2011. So what's this mean for *you*?

When Uranus leaves the sign of Pisces, where it has been for the last seven years, you may not be glad to see it leave. Water sign Pisces is compatible with your sun. That said, Uranus's transit through Aries will keep you on your toes and, often, at the edge of your seat! It will transit your solar fourth house—home, family, your domestic situation and personal environment.

Uranus's job is to break up the status quo, to shake us out of the ruts and routines into which we all fall. If you're in a dead-end relationship, then it will hit you there. If you're in a dead-end job, Uranus will sweep in and turn your professional life inside out. On the other side of it all, you'll have greater freedom. Not only will you have found your genuine voice, but you'll have the freedom to express who you are.

As a cardinal earth sign, you may not be particularly fond of change. So before this transit begins, look honestly through the various compartments of your life. What has become so routine that you can do it with your eyes shut? Where has your life gone stale? Try to initiate changes in these areas before March 11. If you resist change during this transit, it will be thrust upon you—and with far less pleasant results.

The change that Uranus brings about usually occurs abruptly, without warning. You walk into work one day, and you are handed a pink slip. You enter your home—and discover you have been robbed. You enter a restaurant and suddenly lock eyes with a stranger whom you know you are going to marry. Those kinds of abrupt, out-of-the-blue surprises.

During this transit, it's important to maintain your health. Establish a regular exercise program if you don't have one already. Watch your nutrition. Take vitamins if you don't get enough antioxidants in your meals. Break long-standing habits—smoking, overeating, drinking to excess. Meditation can be helpful too, particularly as a way to find the calm center of any storm that's raging around you.

Any courses or workshops you can take in personal growth would be valuable and beneficial. This transit forces you to think differently, outside the box—maybe way outside the box—and to be fearless in exploring what's new and different.

Let's go through a simple checklist to find out where your life feels stale, and so routine that you have ceased to grow.

Career/Job: Are you satisfied with it? Do you wake every morning eager to get to work? Are you doing what you love?

Finances: Are you satisfied with your income?

Family: Is your family life gratifying?

Creativity: Are you satisfied with your creative talents? Is there any area you would like to develop more fully?

Education: Given the time and resources, would you return to college or go to graduate school?

Partnerships: Do your most intimate partnerships bring you peace and happiness?

This list is simple, but it gives you a place to start.

Navigating Successfully

Be sure to check the Web sites listed in chapter 11 and in other areas of this book to find out where Uranus is in a given month. It moves very slowly, so a monthly check should be all you'll need. Then consult your natal chart to find the degree of any planet you have in Aries or where Aries appears in your chart. Uranus's approach to that planet is when the transit is most powerful.

In 2011, Uranus reaches 4 degrees of Aries before it turns retrograde and revisits the first 4 degrees of the sign. By the end of the year, it has returned to 0 degrees and 50 minutes of Aries. In 2012, it reaches 8 degrees of Aries before it retrogrades again, and by the end of the year, it's back to 4 degrees. So let's say you have an Aries moon at 4 degrees. That means the Uranian changes will be happening emotionally, internally.

Look at the woman's chart in chapter 11. She has Aries rising at 19 degrees and 54 minutes. So Uranus won't be hitting her rising until late May 2015. However, it will be approaching an appointment with her rising, and the approach is when these transits are most powerful. As it nears that conjunction, she may suddenly pack up and move to another state or even another country. She may get married, win the lottery, sell a book, and retire. No telling. The events that unfold during this seven-year period will free her from the constraints, restrictions, and routines of the past. Since the rising in the doorway to the natal chart, she will feel as if she has been reborn. A new chapter in her life? You bet.

Here are some simple suggestions to make the journey easier:

Welcome change. We already discussed why this is important.

Take risks. Do this in your daily work and career first, and see what happens. Experiment. Embrace new passions that you discover. Be fearless.

Synchronicities. Be alert for them. During any time when there's a lot of change, when life is in flux, synchronicities or meaningful coincidences tend to occur more frequently. Pay attention to them. They may offer guidance and direction. Check out our blog on the topic, www.ofscarabs.blogspot.com.

Honest appraisal. Take an honest look at your life in terms of where you are rigid or where things have gone flat, stale. Initiate action to make changes.

Liberation

Go back to the simple checklist we discussed earlier. Add or delete items from it. But always ask yourself how you can enjoy greater freedom to pursue your passions and creative interests.

If you want more creative freedom what steps can you take now, before the transit starts, to help bring that about? If you're involved in a repressive relationship, what can you do to change the status quo? If you would like to change careers, do you need more education? Is it necessary to move? Go through each area with a laser-sharp eye.

Look ahead to 2019. Where would you like to be when Uranus enters Taurus?

CHAPTER 18

Neptune in 2011 and Its Impact on Capricorn

During this year, Neptune will occupy two signs—Aquarius and Pisces. It enters Pisces on April 4, retrogrades on June 2, enters Aquarius again on August 4, turns direct on November 9, and moves toward its second appointment with Pisces. You already know what Neptune in Aquarius feels like—you've been living it for the last fourteen years. So let's concentrate on what kinds of experience may unfold during Neptune's transit of Pisces for you personally.

What kinds of adjustments will you have to make this year to get through this transitional period? How will Neptune's transit through Pisces impact your sun sign?

What kinds of experiences should you expect? How can you take advantage of this transit to maximize your own potential?

For the next fourteen years, Neptune will be transiting Pisces and your solar third house. This transit will be very much to your liking because Pisces is a water sign compatible with your earth-sign sun. It's transiting the area of your chart that governs relatives, neighbors and neighborhoods, short-distance travel, education, and your conscious mind.

This transit will deepen your awareness of and concern and compassion for others. Your friends and relatives will become more important to you, and you will do whatever you can to help them out. Your spiritual beliefs both change and deepen. You will reach out to the disenfranchised, the homeless, or to some other group and offer your assistance. You may volunteer for an organization that does charitable work. It's as if you gradually come to understand that what affects one affects many, and you want to do your part to help those who are less fortunate than you.

Neptune rules Pisces, so it's comfortable in this sign and functions just as it should—a kind of free-flowing, ethereal energy. Neptune sometimes creates confusion, usually for lack of information, but can also sweep you along in a dreamy, psychic current of inexplicable happenings, feelings, imaginings.

This transit favors artistic pursuits—music, writing, art, photography, dance. But there's a more evolved texture to any artistic endeavors in which you become involved. It's as if your growing compassion and spirituality spill over into your creative life, and you must depict what you see and feel.

Neptune not only rules our higher and more evolved impulses and feelings, but our blind spots and illusions as well. It rules escapism of all kinds—from drugs and alcohol to fiction, movies, the dance of our imaginations. It's important to stay away from alcohol and drugs during this transit. If you get sick, try herbal remedies and alternative therapies first. Your body will be sensitive to drugs. Also, if you're diagnosed with a serious problem, get other opinions. The confusion with which Neptune is associated can result in misdiagnosis. Read Louise Hay's *You Can Heal Your Life*. Hay's personal story is compelling, and her take on the emotional cause of illness will prompt you to take a deeper look at your own emotions and where you may be blocked or may not be allowing a free flow of energy.

Integral to this journey is discovery. As your intuitive skills increase and deepen, you'll find yourself exploring psychic undercurrents, the realm of your imagination, the world of your dreams. Be sure to keep track of your dreams, which could yield important answers and insights during this transit. Start an online discussion group on dreams—or some other interest you have—on a social networking site like Facebook. Share your journey.

Synchronicity or meaningful coincidence may be a huge part of this transit, particularly if you're paying attention to events that are unfolding from the inside out—your hidden patterns. When you experience a meaningful coincidence, pause to look for and decipher the deeper meaning. Is it leading you in a new direction? Is it a confirmation of something you've been feeling?

Books on quantum physics may interest you—not the science part so much as the layman's explanation of how recent discoveries in the field seem to hint that our lives are written from the inside out. Synchronicity or meaningful coincidence may be the bridge between this inner or implicate order and our external lives.

During this transit, have a physical exercise routine that keeps your body strong and flexible. Watch your nutrition; get plenty of antioxidants. Experiment with different herbal and vitamin supplements. Get a weekly massage, with a focus on your feet, which are ruled by Neptune. The soles of the feet hold many acupuncture points that are important in maintaining health and emotional balance.

Try to get sufficient sleep at night. The better able you are to find the calm center of your life, perhaps through meditation or other mind-body disciplines, the easier this transit will be. If it helps to write about your experiences, then do so. Keep a journal, blog, have discussion groups in your home.

Here are some guidelines to navigate events with greater ease and maximum benefit:

- Nurture your ideals and compassion.
- Be true to yourself. It sounds trite, but it will make this transit easier to navigate and less confusing.

- Never make excuses for your idealism.
- Whenever you find an opportunity to help someone else, do so. This suggestion seems obvious, but so many of us are swept up in the events of our own lives that we feel constantly pressed for time and simply can't be bothered.
- Strive to start each day in an upbeat, optimistic mood. If you find your good mood faltering during the day, then practice what Esther and Jerry Hicks call "rampaging appreciation," where you express appreciation for everything around you.
- Explore what's hidden. From quantum physics to psychic phenomena to the stuff in your own psyche, dive in!
- Live fully in the moment. Don't worry about what hasn't happened yet. Simply stay focused on now. Trust that you're in the right place, at the right time.
- Banish negativity from your thoughts—and thus from your life.

In terms of your idealism, reach for the stars. Believe that one person can bring about enormous change. Try to integrate your ideals into your daily life, but don't get suckered into cults or organizations that promise nirvana or salvation *if* you donate a percentage of your annual earnings. Before joining any group, gather your facts.

Spirituality and Worldview for Capricorn

If you put a hundred strangers in the same room and then ask each of them about their spiritual beliefs, you'll probably get a hundred different answers. Even individuals who follow a traditional religion probably don't adhere to all that religion's teachings. They take a little from here, a little from there.

Even if you're an agnostic or an atheist, there's something for you in here. After all, when you walk outside on a beautiful day, when you hear birds sing, when the flowers are in bloom and everything is green and flourishing, there's a spiritual element to it just in the sheer magnificence.

As you become more sensitive and attuned to the spiritual dimension in life, your external life changes. If you adhere to traditional religious beliefs, then you may become more involved with your church and its activities within the community. If you're not into traditional religion, then your spiritual beliefs may deepen or gradually evolve into some other belief system. Since the transit lasts fourteen years, the evolution of these beliefs is subtle. If you've never studied metaphysics, you probably will now.

Your natal Jupiter often describes the nature of your spiritual quest. So check out the description for your Jupiter in chapter 5. If it's in a water sign—Pisces, Cancer, Scorpio—then your quest will take place on a deeply intuitive level. If your natal Jupiter is in a fire sign—Aries, Leo, Sagittarius—then you will aggressively pursue this quest, looking for the bigger picture. If it's in an air sign—Gemini, Libra, Aquarius—your search will be an intellectual exercise, a constant search that answers a single burning question: *Why?* If your natal Jupiter is in an earth sign—Taurus, Virgo, Capricorn—your search will unfold slowly, with persistence, resoluteness.

What you're really after during the transits of Neptune and Jupiter is a broader and more cohesive and inclusive worldview, a belief system that can carry you through life. Dictionary.com defines a belief system as: "faith based on a series of beliefs but not formalized into a religion; also, a fixed coherent set of beliefs prevalent in a community or society."

Your worldview is typically symbolized by Jupiter. So

let's take a close look at how your belief system may change during this year of transitions. The most important Jupiter transit for you will be the one through Taurus, which will form a beneficial angle to your ninth house. This house governs worldview, and yours will expand tremendously during this yearlong transit. If you travel abroad, there will be something other than business or enjoyment behind the trip. You may be on a quest of some kind, in search of particular types of information, people, experiences.

You may decide to go back to school for additional training. You might even be training others in a topic about which you know a great deal. One way or another, Jupiter's transit in Taurus blows open the door on your worldview and the fresh insights and knowledge that pour in sustain you, fill you.

Dates to Circle

May 11 to June 20. Mars in Taurus travels with Jupiter through your solar fifth house. Your creativity is highlighted. You may discover that creativity is one way to explore and express your worldview.

May 15 to June 9. During this period, when Venus transits Taurus, traveling part of the time with both Jupiter and Mars, you're in a very stable period, with great staying power.

August 21 to September 14. Venus moves through Virgo and your solar ninth house. Beautiful transit for travel, exploration, defining your quest.

November 11 to July 4, 2012. Mars transits fellow earth sign Virgo and your ninth house. Think of this transit as your booster rocket. If you've been dallying, this transit gets you moving.

The more awareness you bring to your life during these periods, the greater your opportunities for broadening your worldview and spirituality and for enriching your existence. You might want to keep track of Mercury's movements during these Jupiter and Uranus transits. As the planet of communication, its transits are important in terms of talking and writing about what you're feeling and experiencing. You can Google Mercury transits and the day's date to find that information.

Keep in mind that during Mercury retrogrades, you may feel somewhat discombobulated, particularly if there's a lot going on in your life. So you'll want to be sure to write and talk with greater clarity about your emotions and experiences. The dates for those are listed in the big-picture section for your sign before the daily predictions.

CHAPTER 19

The Big Picture for Capricorn in 2011

Welcome to 2011, Capricorn! This year is about freedom—creative freedom, personal freedom, professional freedom, glorious freedom in all its forms. It's your year for thinking outside of the box, for following the dictates of your own heart rather than doing something only because you feel obligated.

Let's start with Pluto. Even though Pluto was demoted by astronomers, this powerful planet is still used by astrologers. Three years ago it entered your sign and will be there until early 2024. Pluto's job is to transform from the bottom up, so the effects of this transit will unfold slowly, at deep levels, and will profoundly change your personal life and who you are as an individual. It won't be as if you wake up one morning to suddenly find yourself unrecognizable. But your beliefs about yourself will definitely change.

On a global level, Pluto's impact is evident in the economic challenges that now face the U.S. Most institutions are in the throes of great change—the health-care industry, the petroleum and insurance industries, mortgages/lending, housing, aviation, the Internet, the entire financial system, even the planet. You name it, and Pluto's fingerprint can be found. Pluto knocks down the stuff that no longer works, then asks that you rebuild from the ashes.

Neptune has been in Aquarius since 1998 and on April 4, it enters elusive, mystical Pisces, in your solar third house, a much more positive transit for you than when it was in Aquarius. During this transit, which ends in late January 2026, Neptune forms a beneficial angle to your sun and should bring your ideals, spiritual beliefs, and idealism into greater alignment with how you live your life. This transit brings a decidedly softer focus to your daily life and to the way you communicate your ideas.

Neptune is also the planet of illusion and represents our blind spots. So you may not always have the full information that you need to make informed decisions.

On June 2, Neptune turns retrograde, and slides back into Aquarius for a while, and on November 9, it turns direct again.

Uranus has been in Pisces, your solar third house, for the last seven years. On March 11, it enters Aries and your solar fourth house. This transit lasts until May 2018 and will bring excitement and unpredictability to your domestic and family life. Under the Uranus transit, relationships could begin and end suddenly, your children or other people within your family experience sudden, unpredictable events, and people who may be idiosyncratic or geniuses in their field enter your life. Uranus's job is to shake us out of our ruts and routines so that we embrace the new and the different. It turns retrograde on July 9 and direct again on December 10, but won't return to Pisces for another eighty-four years.

Saturn, the planet that governs the rules of physical existence, begins the year in Libra, in the career sector of your chart. This sociable air sign suggests that you will be networking and connecting more aggressively with people in your work environment. But because Saturn restricts, delays, and governs the rules of physical existence, it's likely that you will approach your professional life with the seriousness it deserves. During this transit, which lasts until October 2012, you may have to assume more responsibility in your home life—for a parent, child, spouse, or partner. If you try to take shortcuts, Saturn thwarts your efforts, and whatever you're trying to do or achieve takes longer than it should.

With Saturn and Uranus opposed to each other for part of the year, there could be a struggle between the old and the new paradigms. On a personal level, this could mean that your established way of doing things no longer works as well as it did, and to achieve what you desire requires new methods, new attitudes. Since Saturn rules your sun sign, its transits and movements have greater bearing for you.

Jupiter is the planet of luck, expansion, and serendipity. It enters fire sign Aries and your solar fourth house on January 22, speeds through it and enters Taurus on June 4. Jupiter turns retrograde on August 30, and then direct again on December 25 and doesn't leave Taurus until June 2012. How does this translate for you? Read on.

Jupiter's transit through Aries should expand your home life in some way—you move to a larger home, you refurbish or add to your existing home, your family expands through the birth of a child, a parent or child moves in—you get the idea. Expansion. Greater breadth. Just remember that Jupiter expands everything it touches. While Jupiter travels with Uranus in Aries after March 11, these two set off major explosions in your domestic environment. Your challenge will be to record all the ideas that pour through you and then use them in some way in your creative endeavors.

Once Jupiter enters Taurus on June 4, your love life and your creative endeavors undergo incredible expansion. No telling how this might unfold for you. But there are a couple things you can count on. If you're not involved when this transit begins on June 4, you probably will be when it ends in early June 2012. And if you're not, it won't matter because you're enjoying yourself too much to give it much thought. That said, your creative adrenaline will be pumping hard and furiously, so take full advantage of it.

Romance/Creativity

The most romantic and creative times for you all year fall between February 4 and March 1, and November 26 and December 20, when Venus transits your sign. Another period falls between May 15 and June 9, when Venus transits Taurus and the romance sector of your chart. Then, of course, until June 12, Jupiter will be transiting your romance sector! Possibilities?

During the Venus transits mentioned above, life in general unfolds with greater ease and harmony, but it's your love life and creative drive that benefit the most. Whether you're involved in a relationship or not, other people find you immensely attractive, and this boosts your self-confidence.

The best time for serious involvement and deepening commitment in an existing relationship occurs when Venus transits your seventh house and Cancer between July 4 and July 28. So if you and your partner get engaged in early February, this period could be when you marry. Just make sure the marriage doesn't happen under a Mercury retrograde! Check the dates below.

Good backup dates: May 11 to June 20, when Mars transits Taurus and your romance sector. Your sexuality is heightened then.

Career

The best times this year for professional endeavors and relationships fall between September 14 and October 9, when Venus transits Libra and your solar tenth house.

Good backup dates: June 9 to July 4, when Venus forms a beneficial angle to your career sector. Life should run more smoothly during these periods. Women are helpful, your professional earnings may increase, and a raise or promotion or recognition by peers is possible. To maximize these transits, focus on what you want—rather than on the lack of what you want.

Best Times For

Buying or selling a home: Between January 22 and June 4, while Jupiter transits Aries and your solar fourth house. Backup dates: April 21 to May 15, when Venus transits the same area.

Family reunions: Any of the dates above.

Financial matters: March 1 to March 27, while Venus transits Aquarius and the financial sector of your chart, and December 20 to January 14, 2012. These dates favor increased income, investments, a raise for you or your partner, breaks with insurance and taxes, and an ease with obtaining mortgages and loans. For discussing financial matters, these dates are good: February 3 to February 21, when Mercury is moving direct in the financial sector of your chart.

Signing contracts: When Mercury is moving direct!

Overseas travel, publishing, and higher-education endeavors: August 21 to September 14, while Venus transits Virgo and your solar ninth house, and anytime Mercury is moving direct.

Mercury Retrogrades

Every year, Mercury—the planet of communication and travel—turns retrograde three times. During this period, it's wise not to sign contracts (unless you don't mind re-negotiating when Mercury is moving direct), to check and recheck travel plans, and to communicate as succinctly as possible. Revise, review, and refrain from buying any big-ticket items or electronics during this time too. Often, computers and appliances go on the fritz, cars act up, data are lost—you get the idea. Be sure to back up all files before the dates below:

March 30–April 23: Mercury retrograde in Aries, your solar fourth house. This one impacts your family and domestic environment.

August 2–August 26: Mercury retrograde in Virgo, your solar ninth house—dealings with foreign countries, your spirituality and worldview, education, and publishing.

November 24–December 13: Mercury retrograde in Sagittarius, your solar twelfth house. You retreat into solitude and delve into your own unconscious.

Eclipses

Solar eclipses tend to trigger external events that bring about change according to the sign and the house in which they fall. Lunar eclipses trigger inner, emotional events according to the sign and house in which they fall. Any eclipse marks both beginnings and endings. The solar and lunar eclipse in a pair falls in opposite signs. If you're interested in detailed information on eclipses, take at look at Celeste Teal's excellent and definitive book, *Eclipses: Predicting World Events & Personal Transformation.*

If you were born under or around the time of an eclipse, it's to your advantage to take a look at your birth chart to find out exactly where the eclipses will impact you.

Most years feature four eclipses—two solar, two lunar, with the set separated by about two weeks. In late December 2010, there was a lunar eclipse in Gemini, so the first eclipse in 2011 will be a solar eclipse. Below are the dates for this year's eclipses and you'll notice a pattern—Gemini/Sagittarius:

January 4: Solar, Capricorn, your first house. New opportunities in your personal life. Should be positive. Mars is close to the eclipse degree, suggesting lots of action and forward thrust.

June 1: Solar in Gemini. New opportunities in your daily work routine and with the maintenance of your health. A good time to join a gym? Sign up for yoga? Rearrange your work hours? Saturn forms a harmonious angle to the degree of this eclipse, suggesting that you benefit by following the rules.

June 15: Lunar, Sagittarius. Emotions surface behind the scenes. Something from the past stirs up feelings.

November 25: Solar, in Sagittarius. The same areas are affected as for the June 15 lunar eclipse, but look for external events and new opportunities.

December 10: Lunar, Gemini. Same area affected as the June 1 solar eclipse, but it's all internal, emotional.

Luckiest Day of the Year

Every year, there's one day when Jupiter and the sun meet up and luck, serendipity, and expansion are the hallmarks. This year, that day falls on April 6, with a conjunction in Aries.

Now let's take a look at what's in store for you, day by day, Capricorn!

CHAPTER 20

Eighteen Months of Day-by-Day Predictions: July 2010 to December 2011

Moon sign times are calculated for Eastern Standard Time and Eastern Daylight Time. Please adjust for your local time zone.

JULY 2010

Thursday, July 1 (Moon in Pisces) The moon is now opposite Mars in Virgo, so there could be something of a struggle while you balance various obligations. A brother or sister or someone who visits from a foreign country could be involved. Just try to go with the flow.

Friday, July 2 (Moon in Pisces) Intuitively, you're on your game today. You may have to rely on your intuition, in fact, to resolve an issue in your neighborhood or community or perhaps with a sibling. If you try to solve things with your left brain, through reason, the results may not be as positive.

Saturday, July 3 (Moon into Aries, 10:45 a.m.) The moon joins both Jupiter and Uranus in Aries, in your fourth house. This appropriate combination for the July Fourth weekend places your focus squarely on family and home. There should be a lot of excitement—and excitable people around you—but it's all about expansion now: expanding your communication venues, expanding your existing relationships, and forging your own path forward.

Sunday, July 4 (Moon in Aries)   Whether you're out of town or sticking close to home, you're intent on doing your thing today, and you hope that everyone else follows along. If you're the host this weekend, you may have to relent a bit and do what the group wants to do. Yes, it probably will run contrary to your own desires. Then again, you can be diplomatic and very much of a team player when you need to be.

Monday, July 5 (Moon into Taurus, 9:30 p.m.)   Uranus turns retrograde in Aries and begins its movement back into Pisces, which occurs on August 13. Once Uranus turns direct on December 5, it moves toward its appointment with Aries again early in 2011. What all this means is that between August 13 and the end of the year you'll have Uranus in a beneficial angle to your sun again, and that will attract unusual people and experiences. Just think back over the last seven years, and you'll have a clearer understanding what to expect during Uranus's last hurrah in Pisces.

Tuesday, July 6 (Moon in Taurus)   You may find yourself eyeing some expensive item today that you would like to buy for someone special in your life. Just be sure the money is in the bank! If it's not, then treat yourself to something less expensive that still satisfies your need for beauty.

Wednesday, July 7 (Moon in Taurus)   With the moon, Mars, and Saturn all in fellow earth signs, you're feeling quite grounded, your ideas feel solid, tangible, and real, and your goals seem to be within your reach. In a few days, Venus will also be in a fellow earth sign, and your heart will be singing. Just take things a moment at a time. If you feel overwhelmed in any area of your life, don't hesitate to delegate. You can relinquish some control. It's really okay.

Thursday, July 8 (Moon into Gemini, 4:51 a.m.) You and a partner in romance or business may embark on some new chapter in your relationship. You may be trying to expand your relationship, services, or product to different markets, and each of you has unique ideas. Open and honest communication about your respective needs and goals will take you farther than working in solitude.

Friday, July 9 (Moon in Gemini) Mercury enters Leo, where it will be until July 27. This transit brings your attention toward how you appear to others, and urges you to examine mundane areas like taxes and insurance. It's a good time to have a will drawn up too.

Saturday, July 10 (Moon into Cancer, 8:38 a.m.) Venus enters Virgo, a very nice transit that lasts until August 6. During this period, your social calendar should be packed. You may be doing more publicity and promotion, and the public is receptive to you and your ideas. If you're not involved, you may meet a potential romantic interest through friends or through a group to which you belong.

Sunday, July 11 (Moon in Cancer) Today's solar eclipse in Cancer should trigger external events that usher in opportunities in partnerships, either romantic or professional. Mars forms an exact and beneficial angle to the eclipse degree, suggesting a lot of frenetic activity around this date. Some possibilities: You land a new job, you and a partner launch your own business, you sell a book or screenplay, you move, or you sell your home.

Monday, July 12 (Moon into Leo, 9:54 a.m.) You feel the change in lunar energy today. You feel confident, but may be a bit more flamboyant than usual, with brighter colors in your clothes, for instance, or more posturing. If you're seeking support for a project, wait until the moon is in a fellow earth sign.

Tuesday, July 13 (Moon in Leo) You're pushing forward along a particular track in life, and then something happens that alters your perception of that path. What do you do? It's likely that you don't panic. Instead, you find a detour around whatever the obstacle might be and move on with the relentlessness for which you're famous.

Wednesday, July 14 (Moon into Virgo, 10:15 a.m.) Now that the moon is entering a fellow earth sign, you'll be in a stronger position to make decisions you avoided or put off. The Virgo moon asks that you be meticulous about emotional details—connect the dots about why you feel as you do. Or connect the dots about why you were avoiding a particular issue.

Thursday, July 15 (Moon in Virgo) If you're feeling restless and nomadic today, it may be time to get out of town. It can be as close to or as far from home as you like. Right now farther will be more satisfying. Another way this energy could manifest itself is in dealing with foreign countries or foreign-born individuals. If you're a writer, it's a good day to contact your editor.

Friday, July 16 (Moon into Libra, 11:25 a.m.) The moon enters the career sector of your chart and could necessitate having to work with several other individuals in a close situation. If anyone in this group bothers you, ask yourself about the traits you find distasteful in this individual. Is it possible these traits may be part of who you are as well?

Saturday, July 17 (Moon in Libra)   Among your peers, you're perceived as the person who gets things done. It isn't just that your physical energy is excellent, but that you're an exceptionally organized and efficient person who gets the most done in the least amount of time. So today capitalize on that, and don't allow others to distract you from the task at hand.

Sunday, July 18 (Moon into Scorpio, 2:43 p.m.)   With Venus, Mars, Pluto, and the moon in earth signs or signs that are compatible with yours, you have a distinct advantage over the competition. Your pragmatic approach to projects, situations, relationships, and events is impossible to dispute. On a personal level, there could be some inner tension between your professional and family obligations. But you'll deal with it just as you do with everything else.

Monday, July 19 (Moon in Scorpio)   Bottom lines— that's what you're all about today. You may be digging into the employment or work history of an employee or someone you're thinking about hiring. You eventually find what you're looking for and could discover that your hunch was right.

Tuesday, July 20 (Moon into Sagittarius, 8:49 p.m.) Here it is again, that Sagittarius moon. By now you have some idea of the possibilities it presents. Forget connecting the dots. Forget looking at the trees. Today, you're in search of the forest. Once you've got that big picture in your mind, you can implement whatever you need to in order to achieve the goal.

Wednesday, July 21 (Moon in Sagittarius)   Things are in flux. And that's fine with you. With the Sagittarius moon, you're able to remain emotionally flexible and to blend with your surroundings. You become the mirror through which others recognize their own truths.

196

Thursday, July 22 (Moon in Sagittarius)   You're dealing with loose ends, leftovers, and trying to figure out what to do with the overflow of e-mail. Your drawers may be stuffed with papers that need your attention. Can you get it all done today? Try. Tomorrow, the moon enters your sign, and you need to start fresh.

Friday, July 23 (Moon into Capricorn, 5:40 a.m.) Whether you're planning a trip, taking care of kids, diving into work and creative projects, or just hanging out with friends, it's your day. You feel anchored in your own skin. Can it get any better than this?

Saturday, July 24 (Moon in Capricorn)   The moon and Pluto team up again and have both Venus and Mars in the earth-sign court as well. This could be another one of those days when things all click into place, seemingly of their own volition, with hardly any effort from you. So enjoy it. You've earned a day like this!

Sunday, July 25 (Moon into Aquarius, 4:39 p.m.) Today's full moon in Aquarius brings news and insights about finances. Both Uranus and Jupiter form beneficial angles to the degree of this moon, indicating that the news is positive and could result in a check in your mailbox!

Monday, July 26 (Moon in Aquarius)   This moon is opposed to Mercury in Leo, so your mind is moving in one direction and your emotions in another. But the contrast may be good for you, if you can look at it in that light. Contrast helps define what you want. What you desire. And once you know that, you can make attitude and thought adjustments to create more of what you want.

Tuesday, July 27 (Moon in Aquarius)   Mercury enters Virgo, and yesterday's angst is history. You're in the groove again, doing, plotting, planning, and examining details. You may not even be after a particular result. You're just digging around and gathering information and opinions.

Wednesday, July 28 (Moon into Pisces, 5:00 a.m.) All the digging you did yesterday and whatever you unearthed can be put to good use today. Take your cues from your immediate environment. Look for metaphors in whatever happens. Do these metaphors reflect your inner thoughts and beliefs in some way?

Thursday, July 29 (Moon in Pisces) Mars enters Libra and will be transiting the career sector of your chart until September 14. During this period, all professional concerns are energized. Your career is the central focus. You may be working longer hours, perhaps to meet a deadline. Or, if you've been dissatisfied with your job and have sent out résumés, you could land a job that would be more satisfying.

Friday, July 30 (Moon into Aries, 5:42 p.m.) The moon links up with Uranus and Jupiter in your fourth house. Nice that it happens on a Friday, when all this energy can be put to excellent use—to enjoy yourself or to get back in touch with your family. In fact, a party may be in order.

Saturday, July 31 (Moon in Aries) A parent or someone else within your most intimate circle has suggestions and insights that you should listen to. Or this person needs your help and support for some reason. Whichever it is, take this person along with you today— get out of town!

Sunday, August 1 (Moon in Aries)   Change may be in the air. If you have children, they may be preparing to return to school. You may be planning a final vacation fling for summer. If so, travel on either side of the next Mercury retrograde dates: August 20 to September 12. It will be retrograde in Virgo, in your ninth house of overseas travel.

Monday, August 2 (Moon into Taurus, 5:13 a.m.)   In a few days, Venus will join Mars in Libra, a certain recipe for romance. Since the two planets will be transiting your career sector, this could indicate the advent of a relationship with a coworker or boss. It can be risky to mix business and pleasure.

Tuesday, August 3 (Moon in Taurus)   Sensuality is often a part of the Taurus moon. Today's dose of sensuality could be something as simple as the feel of silk against your skin or the warmth of the sun against your face. Or it could be as complex as the foods you prepare to seduce someone!

Wednesday, August 4 (Moon into Gemini, 1:54 p.m.) As the poem says, you've got miles to go before you sleep. It's part of that relentless work ethic that you have, always moving and doing. You always have some sort of goal, even when you're vague about what it is.

Thursday, August 5 (Moon in Gemini)   If you've got a child headed off to college this fall, you may be running around, buying supplies for the dorm, gathering the final paperwork, and basically consolidating things to get the job done more quickly. The point is information—culling it and disseminating it. Again, look for cues within your environment about the path you're on.

Friday, August 6 (Moon into Cancer, 6:50 p.m.)   Venus joins Mars in Libra, in your tenth house. In addition
to the romantic implications, this is a nice creative match
that could result in some sort of joint project with a peer
or boss. The creative component should be quite powerful and could appeal to a number of people across the
board.

Saturday, August 7 (Moon in Cancer)   With the
moon in cardinal sign Cancer, Venus, Mars, and Saturn
all in cardinal sign Libra, and your natal sign in cardinal
sign Capricorn, you are in very rare form indeed. There's
a lot of pressure on you to succeed. It may not even be
external pressure, but some sort of inner pressure cooker.
Once you pop off the lid, watch out!

Sunday, August 8 (Moon into Leo, 8:23 p.m.)   It's
that time of month again when the day can go one of
several ways. You can tend to mundane stuff like taxes,
insurance, and paying bills. Or you can delve into the
truly mysterious realms of reincarnation, life after death,
communication with the dead, and the like.

Monday, August 9 (Moon in Leo)   Today's new moon
in Leo ushers in new opportunities to research the really
big cosmic questions. Seek the kind of wisdom and knowledge you need for this new journey. Or if that doesn't interest you, head out and enjoy the summer weather.

Tuesday, August 10 (Moon into Virgo, 8:02 p.m.)   If
you're a writer in search of a publisher, today's lineup
of planets favors submissions or news about a submis-
sion you've made. If you're traveling overseas, the day
should be very good, indeed, with lot of stimulation for
heart and head and soul.

Wednesday, August 11 (Moon in Virgo)   As your
summer winds down, you could be feeling that nostalgia

or whatever it is that people sometimes feel about the passage of time and of summer. But instead of looking back, be rooted in the moment and look forward. What would you like to see for yourself?

Thursday, August 12 (Moon into Libra, 7:44 p.m.) The moon joins Mars and Venus in Libra, in your tenth house. This trio certainly ramps up your professional energy and your focus on career matters. With Mars, you have the physical stamina to work long and hard. Venus causes events to unfold more smoothly. And the moon provides the emotional nourishment you need to get to where you want to go.

Friday, August 13 (Moon in Libra) You're a team player today. You almost have to be with the lineup of planets in Libra. But the team may not stick around at work. It may decide to hit the closest restaurant or pub to celebrate Friday. And there, in a casual setting, the various elements all come together. Everyone on the team has a part to play, and the combination of ideas proves productive.

Saturday, August 14 (Moon into Scorpio, 9:27 p.m.) Your sexuality is heightened today and plays a major part in what you do. If you're involved, you'll be spending the day with your partner. If you're not involved, then you may be sequestered in your office, writing that steamy romance novel.

Sunday, August 15 (Moon in Scorpio) If you're planning to purchase a new computer or laptop, do it before August 20, when Mercury turns retrograde in Virgo. And you might consider buying a backup external hard drive on which to store documents, photos, and any other computer files that are of the utmost importance to you.

Monday, August 16 (Moon in Scorpio)   If you have any health issues, look for the inner triggers for illness and unhappiness. Take a deeper, more penetrating look at your own life. That's something the Scorpio moon does very well.

Tuesday, August 17 (Moon into Sagittarius, 2:35 a.m.) It's a good day to communicate with clients, coworkers, and employees through e-mail. If you have to go into work, fine, but keep your mouth shut. The Sagittarius moon can bring out your sharp wit, which may not be appreciated by the people around you. If you can confine communication to the written word, you'll be better able not to offend anyone.

Wednesday, August 18 (Moon in Sagittarius)   Start backing up those computer files. Mercury turns retrograde the day after tomorrow. You might want to buy a flash drive as a second backup. Think it's redundant? You won't think that if your computer crashes.

Thursday, August 19 (Moon into Capricorn, 11:18 a.m.) The moon enters your sign, and over the course of the next two days, the world is at your feet. Make good use of this energy. You should start planting seeds now for the fall, which will carry you to the end of the year. Back up computer files!

Friday, August 20 (Moon in Capricorn)   Mercury turns retrograde in Virgo, in your ninth house, and stays like that until September 12. You know the drill by now, and hopefully, you've taken steps before today to protect your computer files. On other fronts, it's a great time to dive into anything that needs to be revised, reviewed, or rewritten.

Saturday, August 21 (Moon into Aquarius, 10:38 p.m.) Every month for several days, the moon is conjunct to

Neptune, and the two planets urge you to think about money and idealism. In addition, with Pluto in your sign now, you may witness the collapse of established institutions and try to figure out how to create a safe haven for *your* money. The secret lies in what you think and feel about money.

Sunday, August 22 (Moon in Aquarius) Keep abreast of politics. Even if you're apolitical and prefer to believe it's got zero to do with your daily life, think again. The Internet, political blogs, and TV political commentary have changed the landscape. Legislation, the decisions of the Supreme Court, and the activities of the Congress all impact your life.

Monday, August 23 (Moon in Aquarius) The deal seems simple. It also may seem too good to be true. And if that's the case, run in the opposite direction. You know the routine—you're supposed to get something for practically nothing. Remember your cardinal rule: Nothing is free.

Tuesday, August 24 (Moon into Pisces, 11:11 a.m.) Today's full moon in Pisces brings news concerning a communication project and insights into how your conscious mind works. Pluto forms a close and beneficial angle to this moon, so the insights should be quite positive and powerful for you.

Wednesday, August 25 (Moon in Pisces) Whenever the moon is in Pisces, your intuition is exceptional, and it's easier to zip through issues, agendas, situations, and events because you draw on information and insights in nontraditional ways. Sometimes, you can grasp the fuller picture by conceptualizing it in your imagination. Try not to shy away from this kind of knowing. It benefits you.

Thursday, August 26 (Moon into Aries, 11:49 p.m.)
The moon joins Jupiter in your fourth house. Pretty soon, Jupiter will retrograde back into Pisces, but while it's here, make full use of it. Plan to expand your personal space in some way. If you own your home, look for ways to expand the space you have. If you're renting, add mirrors or use colors that create the illusion of more space.

Friday, August 27 (Moon in Aries)   Continuing yesterday's theme, you may want to buy a feng shui book or talk to someone who's an expert in it and practice some of the techniques on different areas of your life. What areas would you like to enhance: creativity, prosperity, family, career, or reputation? Sounds like you have a renovation project on your hands.

Saturday, August 28 (Moon in Aries)   As you're working your way toward the Labor Day weekend, it's smart to take a few moments for reflection. Have you done what you intended to do so far this year? Have certain areas of your life improved? Are you happy? If the answer to any of these questions is no, then you've got your work cut out for you for the last four months of 2010.

Sunday, August 29 (Moon into Taurus, 11:36 a.m.)
Time to join a gym, create an exercise routine you'll stick to, sign up for yoga classes, or start running or walking or something. On the other hand, if you already have your exercise routine, you're ahead of the game and now need to ask yourself how you can enhance it. The Taurus moon makes you more aware of your physical appearance, so if your body is in good shape, what about the rest of you? New wardrobe in your future? New skin creams?

Monday, August 30 (Moon in Taurus)   About those skin creams mentioned yesterday: Do some online research. Figure out your skin type; see what products apply to you. This will make the Taurus moon joyful. It's the sort of thing Taurus really enjoys.

Tuesday, August 31 (Moon into Gemini, 9:20 p.m.)   If you have a close Virgo friend or a family member whose birthday is today, do something special for this person. He or she would enjoy the gesture and probably has insights and commentary you need to hear.

SEPTEMBER 2010

Wednesday, September 1 (Moon in Gemini)   Chatty Gemini moon always seeks someone to talk to. The urge can be satisfied in any number of ways—face-to-face, through e-mail, by phone, or through writing. In fact, writing might be the best way today. You can vent on paper or in a computer file. You can imagine your audience and address them in your mind.

Thursday, September 2 (Moon in Gemini)   Mercury is still retrograde, but even so, it's possible to communicate whatever you need to say to a coworker or employee, as long as you're clear and concise in what you're saying. Maybe e-mail is the best alternative. That way you can think about what you want to say.

Friday, September 3 (Moon into Cancer, 3:51 a.m.) The moon enters your opposite sign, so once again your focus shifts to others. If you're not married, the others could be your friends. If you're involved or married, the other would be your partner. If you're in business with someone else, the other could be your business partner. This person may need emotional support at this time.

Saturday, September 4 (Moon in Cancer)   If you're traveling over this long Labor Day weekend, it's best to maintain flexibility and your sense of humor. Not only is this one of the busiest travel times, but Mercury is retrograde. If you do experience an abrupt change in plans, go with the flow.

Sunday, September 5 (Moon into Leo, 6:46 a.m.) As the moon enters Leo today, you may feel the need for recognition from peers, family, and friends. Even if you aren't entirely clear what you should be recognized for, the feeling persists. But the bottom line here is that you don't need the approval of others to validate your work, your being, or your existence.

Monday, September 6 (Moon in Leo) If you've got decisions to make about insurance or taxes, delay until tomorrow, when the moon will be in fellow earth sign Virgo. Or, better yet, wait until the new moon in Virgo on September 8. If you're launching something new or have ideas to pitch, wait until the new moon as well.

Tuesday, September 7 (Moon into Virgo, 6:54 a.m.) Tomorrow, there's not only a new moon, but Venus enters Scorpio. This transit will last through the end of the year, because Venus will retrograde between October 8 and November 18. But while it's moving direct, romance may be as close as your backyard or your own neighborhood. This transit bolsters your self-confidence and your appeal to others.

Wednesday, September 8 (Moon in Virgo) Today's new moon in Virgo attracts opportunities to travel abroad, to do business with foreign countries, and to broaden your spiritual knowledge, and opportunities for higher education. Whether you're a teen bound for college, already in college, or an adult who wants to return to college, this new moon should be beneficial for you.

Thursday, September 9 (Moon into Libra, 6:02 a.m.)
With the new moon in Virgo yesterday and today's moon in the career sector of your chart, you should be seeing results of seeds you planted weeks or even months ago. Don't make any moves until after September 12, when Mercury turns direct.

Friday, September 10 (Moon in Libra)   The moon, of course, is now traveling with Saturn through the career sector of your chart. While the combination can sometimes feel oppressive and serious, there's an upside to it. Saturn strengthens whatever professional structures you have in place and allows you to work well within the parameters you've established.

Saturday, September 11 (Moon into Scorpio, 6:22 a.m.)
Here it is again, that intense Scorpio moon. By now you have a pretty clear idea how you feel on these particular days. This moon should bring insights into your closest friendships or into some wish or dream that you hold. One thing is for sure. If you encounter a naysayer who says that your dreams are unrealistic, you'll have the inner certainty to just laugh it all off.

Sunday, September 12 (Moon in Scorpio)   Mercury turns direct today in Virgo. Pack your bags and get out of town. What's especially nice about this movement is that Mercury, the moon, and Uranus are all in signs compatible with your sun sign. This combination brings heightened intensity and excitement to anything you undertake today.

Monday, September 13 (Moon into Sagittarius, 9:52 a.m.)   Pluto turns direct in your sign. The effects will be subtle, but fairly soon you should begin to notice that whatever has been stalled in your personal life should begin to move forward once again. You'll be able to integrate your own power successfully into whatever you do without being obnoxious or dictatorial about it.

Tuesday, September 14 (Moon in Sagittarius) Mars enters Scorpio, where it will be until October 28, and joins Venus in your eleventh house. This transit is certain to energize your social life and to act as a booster for the achievement of at least some of your wishes and dreams. Even if you don't achieve them now, you'll make significant strides.

Wednesday, September 15 (Moon into Capricorn, 5:30 p.m.) The moon enters your sign this afternoon and joins Pluto, now moving direct, in your first house. You should notice the difference of this combination now, the first time it's happened (with Pluto direct) since April 6. You'll feel more powerful and centered, and you should be able to make swifter, more focused decisions.

Thursday, September 16 (Moon in Capricorn) You're grounded today. Feels good, doesn't it? Just be sure that you don't overstep your boundaries with bosses, peers, or others who have authority over you. With the planets lined up like this in your favor, there can be a tendency to believe that no matter what you do, nothing will go wrong.

Friday, September 17 (Moon in Capricorn) In love, as in life, you like to be the captain of the ship. And today that tactic probably will work well for you. But tomorrow, it may not. So don't burn any bridges. And be careful what you wish for.

Saturday, September 18 (Moon into Aquarius, 4:35 a.m.) It's one of those days when you're fairly detached emotionally, which makes it good for dealing with emotional stuff. You'll have the distance you need. Since the issue could involve money, a subject about which you can be emotional, dive into your financial records. Get every-thing straightened out to your satisfaction. Figure out your financial goals.

•

Sunday, September 19 (Moon in Aquarius)   You're coming up on a full moon in Aries, and you may notice increased activity and perhaps a bit of chaos at home. Not to worry. If you're warned, you can be forearmed and deal with whatever comes up. But mark September 23 on your calendar.

Monday, September 20 (Moon into Pisces, 5:15 p.m.) With both Mars and Venus in Scorpio, your love life and creativity should be humming along very much to your satisfaction. Romance, in fact, may be as close as the house next door, or a flirtation could be heating up with someone you meet through a relative.

Tuesday, September 21 (Moon in Pisces)   Lucky you. With both Jupiter and Uranus back in Pisces for the rest of the year, any time the moon enters Pisces should be exciting, expansive, and generally a good luck day. So do something special today for yourself and for the people in your immediate environment. Practice ap-preciation. The more often you do that, the more likely it is that the universe will send more stuff your way to appreciate!

Wednesday, September 22 (Moon in Pisces)   Your head longs to go in one direction, your heart in an-other. It's the classic dilemma for the Pisces moon. So who wins: the head or the heart? You can't satisfy both. This is where you have to test your desires against your intuition.

Thursday, September 23 (Moon into Aries, 5:47 a.m.) Today's full moon in Aries is at zero degrees, a rather powerful full moon that stimulates three other areas in your chart. You become the intrepid explorer and may find that by handling a challenge differently from the way you usually do, things are settled much more quickly.

Friday, September 24 (Moon in Aries)   Combine the Aries moon with both Venus and Mars in passionate Scorpio, and you've got high-tension emotions. The Aries moon can be volatile, restless, and sharp-tongued. It can also be jealous. So walk a careful line. If you feel yourself getting jealous, breathe. Try to understand why you feel threatened. Don't lash out.

Saturday, September 25 (Moon into Taurus, 5:17 p.m.) Here's that beautiful Taurus moon again, all prepared to stir your sensuality, your romanticism, and your sexuality. Even if you're not involved right now, you probably will be before the end of the year. In terms of creativity, this moon brings new insights into a current project and the emotional stamina to see it through to the end.

Sunday, September 26 (Moon in Taurus)   Today is all about fun and pleasure. Make sure that any activity today is one in which you engage because you want to and not out of a sense of obligation. These Taurus moon days are supposed to open you up to your own desires so that you act on them.

Monday, September 27 (Moon in Taurus)   Mars and Venus are opposed to this moon, meaning they are in Taurus's opposite sign. That can create some tension between your desires and your outward actions, your needs and the needs of a partner. It's often a fine balance. But you manage to find it.

Tuesday, September 28 (Moon into Gemini, 3:12 a.m.) If you live in the northern hemisphere, are you still enjoying warm, beautiful weather? Take notice of your environment. Then communicate what you feel to others.

Wednesday, September 29 (Moon in Gemini) Things at work seem to loosen up a bit today, and you have a chance to socialize with coworkers or employees. You may be surprised to discover the commonalities that you share with the people you work alongside of day after day. It would behoove you to begin keeping a journal. Nothing fancy. A paragraph a day about your inner world.

Thursday, September 30 (Moon into Cancer, 10:47 a.m.) The moon enters your opposite sign. This can be a low point in the month for you, so it's important to get enough rest and to eat right. Your digestive system is ruled by the moon and Cancer, so if your stomach is bothering you, perhaps a change in diet is in order.

OCTOBER 2010

Friday, October 1 (Moon in Cancer) With the moon still in your opposite sign, the month gets off to a hectic start. It seems you've got a lot to do and not much time in which to do it. But instead of taking your work home with you this weekend, try leaving everything at the office and resolve to enjoy yourself for the next two days.

Saturday, October 2 (Moon into Leo, 4:22 p.m.) You may be helping out someone else today. This person could be moving or need help with taxes or insurance issues. Whatever it is, you're delighted to lend a helping hand and may be back tomorrow to finish up the job.

Sunday, October 3 (Moon in Leo) Mercury enters Libra, and the career area of your chart, where it will be until October 20. During this period, you may be

211

meeting more frequently with bosses and peers and could be traveling for business. This is a great time to pitch ideas, to boost your sales, and to generally consolidate your mental energy toward career and professional matters.

Monday, October 4 (Moon into Virgo, 5:00 p.m.) In a few days, Venus will turn retrograde in Scorpio, in your eleventh house. There are a couple of ways to prepare for this. If you're in the market for a computer, a car, or any other big-ticket item, buy before October 8. While it's possible to get good deals sometimes under a Venus retrograde, you may have to jump through hoops to do it. Best to buy now or wait until after November 18.

Tuesday, October 5 (Moon in Virgo) Hungry for adventure or a break in your routine? Feeling a bit of wanderlust? Then today is the day to head out of town by car, train, plane, or even on foot. You're primed for new experiences, and even though you don't actually have to leave town to have them, it's guaranteed to stir up your perceptions.

Wednesday, October 6 (Moon into Libra, 3:52 p.m.) The moon joins Mercury and Saturn in Libra, in your tenth house. The combination of planets snaps your focus to professional matters, teamwork, and social structures and relationships. With Saturn in your career court, any offers you receive deserve serious consideration.

Thursday, October 7 (Moon in Libra) Today's new moon in Libra should attract professional opportunities: a new job, a new career path, new contacts, a move, a promotion, a raise, a sale, an audition. You get the idea. Both Saturn and Mercury form wide conjunctions to this new moon, suggesting contracts, discussion, and debate and the new, stronger structures within which to work.

Friday, October 8 (Moon into Scorpio, 3:52 p.m.)
Venus turns retrograde in Scorpio, in your eleventh house. One possible repercussion for this retrograde is that former lovers or ex-spouses appear in your life. Or old friends you haven't seen in years suddenly get in touch. It's also possible that someone you consider a friend becomes something much more.

Saturday, October 9 (Moon in Scorpio)   The moon joins Venus retrograde in your eleventh house. If you hang out with friends or meet with a group to which you belong, there could be some bumps and bruises in personal relationships—the wrong words said at the wrong time, or a silly misunderstanding gets blown out of proportion. You may decide to beautify your surroundings in some way. Be careful about buying any expensive items to do this!

Sunday, October 10 (Moon into Sagittarius, 6:09 p.m.)
Tie up loose ends, complete projects, finish up answering your e-mails, and schedule appointments with your health-care practitioners. Today, tomorrow, and Tuesday are the days to do whatever has been placed on a back burner. Clear the decks. You're preparing yourself for the moon entering your sign on Wednesday.

Monday, October 11 (Moon in Sagittarius)   You're delving into your own psyche, looking for your true motives. Or you may be digging around in your own unconscious, looking for clues to a past life. Or you're making plans for your Halloween costume. Maybe a crazy astrologer?

Tuesday, October 12 (Moon in Sagittarius)   Your quest for deeper answers spills over into other areas of your life. You're at a bookstore and a particular book falls at your feet. You turn on the radio, and the first thing you hear actually answers a question that's been bugging you. Synchronicities abound.

Wednesday, October 13 (Moon into Capricorn, 1:17 a.m.) The moon enters your sign, and for the next two and a half days, you're in charge. Whenever the moon is in your sign, you may feel that you're the only one who can get the job done or meet the deadline. Or that you have to do everything. Resist that kind of thinking. Delegate.

Thursday, October 14 (Moon in Capricorn) The moon forms beneficial angles to Mars, Jupiter, Uranus, Pluto, and Venus. With this sort of lineup, things aren't just exciting. Your life may be moving at the speed of light, with events unfolding so quickly that you can barely keep pace. But keep pace you do, of course, because few signs in the zodiac have your gift for getting things done.

Friday, October 15 (Moon into Aquarius, 11:24 a.m.) If you're feeling a financial pinch right now, it's probably only in your mind. What's really going on is that you're aware of what you need to feel emotionally secure. Is it a certain amount of money in the bank, a solid family life, or friends or a partner upon whom you can depend? Answer these questions.

Saturday, October 16 (Moon in Aquarius) If you don't have to work weekends, then get together with friends and brainstorm for new ways to make money. You're feeling entrepreneurial today, and chances are that the people around you are as well. With that kind of energy humming through the air, indulge in some group brainstorming. Be as outrageously creative as you dare!

Sunday, October 17 (Moon into Pisces, 11:52 p.m.)
Enjoy. That's the day's message. The moon joins Uranus and Jupiter in your third house. One of the best uses for this energy is to feed your intellect by attending a seminar or workshop or just settling in with a great book. You're a psychic sponge today, so be sure to associate only with upbeat, positive people.

Monday, October 18 (Moon in Pisces)   There's usually an air of unpredictability with Uranus involved in an astrological lineup, and today is no exception. But because Uranus forms such a beneficial angle to your sun and is conjunct to expansive Jupiter, the unknown works in your favor. You attract unusual people and experiences, and in some way, these people or experiences expand your understanding of your world. You're finally beginning to understand your place in the scheme of things.

Tuesday, October 19 (Moon in Pisces)   Intuitively, you're paying closer attention to what you think. Sounds contradictory, doesn't it? But it really isn't. You're able to catch yourself now when some negative loop keeps playing in your head—something that probably has no basis in reality but for which you feel you should be prepared. Remember that you get what you concentrate on.

Wednesday, October 20 (Moon into Aries, 12:24 p.m.)
Mercury enters Scorpio and your eleventh house, where it will be until November 8. During this transit, you really do become a psychic sponge, absorbing information intuitively, and homing right in on the bottom line concerning issues and in relationships that are important to you. Friends take a more central role during this transit.

Thursday, October 21 (Moon in Aries)   You're on your own track today, wearing blinders that block your peripheral vision. It's likely that whatever you're doing requires a concentrated focus and determination, but you may have to remove those blinders before the end of the day to get some sense of how far you've gone.

Friday, October 22 (Moon into Taurus, 11:31 p.m.)
Expect news or some sort of culmination related to your family, your home, and your roots. Neptune forms a close and beneficial angle to this moon, indicating that you may not have all the information you need to make an informed decision.

Saturday, October 23 (Moon in Taurus)   It's smart to remind yourself that the Taurus moon days are the universe's gifts to you. It's as if some higher power is making it clear that it's okay to take a day off and have fun. So with that in mind, let this be a day with nothing scheduled.

Sunday, October 24 (Moon in Taurus)   You're learning that it's fine to live rooted in the moment. Yes, we all still need plans and goals and dreams toward which we can strive. But the moment is the only certainty, and the more present you are, the greater your sense of fulfillment and joy. And the more joyful you are, the more likely it is that you'll experience more joyful events and relationships.

Monday, October 25 (Moon into Gemini, 8:48 a.m.)
If you absolutely love what you do, it puts you leagues ahead of most people. It also helps you to maintain a positive attitude and belief in your own abilities, which then makes it easier to attract more experiences that feed this joy. But if you *are* looking for a job, today is the day to submit résumés and begin networking. Maintain your confidence. Keep believing in yourself. See yourself in the job you want.

Tuesday, October 26 (Moon in Gemini)   Jupiter is still moving retrograde through Pisces, making it likely that today you'll be communicating with a relative. If you and this person don't get along well, it's time to mend the relationship so that you both can move forward.

Wednesday, October 27 (Moon into Cancer, 4:15 p.m.) This moon forms a harmonious angle with both Venus and Mars in Scorpio. It boosts your intuitive abilities and also your nurturing qualities. But are you nurturing someone else out of a sense of obligation or because it's what you want to do?

Thursday, October 28 (Moon in Cancer)   Mars moves into Sagittarius and your twelfth house, where it will be until December 7. During this transit, you're urged to delve into your own unconscious. Therapy and meditation are excellent ways to do this. But so are dream recall, some sort of mind-body discipline like yoga, and even taking workshops in the development of psychic abilities.

Friday, October 29 (Moon into Leo, 9:39 p.m.)   This evening, the moon enters Leo and forms a beneficial angle with Mars in Sagittarius. You may be somewhat short-tempered or, at the very least, more irritable. Try not to take your irritability out on the people around you. Use the energy to do something constructive.

Saturday, October 30 (Moon in Leo)   You may be looking for end-of-the-year tax cuts. But it's best to wait until after Venus turns direct again on November 18 if you're buying expensive items that you can write off on your taxes. For now, just discuss your options with an accountant or someone with expertise in this area.

Sunday, October 31 (Moon in Leo)   Happy Halloween! Today, it all comes down to fun and games. If you have kids, then get into the Halloween celebrations. Even if you don't have kids, celebrate in some way.

NOVEMBER 2010

Monday, November 1 (Moon into Virgo, 12:51 a.m.)
As you enter the final two months of the year, the Virgo moon asks you to evaluate where you have been this year, what you have learned, and where you're headed now. In other words, it's time to take stock. If you're feeling really detail-oriented, you may want to open a computer file and take notes.

Tuesday, November 2 (Moon in Virgo)   In-laws or an out-of-town visitor may show up today. Whether the visit is expected or unexpected, you may feel pressured to take some time off work and show them around. Remind yourself that it's okay *not* to work around the clock.

Wednesday, November 3 (Moon into Libra, 2:19 a.m.)
Before Saturn leaves Libra in 2012, you should see progress in your professional life—a raise, a promotion, or recognition by peers or bosses. But Saturn can also cause delays.

Thursday, November 4 (Moon in Libra)   You may be juggling a lot of different balls today. Work, home, personal life, and everything in between. The balance you're seeking may elude you. But if you can keep your eye on the goal, then by tomorrow the balls all fall into place.

Friday, November 5 (Moon into Scorpio, 3:16 a.m.)
If you celebrate Thanksgiving, then you may be in discussions with friends and family members about who will host the festivities and who will bring which piece

of the dinner. If you have to fly to your destination for Thanksgiving, know that Mercury will be in direct motion, always a bonus. But traveling over the Christmas holidays may be another matter. Mercury will be retrograde from December 10 to December 30.

Saturday, November 6 (Moon in Scorpio) Today's new moon in Scorpio should attract new friends and groups into your life. You'll have opportunities to develop your intuitive ability, to conduct research and investigation, and to expand your creative venues. Neptune also turns direct today in Aquarius, in the financial sector of your chart. The impact of this movement will be subtle, but you'll begin to find ways to integrate your spirituality more readily into the way you earn your living.

Sunday, November 7—Daylight Saving Time Ends (Moon into Sagittarius, 4:28 a.m.) Communion with your hidden self is part of what unfolds today. It's possible that you finally understand what has motivated you in a relationship or situation. Whether or not you like what you find is really irrelevant. The important thing is that a question is answered.

Monday, November 8 (Moon in Sagittarius) Mercury enters Sagittarius and your twelfth house, where it will be until November 30. This transit certainly favors writers and writing and communication of all kinds. It would be a good time to get involved with publicity and promotion for your company's service or product. There could be some travel related to something you're working on.

Tuesday, November 9 (Moon into Capricorn, 9:37 a.m.) The transition is palpable. Midmorning, you suddenly are in your element again. The moon enters your sign once more. Work like a maniac, because that last

Mercury retrograde this year will be in your sign, and that will be a time for lying low and sticking close to home!

Wednesday, November 10 (Moon in Capricorn) Organization is the key. It doesn't matter whom or what you're organizing—you do it with your usual efficiency and drive. People around you marvel at how easy you make it all seem.

Thursday, November 11 (Moon into Aquarius, 6:33 p.m.) If possible, take some time today for reflection. You'll have the emotional detachment to do it, which will make it easier to deal with anything you discover that you don't like. But you tend to be tough on yourself and may ask for input from a trusted family member or friend.

Friday, November 12 (Moon in Aquarius) Vision is a quality of the Aquarius moon. Today you can put this quality to good use by trying to figure out where to invest your money. In the end, you may opt for what seems safest.

Saturday, November 13 (Moon in Aquarius) You know your priorities. You live according to your priorities. But today, the priorities may get switched around somewhat. A challenge surfaces at home, at work, or with a partner, and you have to deal with it.

Sunday, November 14 (Moon into Pisces, 6:25 a.m.) E-mails are flying back and forth through cyberspace as everyone in your environment gets dates and times for arrival set for the long Thanksgiving weekend. It may be that this year's table is open to neighbors and people in your community who live too far from their own families to go home.

Monday, November 15 (Moon in Pisces)   With Mars now in jubilant Sagittarius, your sex life could be heating up, but behind the scenes, in a relationship that may have an element of secrecy to it. That's fine. Unless you're being secretive because the relationship is illicit. Then you have to ask yourself if all the sneaking around is really worth it.

Tuesday, November 16 (Moon into Aries, 7:00 p.m.) This evening, the moon enters your fourth house, and things at home suddenly seem to be on an unexpected track. It throws you off your game. But by the end of tomorrow, you find a unique and creative way to deal with whatever it is.

Wednesday, November 17 (Moon in Aries)   You're emotionally charged today, a knight armed for battle. Things could be somewhat volatile with someone close to you, so it might be best to sit out a round or two. In fact, wait until Friday to deal with this. The moon will be in Taurus then.

Thursday, November 18 (Moon in Aries)   Both Venus and Jupiter turn direct today, certainly a cause for celebration. You now have a much clearer idea about what you're looking for romantically and creatively. Both Venus and Jupiter now head toward their appointment with Aries early in 2011, so enjoy these two planets traveling in harmony with your sun sign through the end of the year. Life will unfold more smoothly.

Friday, November 19 (Moon into Taurus, 6:05 a.m.) Any decision you put off should be tackled now, while the moon is in fellow earth sign Taurus. Your resolve will be helpful in dealing with whatever the issue is. Also, other earth-sign individuals may be helpful now— anyone with a Taurus, a Capricorn, or a Virgo sun. On the romantic front, it's the day to plan something special with the person who is most special to you.

Saturday, November 20 (Moon in Taurus)   You could be feeling the effects of tomorrow's full moon already. If so, then your day is sure to be fast-paced, with e-mail filling your in-box, your phone ringing constantly, and your calendar getting crowded. You're in demand.

Sunday, November 21 (Moon into Gemini, 2:46 p.m.) Today's full moon in Gemini should be splendid for you. It falls in your fifth house of romance and creativity, so in those areas, there should be news and some sort of culmination. Perhaps you and a partner decide to take your relationship to a deeper level of commitment. Maybe you decide it's time to start a family. With friendly angles from both Jupiter and Uranus, excitement and serendipity are sure to be part of the events.

Monday, November 22 (Moon in Gemini)   Network. Even if you're not up to it, do it anyway. It will benefit you in the long run and take your mind off other issues and concerns. Besides, once you start socializing and talking with people, you find that you enjoy it.

Tuesday, November 23 (Moon into Cancer, 9:14 p.m.) If you're taking time off this week to head out of town for Thanksgiving—or to prepare for the arrival of guests— then you may be in a frenetic mood today. Rushed. Trying to get stuff done. Relax. You have a partner who is willing to help or employees and coworkers who are eager to get involved.

Wednesday, November 24 (Moon in Cancer)   Mom or her surrogate in your life plays a part in the day's events. Or you may be nurturing someone else. Regardless, there's a strong home-and-hearth component to the day, right in time for Thanksgiving.

Thursday, November 25 (Moon in Cancer) Happy
Thanksgiving! In the celebration of a long weekend, remember to be appreciative of all that you have. Surrounded
by good friends or family or even caring strangers.

Friday, November 26 (Moon into Leo, 2:01 a.m.)
This moon forms a beneficial angle to Mars in Sagittarius. So you've got plenty of physical energy and the
focus to see a project or anything through to the end.
You have the big picture for sure and may only have to
connect the dots to bring it all together. When the moon
enters Virgo on Sunday, you'll have a clearer sense of
everything.

Saturday, November 27 (Moon in Leo) Still looking
for some end-of-the-year tax breaks? It's favorable to
buy those big-ticket items now that Venus is direct. Do
it before December 10, when Mercury turns retrograde
in your sign, or after December 30, when it turns direct
again. But that might be cutting it all a bit too close.

Sunday, November 28 (Moon into Virgo, 5:34 a.m.)
Here's the connect-the-dots day. Regardless of where
your focus is, it's important to tend to details. Read the
small print. Listen to your intuition. Quite often, you
intuitively pick up things that your left brain misses or
overlooks.

Monday, November 29 (Moon in Virgo) As you
head into the last month of the year, do a retrospective,
just as you did at the end of last month. Are you happy
with where you are right this moment? What would you
like to achieve during December? Start thinking about
your goals for 2011.

Tuesday, November 30 (Moon into Libra, 8:16 a.m.)
Mercury enters your sign. Except for the retrograde period, you'll enjoy this transit. Your mind is sharp, quick,

organized, and focused. You may want to start organizing your New Year's festivities before Mercury turns retrograde on December 10. Otherwise, things are sure to change.

DECEMBER 2010

Wednesday, December 1 (Moon in Libra) Have you met your career goals for the year? If not, what can you do before the end of the year to move things closer to your goal? You'll be dealing with those kinds of questions today and may be talking about these very issues with coworkers and friends.

Thursday, December 2 (Moon into Scorpio, 10:44 a.m.) The moon forms a beneficial angle to Mercury in your sign, bringing an intuitive element to your conscious thoughts. It's easier to plan and strategize now, and if you can do this in an intuitive way, taking your cues from your environment and the people around you, so much the better.

Friday, December 3 (Moon in Scorpio) The moon links up with Venus. Your love life, creativity, and even your kids play into the day's events. Intense experiences and emotions are the norm. You have the ability today to delve deeply into anything you do, read, think, investigate, and feel.

Saturday, December 4 (Moon into Sagittarius, 2:00 p.m.) If the holidays are pressing down against you like a ton of bricks—shopping, guests arriving, plans, or whatever—today is perfect for getting off by yourself and putting things in order. In fact, tomorrow's new moon should bring more opportunities to do exactly that.

Sunday, December 5 (Moon in Sagittarius) The new moon in Sagittarius should usher in opportunities for overseas travel, education, and working behind the scenes in some capacity. Saturn forms a beneficial angle to this moon, indicating that these opportunities are serious and deserve your consideration. Uranus also turns direct in Pisces. The impact of this movement probably will be subtle, but you should notice a difference in your daily life experiences. Fewer snafus!

Monday, December 6 (Moon into Capricorn, 7:17 p.m.) Mercury turns retrograde on December 10, so start making backups of your computer files, finalize your travel plans and your plans for New Year's Eve, and buy whatever items you need for end-of-the-year tax write-offs. Since Mercury will be turning retrograde in your sign, be sure to have backup plans for everything!

Tuesday, December 7 (Moon in Capricorn) Mars enters your sign today, joining Mercury and Pluto in your first house. This lineup of planets, particularly Mars and Pluto traveling together, really acts as a booster rocket for whatever you're doing. You're in a powerful position to get things done, to push your agenda forward, and to organize and implement. This is especially true from now to December 10, when Mercury turns retrograde.

Wednesday, December 8 (Moon in Capricorn) With so many planets lined up in your favor today, you really have to work at making a wrong move! A partner—romantic or business—is helpful in whatever you're working on. Resist the urge to do it all yourself. Delegate.

Thursday, December 9 (Moon into Aquarius, 3:32 a.m.) Time to back up computer files, sign contracts, and finalize travel and New Year's Eve plans. Mercury turns retrograde in your sign tomorrow. It might also be a good idea if you can wind up your holiday shopping today, especially if you're buying expensive items. You don't want to be in the return lines on December 26.

Friday, December 10 (Moon in Aquarius)   Mercury turns retrograde in Capricorn and stays that way until December 30. You've got plenty of other good stuff going on, what with Mars in your sign, providing all the physical energy you need, and Venus still in Scorpio. The angle Mars and Venus make to each other is beneficial and should add smoothness and heightened sexuality to any romantic relationship.

Saturday, December 11 (Moon into Pisces, 2:41 p.m.) Today through Monday will be the last time this year that the moon hooks up with Jupiter and Uranus in Pisces. Take advantage of the energy while you can. Get into a creative project. Mend fences with a relative. Forgive, forget, and move on.

Sunday, December 12 (Moon in Pisces)   Intuitively, you're right on the money about an issue or situation. But to convince someone else that you understand what's going on, you may have to gather facts to back up your intuition. Not a problem. You know exactly where to find what you need.

Monday, December 13 (Moon in Pisces)   Venus and the moon form beneficial angles to each other and to Mars, Pluto, and Mercury in your sign. This combination is so favorable to anything you do, think, or plan that things should manifest in a positive way despite Mercury's retrograde. You simply have to remain focused on your intents and desires.

Tuesday, December 14 (Moon into Aries, 3:15 a.m.)   Today favors picking up last-minute holiday items or planning an office party or just generally trying to get things together for the holidays. You're the planner, and that's true whether you're planning at work or at home, and yes, today you're the problem solver as well.

Wednesday, December 15 (Moon in Aries)　Your ideas flow forth with such shocking ease that you wonder where they're coming from. Record them. When a creative tap like this one opens up, you want to be sure the ideas don't get away! Some of the ideas could be triggered by a conversation with a family member or with someone else in your personal environment.

Thursday, December 16 (Moon into Taurus, 2:49 p.m.) Venus and the moon are opposed to each other. It's not as serious as it sounds, but can lead to excesses— hammering at an old issue, too much partying, losing sleep, and all the things many of us do around the holidays. Strive for balance.

Friday, December 17 (Moon in Taurus)　Despite yesterday's warning, the Taurus moon really is about enjoying yourself, in whatever form that takes. If you have children, then today may be their last school day until the New Year. Perhaps it's time to gather up the kids and enjoy yourself with them.

Saturday, December 18 (Moon into Gemini, 11:38 p.m.) Right now, every planet except for Mercury is moving in direct motion. So despite Mercury's mischievousness, you're able to zip through your day at your usual pace. You connect with old friends through e-mail or a blog or chat room. Information is shared, and it happens to be exactly what you're looking for. Serendipity!

Sunday, December 19 (Moon in Gemini)　Haven't you earned a day off? Yes, you have. So pat yourself on the back, kick back, and get lost in a good book. Or go see a movie. Take a nap. Do whatever you want.

Monday, December 20 (Moon in Gemini)   Your local bookstore could be your favorite haunt today. Whether you're browsing or doing last-minute holiday shopping, there's something about the smell and feel and texture of books that excites you, that stokes your imagination. If you're buying for coworkers, make sure the books fit the people.

Tuesday, December 21 (Moon into Cancer, 5:22 a.m.) Today's full moon in Gemini highlights something in your daily work routine. If you've applied for a new job or put in for a promotion, then today you may receive news about it. Saturn forms a wide but beneficial angle to this moon, indicating that any offers or news you receive are solid, real, and serious.

Wednesday, December 22 (Moon in Cancer) Whether you're traveling for the holidays or staying close to home, it's about this time every year (or sooner) when life gets busy. You flourish when you're busy. You even flourish in chaos. But you also like to call the shots, to be in control of the situation, and today you may not be. Try not to obsess about it. Go with the flow. You'll be happier.

Thursday, December 23 (Moon into Leo, 8:51 a.m.) You may be wrestling with insurance and tax issues today. It's not what you want to do during the holidays, but best to get it out of the way so you can enjoy the rest of the holidays. Be forewarned that because Mercury is retrograde, you may be doing the same thing again on December 30.

Friday, December 24 (Moon in Leo)   Whether you celebrate Christmas or not, it's a good time to take a look around and appreciate everything you have. Whether it's family, friends, a home, good health, or prosperity, be grateful. Show your appreciation for the people around you.

Saturday, December 25 (Moon into Virgo, 11:15 a.m.)
Merry Christmas! Whether you celebrate today or not, there's a need to pay attention to details. It may have to do with people's relationships to one another, how they treat each other, what they say or don't say. You may find yourself mediating or explaining.

Sunday, December 26 (Moon in Virgo)   Avoid the malls. Sleep in. Burn off some of that energy from Mars in your sign. This could mean doing something physical—skiing, taking a walk, or going to the gym. Honor Jupiter's final fling in Pisces by giving back to your neighborhood or community in some way.

Monday, December 27 (Moon into Libra, 1:39 p.m.)
If you go into work today, there will be a team effort of some kind to push through a product, agenda, or idea before the end of the year. If you've taken time off from work, you may have the same challenge facing you, but on the home front.

Tuesday, December 28 (Moon in Libra)   You're the arbitrator today, the one who mitigates, the one who stands in the other person's shoes, feeling and seeing what he or she does. It deepens your understanding of the conflicts between people that are often founded on nothing more than misunderstandings.

Wednesday, December 29 (Moon into Scorpio, 4:50 p.m.)
The moon joins Venus in Scorpio and brings your creativity into sharp relief. Since Mercury will be retrograde until tomorrow, don't pitch ideas or submit any creative projects until December 31. Better yet, wait until next year.

Thursday, December 30 (Moon in Scorpio)   Mercury turns direct. Before you rush to the phone or the computer to firm up plans for tomorrow night, if you don't have plans yet, wait until tomorrow morning, when Mercury is stabilized. If you don't want to wing it that way, then take your chances! But maintain flexibility. You'll need it.

Friday, December 31 (Moon in Scorpio)   Reflect back on the year. Then look forward. Standing where you are right this second, what would you change? There's no right or wrong answer. Only honesty is required!

HAPPY NEW YEAR!

JANUARY 2011

Saturday, January 1 (Moon in Sagittarius)   The year begins with the moon in your twelfth house. After last night, you're probably ready for a relaxed day behind the scenes, especially if you were out late celebrating. Take time to reflect and meditate. Come up with some goals for 2011, if you haven't done so already. Unconscious attitudes can be difficult. Keep your feelings secret.

Sunday, January 2 (Moon in Sagittarius)   Your intuition is heightened. Spiritual values arise. Write in a journal or on a blog. You're restless, impulsive, and inquisitive. You see the big picture, not just the details. There's passion in relationships.

Monday, January 3 (Moon into Capricorn, 2:39 a.m.) It's a number 8 day, your power day. Focus on a power play. Unexpected money arrives. You can go far with your plans and achieve financial success. Be aware that you're playing with power, so try not to hurt anyone.

Tuesday, January 4 (Moon in Capricorn)   There's a new moon in your first house, and also the sun and Mars enter your first house. New opportunities for personal development come your way. You're feeling physically vital, more energetic and confident, and definitely more assertive. You're letting go of the old and taking on the new. You have a stronger understanding this month about who you are and where you are going.

Wednesday, January 5 (Moon into Aquarius, 11:08 a.m.) Cooperation is highlighted. Use your intuition to get a sense of the day. A partnership, either personal or professional, plays an important role. Be kind and understanding. Don't make waves. Just go with the flow.

Thursday, January 6 (Moon in Aquarius) The moon is in your second house. So it's a good day for dealing with money issues. Pay what you owe, and collect what others owe you. You tend to equate your financial assets with emotional security. Look at your priorities in handling your income.

Friday, January 7 (Moon into Pisces, 9:57 p.m.) With Venus moving into your twelfth house, you'll enjoy working on your own this month. You'll feel comfortable in your solitude. After all, you have a secret to guard. Your emotions are strong, but they're below the surface.

Saturday, January 8 (Moon in Pisces) The moon is in your third house. Your mental abilities are enhanced, and you have an emotional need to reinvigorate your studies, especially regarding matters of the past. You're attracted to historical or archaeological studies. You write from a deep place. It's a good day for journaling. Female relatives play a role.

Sunday, January 9 (Moon in Pisces) You're creative and imaginative. You're feeling inspired. You respond emotionally to whatever is happening. Your

feelings of compassion and tenderness can help heal a
friend or loved one.

Monday, January 10 (Moon into Aries, 10:24 a.m.)
It's a number 7 day, a mystery day. You launch a journey into the unknown. Secrets, intrigue, and confidential information play a role. You work best on your own.
Knowledge is essential to success. Gather information,
but don't make any absolute decisions until tomorrow.

Tuesday, January 11 (Moon in Aries)   The moon is
in your fourth house. Spend time with your family and
loved ones. Stick close to home if possible. Retreat to a
private place to meditate. You're dealing with the foundations of who you are and whom you are becoming. A
parent plays a role.

Wednesday, January 12 (Moon into Taurus, 10:37 p.m.)
Finish whatever you've been working on. Clear up odds
and ends. Take an inventory of where things are going in
your life. Make room for something new. Get ready for
your new cycle.

Thursday, January 13 (Moon in Taurus)   With
Mercury moving into your first house for the rest of the
month, you communicate well, and you are open to talking about your feelings and how you feel. That's especially true if you're dealing with a health matter. You're
mentally restless and looking for new information that
could help you understand a personal matter. Express
yourself in writing.

Friday, January 14 (Moon in Taurus)   Be yourself.
Be emotionally honest. In love, there's greater emotional depth to a relationship. Be aware that a loved one
might need a bit more attention than usual. Your emotions tend to overpower your intellect. But your creative
juices are flowing.

Saturday, January 15 (Moon into Gemini, 8:23 a.m.)
Mars moves into your second house of money. That means you're apt to be spending your time this month pursuing ways of increasing your income. Because of your aggressive and competitive stance, you see ways of making money that others overlook. Take a chance.

Sunday, January 16 (Moon in Gemini)   The moon is in your sixth house. Your personal health occupies your attention. Maintain emotional balance. Help others, but don't deny your own needs.

Monday, January 17 (Moon into Cancer, 2:30 p.m.)
Promote new ideas; follow your curiosity. Freedom of thought and action is key. Think outside the box. Take risks; experiment. Variety is the spice of life.

Tuesday, January 18 (Moon in Cancer)   The moon is in your seventh house. The focus is on relationships, business and personal ones. You comprehend the nuance of a situation, but it's difficult to go with the flow. You feel a need to be accepted, but be careful that others don't manipulate your feelings.

Wednesday, January 19 (Moon into Leo, 5:17 p.m.)
There's a full moon in your seventh house, and Jupiter forms a fantastic and exact angle. That means you gain insight and illumination related to partnerships. You understand what was going on. The air is cleared, and you have a chance to expand your plans. Meanwhile, Uranus also forms a harmonious angle. Watch out for sudden changes in plans in coming weeks. Go with the flow.

Thursday, January 20 (Moon in Leo)   The moon is in your eighth house. That means you reap what you've sown related to psychic exploration. Your intuition is enhanced. You see what's coming much better. You

233

could be involved in managing joint finances or shared possessions. You're a go-getter, Capricorn.

Friday, January 21 (Moon into Virgo, 6:11 p.m.)   Finish what you started. Visualize the future; set your goals, and then make them so. Clear up odds and ends. Take an inventory of where things are going in your life. Make a donation to a worthy cause.

Saturday, January 22 (Moon in Virgo)   Jupiter moves into Aries, your fourth house. That means that over the next six months, you'll be able to expand whatever you initiate. That's particularly true if you're working out of your home or working on home improvements. Look at who you are and whom you are becoming.

Sunday, January 23 (Moon into Libra, 7:00 p.m.) It's a number 2 day, putting the spotlight on cooperation. Help comes through friends and loved ones, especially a partner. Don't make waves. Don't rush or show resentment. Let things develop. There could be some soul-searching related to a relationship.

Monday, January 24 (Moon in Libra)   The moon is in your tenth house. Your professional life is energized. You make a strong emotional commitment to your profession or to a role in public life. You gain recognition and prestige along with material success.

Tuesday, January 25 (Moon into Scorpio, 9:16 p.m.) It's a number 4 day. Your organizational skills are highlighted. Control your impulses. Fulfill your obligations. You're building foundations for an outlet for your creativity.

Wednesday, January 26 (Moon in Scorpio)   Saturn goes retrograde in your tenth house and stays there until June 12. That means that things related to your career probably slow down. For example, you could encounter delays in projects you want to launch. You might start to rethink or revise your career goals.

Thursday, January 27 (Moon in Scorpio)   The moon is in your eleventh house. Group activities work in your favor, even if you're a nonjoiner. You assist the group and—surprise—the group helps you in return. Friends also play an important role. Focus on your wishes and dreams, but make sure that your goals remain an expression of who you really are.

Friday, January 28 (Moon into Sagittarius, 1:55 a.m.) It's a number 7 day. You could be pursuing a mystery or investigating the unknown. Knowledge is essential to success. Secrets, intrigue, and confidential information play a role. Go with the flow. Maintain your emotional balance.

Saturday, January 29 (Moon in Sagittarius)   With the moon in your twelfth house, yesterday's energy flows into your Saturday. You feel best working on your own, remaining behind the scenes. Secret information comes into play, and you're intent on keeping it yourself. Unconscious attitudes can be difficult. So can relations with women.

Sunday, January 30 (Moon into Capricorn, 9:04 a.m.) Clear your desk for tomorrow's new cycle. Visualize the future; set your goals, and then make them so. Look beyond the immediate. Use the day for reflection, expansion, and concluding projects.

Monday, January 31 (Moon in Capricorn)   The moon is on your ascendant. Start something new. Your appearance and personality shine. Your feelings and thoughts are aligned. The way you see yourself is the way others see you. You're recharged for the month ahead, and this makes you more appealing to the public.

FEBRUARY 2011

Tuesday, February 1 (Moon into Aquarius, 6:21 p.m.)
It's a number 8 day, your power day and your day to play it your way. It's a good day to buy a lottery ticket. Take a chance. Look for a windfall. Business dealings go well.

Wednesday, February 2 (Moon in Aquarius) There's a new moon in your second house. Look for new money-making opportunities. You equate your financial assets with emotional security. Watch your spending. You take pride in your possessions, but it's not a good day to add to them.

Thursday, February 3 (Moon in Aquarius) Mercury moves into your second house, adding energy to your moneymaking efforts. Ideas are abundant, and you're very conscious of your values. You also communicate well—speaking or writing—and you are persuasive. You attract the attention and interest of others, especially related to a business plan.

Friday, February 4 (Moon into Pisces, 5:24 a.m.)
Venus moves onto your ascendant for the next three weeks. That means your appearance impresses, and your personality shines this month. Your personal grace and friendly demeanor are pleasing to others. You are outgoing and have a positive outlook. It's easy to make friends this month, and any contacts you make will benefit you later.

Saturday, February 5 (Moon in Pisces) The moon is in your third house. You can be quite opinionated, especially when talking with family members or neighbors. Try to stay in control of your emotions. You tend to be affected by the past. Best to let it go.

Sunday, February 6 (Moon into Aries, 5:46 p.m.)
Your organizational skills are called upon, Capricorn. Stay focused on whatever you're doing. Be methodical and thorough. Don't get sloppy. You're building a creative base for the future.

Monday, February 7 (Moon in Aries) The moon is in your fourth house. Spend time with your family and loved ones. Stick close to home if possible. A parent or parents could play a role. You're dealing with the foundations of who you are and whom you are becoming. It's a good day for dream recall.

Tuesday, February 8 (Moon in Aries) Initiate projects, launch new ideas, and brainstorm. Emotions could be volatile. You're passionate but impatient. You're active and physical. Be careful to avoid reckless behavior. A sports event could be highlighted.

Wednesday, February 9 (Moon into Taurus, 6:23 a.m.)
It's a number 7 day, a mystery day. You set off on a journey into the unknown. Secrets, intrigue, and confidential information play a role. Be aware of decisions made behind closed doors. You figure out what's going on and wonder why others aren't as aware. You detect deception and recognize insincerity with ease. That said, make sure that you see things as they are, not as you wish them to be.

Thursday, February 10 (Moon in Taurus) Your emotions tend to overpower your intellect. Be yourself. Be emotionally honest. In love, there's greater emotional depth to a relationship. You feel strongly attached to loved ones, particularly children. But eventually you need to let go.

Friday, February 11 (Moon into Gemini, 5:22 p.m.)
Look beyond the immediate. Finish what you started. Visualize the future; set your goals, and then make them so. Complete a project and make room for something new.

Saturday, February 12 (Moon in Gemini)   The moon is in your sixth house. It's a service day. Help others, but don't deny your own needs. Keep your resolutions about exercise, and watch your diet. Attend to details related to your health.

Sunday, February 13 (Moon in Gemini)   You're mentally quick, and you communicate well. Get together with friends and relatives. A change of scenery—maybe a short car trip for a visit—gives you a new perspective. In any discussion, you have the ability to see both sides of the issue.

Monday, February 14 (Moon into Cancer, 12:50 a.m.)
Yesterday's energy flows into your Monday. You're innovative and creative; you communicate well. You keep everyone in balance, and you are well liked. Enjoy the harmony, beauty, and pleasures of life. Remain flexible. Intuition is highlighted.

Tuesday, February 15 (Moon in Cancer)   With the moon in your seventh house, the focus turns to relationships, both personal and business. You communicate well and get along with others. You can fit in just about anywhere. You comprehend the nuances of a situation.

Wednesday, February 16 (Moon into Leo, 4:15 a.m.)
Promote new ideas; follow your curiosity. Approach the day with an unconventional mind-set. Release old structures; get a new point of view. Think outside the box. Think freedom, no restrictions.

Thursday, February 17 (Moon in Leo)   The moon is in your eighth house. Your experiences are more intense than usual, especially when dealing with matters related to your home. Meditate, especially at home, or study a metaphysical subject, such as life after death or reincarnation.

Friday, February 18 (Moon into Virgo, 4:40 a.m.) With the full moon in your eighth house, you gain insight and illumination related to mortgages, taxes, or insurance. In essence, you reap what you've sown. Alternately, you gain a better understanding of the goals of a large social movement in which you are invested emotionally or socially.

Saturday, February 19 (Moon in Virgo)   The moon is in your ninth house. You're a dreamer and a thinker. You may feel a need to get away. Plan a long trip. Sign up for a workshop or seminar. Publicize and advertise whatever you're doing. If you're involved with a publishing project, expect some answers—positive ones.

Sunday, February 20 (Moon into Libra, 4:01 a.m.) Use the day for reflection, expansion, and concluding projects. Clear up odds and ends. Take an inventory of where things are going in your life. Visualize the future; set your goals, and then make them so.

Monday, February 21 (Moon in Libra)   With Mercury moving into your third house, you are witty and clever. You express yourself clearly and can talk about a variety of subjects, though not in great depth. You're also adaptable to changing circumstances.

Tuesday, February 22 (Moon into Scorpio, 4:29 a.m.) With Mars joining Mercury in your third house, you get somewhat aggressive in presenting your ideas, especially about the past. Unless you catch yourself, you're likely to get into arguments with family members or neighbors. You tend to have little patience with those who don't agree with you. Participate in competitive games that require acute mental concentration.

Wednesday, February 23 (Moon in Scorpio) The moon is in your eleventh house. Friendships take on more structure, Capricorn. If you get involved in a group or a charitable cause, everything is structured and has a schedule. Take time to focus on your wishes and dreams.

Thursday, February 24 (Moon into Sagittarius, 7:46 a.m.) Get organized, Capricorn. You're a natural. Clean out a closet or straighten up your desk. Like yesterday, keep your goals in mind, and follow your ideas. Be tenacious. You tend to stay with the tried and true. It's not a day for experimentation or new approaches.

Friday, February 25 (Moon in Sagittarius) You work behind the scenes, possibly at a home office. E-mails or text messages play a role. So does a private discussion with someone you trust. It's a good day for meditation or a therapy session. Avoid any self-destructive tendencies, confrontations, and conflict. Think carefully before you act. Be aware of hidden enemies.

Saturday, February 26 (Moon into Capricorn, 2:32 p.m.) Service to others is the theme. You offer advice and support. Diplomacy, rather than confrontation, wins the day. Be sympathetic and kind, generous and tolerant. Do a good deed for someone. But know when to say enough is enough.

Sunday, February 27 (Moon in Capricorn) The moon is in your first house. You're sensitive to other people's feelings. You feel moody one moment, happy the next, then withdrawn and sad. It's all about your emotional self. Your feelings and thoughts are aligned. You're dealing with your emotional self, the person you are becoming.

Monday, February 28 (Moon in Capricorn) Your ambition and drive to succeed are highlighted. Your responsibilities expand. You may feel stressed, over-worked. Don't ignore your exercise routine. Be conservative. Don't speculate or take any unnecessary risks. Maintain emotional balance.

MARCH 2011

Tuesday, March 1 (Moon into Aquarius, 12:15 a.m.) Venus moves into your second house. You love the idea of making a lot of money, and you could do so through a creative endeavor. You love the good things in life. You're pleased with your belongings and the memories associated with them.

Wednesday, March 2 (Moon in Aquarius) You have a greater sense of freedom. You're dealing with new ideas, new options, and originality. You get a new perspective, especial one related to moneymaking ideas. Play your hunches. Look beyond the immediate.

Thursday, March 3 (Moon into Pisces, 11:48 a.m.) Use your intuition to get a sense of your day. Don't make waves. Don't rush or show resentment. Let things develop. Cooperation is highlighted. Be kind and understanding.

Friday, March 4 (Moon in Pisces) There's a new moon in your third house. That means new opportunities related to your ideas, especially those that are connected to matters from the past. Put it all down in writing. You won't regret it! That's especially true because Mercury and Mars are in your third house. Siblings or neighbors could play a role in your plans.

Saturday, March 5 (Moon in Pisces)   You're feeling inspired with all these new opportunities turning up. Imagination is highlighted. Watch for synchronicities. Keep track of your dreams, including your daydreams. Ideas are ripe. Universal knowledge and deep healing are key.

Sunday, March 6 (Moon into Aries, 12:15 a.m.) Think freedom, no restrictions. Change and variety are highlighted. Let go of old structures and find a new point of view. Promote those new ideas; follow your curiosity.

Monday, March 7 (Moon in Aries)   Spend time with your family and loved ones. Stick close to home, if possible. Work at home. You're dealing with the foundations of who you are. A parent plays a role.

Tuesday, March 8 (Moon into Taurus, 12:53 p.m.) It's another 7 day, a mystery day. You could be actively investigating a matter of importance to you. There could be secret dealings involved. You're a spy for your own cause. Knowledge is essential to success. Gather information, but don't make any absolute decisions until tomorrow.

Wednesday, March 9 (Moon in Taurus)   Mercury moves into your fourth house. There's a lot of activity in the home related to education. You could be helping a child with homework, considering homeschooling, or looking into colleges for an older child. Things are definitely active and changing in your home life. Try to take time to relax.

Thursday, March 10 (Moon in Taurus)   The moon is in your fifth house. You're emotionally in touch with your creative side. There also could be more involvement with kids. You feel strongly attached to loved ones, particularly children. You're more protective and nurturing, but try to avoid being too controlling. Pets could play a role, possibly involving a visit to the vet.

Friday, March 11 (Moon into Gemini, 12:32 a.m.) Uranus moves into your fourth house. You're looking for more freedom in your home environment. You feel a need to come and go as you please. You're turning away from the traditional idea of family life. However, by following that path, there's a good possibility of sudden upsets in your home life over the next seven years.

Saturday, March 12 (Moon in Gemini) The moon is in your sixth house. It's a service day. Others rely on you for help. You improve, edit, and refine the work of others. Help others, but don't deny your own needs, and don't let your fears hold you back.

Sunday, March 13—Daylight Saving Time Begins (Moon into Cancer, 10:30 a.m.) It's a number 3 day. Relax, enjoy yourself, and recharge your batteries. Have fun in preparation for tomorrow's discipline and focus. You can influence people with your upbeat attitude. In romance, you're an ardent lover and loyal.

Monday, March 14 (Moon in Cancer) The moon is in your seventh house. You get along well with others now. You can fit in just about anywhere. Loved ones and partners are more important than usual. Take time to consider how others see you. You're in the public eye.

Tuesday, March 15 (Moon into Leo, 3:34 p.m.) You tend to drop your usual sense of order and discipline, Capricorn. Variety is the spice of life for you. Think outside the box. You're courageous and adaptable. A change of scenery would work to your advantage. You could be moving to a new location. You're seeking new horizons.

Wednesday, March 16 (Moon in Leo) The moon is in your eighth house of shared resources and investments. Your experiences are more intense than usual. You have a strong sense of duty, and you feel obligated to fulfill your promises. Security is an important issue with you. Deal with mortgages, insurance, and investments.

Thursday, March 17 (Moon into Virgo, 4:53 p.m.) It's another mystery day. You journey into the unknown. You're a searcher, a seeker of truth. You investigate, analyze, or simply observe what's going on. You quickly come to a conclusion and wonder why others don't see what you see. You work best on your own.

Friday, March 18 (Moon in Virgo) The moon is in your ninth house. You're a dreamer and a thinker. You may feel a need to get away. You yearn for a new experience. Plan a long trip, or sign up for a workshop or seminar. A foreign-born person could play a role in your day.

Saturday, March 19 (Moon into Libra, 4:03 p.m.) There's a full moon in your ninth house. Your ideas come to fruition. You are provoking change, and others are finally listening to you. Even though you have a tendency to change your mind, your suggestions are taking root. Plan a getaway. You've done as much as you can for the time being.

Sunday, March 20 (Moon in Libra) The moon is in your tenth house. You're feeling ambitious, pushing ahead in your career, even on a Sunday. You've got your eye on a promotion. Aim high!

Monday, March 21 (Moon into Scorpio, 3:17 p.m.) Cooperation is highlighted. After yesterday's high energy, it's best to back off. Don't make waves. Don't rush or show resentment. Focus on your direction, your motivation. Where are you going and why? Your intuition focuses on relationships.

Tuesday, March 22 (Moon in Scorpio) The moon is in your eleventh house. You have deeper contact with friends. You find strength in numbers, meaning through friends or a group. Focus on your wishes and dreams. You could find a new direction by joining a group of like-minded individuals.

Wednesday, March 23 (Moon into Sagittarius, 4:46 p.m.) It's a number 4 day. That means your organizational skills are called upon, Capricorn. Persevere to get things done. Hard work is called for. Be methodical and thorough. Tear down the old in order to rebuild. You're developing a creative base for the future.

Thursday, March 24 (Moon in Sagittarius) The past is affecting you. There's a tendency to block out your emotions to avoid unwanted feelings. But, if you do that, you'll find these feelings will get stronger. Try to meditate; get centered. It's a day for working behind the scenes.

Friday, March 25 (Moon into Capricorn, 9:58 p.m.) Service to others is the theme. Others come to you for help, and you need to be diplomatic. You offer advice and support. Be sympathetic and kind, generous and tolerant, but avoid scattering your energies. Buy something for your house.

Saturday, March 26 (Moon in Capricorn) The moon is on your ascendant. That means the way you see yourself is the way others see you. You're getting recharged for the month ahead, and this makes you more appealing to the public. You're physically vital, and you can expect relations with the opposite sex to go well.

Sunday, March 27 (Moon in Capricorn)   Venus moves into Pisces. You're creative and imaginative. Your artistic abilities are enhanced. You respond with heart and passion to whatever is happening. Keep track of your dreams, including your daydreams. Ideas are ripe.

Monday, March 28 (Moon into Aquarius, 7:01 a.m.) It's a number 9 day. It's a great time for completing projects and getting ready for something new. Clear up odds and ends. Take an inventory of where things are going in your life. Make a donation to a worthy cause. Look beyond the present.

Tuesday, March 29 (Moon in Aquarius)   The moon is in your second house. You feel strongly about a money issue. Finances and material goods are important to you and give you a sense of security. You identify emotionally with your possessions or whatever you value.

Wednesday, March 30 (Moon into Pisces, 6:39 p.m.) Mercury goes retrograde in your fourth house and stays there until April 23. That means you can expect some delays and glitches in communication over the next three weeks, especially with family members and domestic matters. When explaining your ideas, be sure to make yourself clearly understood. There also could be some delays related to a home-repair project.

Thursday, March 31 (Moon in Pisces)   The moon is in your third house. You write from a deep place. It's a good day for journaling or working on any writing project. Your thinking can be unduly influenced by the past.

Friday, April 1 (Moon in Pisces)   The moon is in your third house. Take what you know and share it with others. However, keep conscious control of your emotions when communicating. That's especially true when dealing with relatives or neighbors.

Saturday, April 2 (Moon into Aries, 7:17 a.m.)   Mars moves into your fourth house. You're physically vital, and it's a good time for do-it-yourself repair work on your home. There's strong energy in your home environment. You have an aggressive drive for security. There's also a tendency to get into arguments with family members.

Sunday, April 3 (Moon in Aries)   There's a new moon in your fourth house, and that means there are new opportunities related to your home. That could mean you sell your house or buy a new one. It could relate to a home-based business. Whatever it is, you have a chance to expand.

Monday, April 4 (Moon into Taurus, 7:47 p.m.) Neptune moves into your third house. For the next two months, before Neptune goes retrograde, your intuition will be heightened. Your higher awareness will expand. You also could be involved with the media or advertising.

Tuesday, April 5 (Moon in Taurus)   The moon is in your fifth house. Creativity is emphasized. Be yourself. Be emotionally honest. In love, there's great emotional depth to a relationship. You feel strongly attached to loved ones, particularly children. But eventually you need to let go.

Wednesday, April 6 (Moon in Taurus)   Be practical and try to maintain your self-control. Cultivate new ideas, but make sure that they're down-to-earth. Health and physical activity are highlighted. Use your common sense, and deal with any money issues.

Thursday, April 7 (Moon into Gemini, 7:22 a.m.) You work best on your own. Secrets, intrigue, and confidential information play a role. You investigate, analyze, or simply observe what's going on. You detect deception and recognize insincerity with ease. Maintain your emotional balance.

Friday, April 8 (Moon in Gemini)   Pluto goes retrograde in your first house and stays that way until September 16. That means you could be rehashing old power issues or personal matters—stuff that you thought was resolved. You're dealing with your emotional self, the person you're becoming.

Saturday, April 9 (Moon into Cancer, 5:02 p.m.)   It's a number 9 day. That means it's a good day to clear up odds and ends and get ready for something new. Visualize for the future. Set your goals, and then make them so. Strive for universal appeal. You're up to the challenge.

Sunday, April 10 (Moon in Cancer)   The moon is in your seventh house. The focus turns to personal relationships, business and personal ones. Loved ones and partners play a role. A legal matter, possibly a marriage, comes to your attention. You comprehend the nuance of a situation, but you've got some concerns.

Monday, April 11 (Moon into Leo, 11:37 p.m.)   Help comes through friends. A partner or lover plays a role. Focus on your direction, your motivation. Where are you going and why? The spotlight is on cooperation. Show your appreciation to others. Partners are highlighted.

Tuesday, April 12 (Moon in Leo)   If you are planning on making a major purchase, make sure that you and your partner are in agreement. Otherwise, you could encounter intense emotional resistance. Sex and power issues may play a role, and shared belongings come into play. You could also be exploring the deeper mysteries of life, including past lives.

Wednesday, April 13 (Moon in Leo)   You're creative and passionate, impulsive and honest. Romance feels majestic. Dress boldly. Showmanship is emphasized. Strut yourself. Drama is highlighted, perhaps involving children.

Thursday, April 14 (Moon into Virgo, 2:41 a.m.) Change and variety are highlighted, no matter how much you might resist it. Let go of old structures, Capricorn. Get a new point of view. Think outside the box. Take risks; experiment.

Friday, April 15 (Moon in Virgo)   You're feeling as if you need to get away. Your mind is active, and you yearn for new experiences. A friend plays an important role in your day. Plan a trip or sign up for a seminar or workshop. A foreign country or person of foreign birth could play a role.

Saturday, April 16 (Moon into Libra, 2:59 a.m.)   It's another mystery day. You're a searcher, a seeker of truth. Be aware of decisions made behind closed doors. You detect deception and recognize insincerity with ease. Express your desires, but avoid self-deception. Maintain your emotional balance.

Sunday, April 17 (Moon in Libra)   There's a full moon in your tenth house. You gain a big boost in prestige related to your profession. You harvest what you've sown. Business dealings go well. Your life is more public than usual. You're more emotional and warm toward coworkers.

Monday, April 18 (Moon into Scorpio, 2:20 a.m.)
Finish whatever you've been working on, but don't start anything new. Clear your desk for a new cycle. Set your goals and make them so. Strive for universal appeal. Use the day for reflection, expansion, and concluding projects.

Tuesday, April 19 (Moon in Scorpio)   The moon is in your eleventh house. You find strength in numbers and meaning through friends and groups. You're passionate about a cause. Work for the common good, but keep an eye on your own wishes and dreams.

Wednesday, April 20 (Moon into Sagittarius, 2:51 a.m.)
Use your intuition to get a sense of your day. Be kind and understanding. Your intuition is on relationships. Focus on your direction, your motivation. Where are you going and why? The spotlight is on cooperation.

Thursday, April 21 (Moon in Sagittarius)   Venus moves into your fourth house. You take great pride and joy in your home life. You add some artistic touches to the decor. Your home is also your love nest, and that works out well over the next three weeks.

Friday, April 22 (Moon into Capricorn, 6:26 a.m.)
Make an effort to stay focused on your work. Emphasize quality. Be methodical and thorough. You're building foundations for an outlet for your creativity.

Saturday, April 23 (Moon in Capricorn)   Mercury goes direct in your fourth house. That means any confusion and miscommunication at home recede into the past. Things move more smoothly. You get your message across, and everything works better, including computers and other electronic equipment. Any delays you experienced on a home-repair project are over.

Sunday, April 24 (Moon into Aquarius, 2:00 p.m.)
It's a number 6 day. Service to others is the theme. Be sympathetic and kind, generous and tolerant. Diplomacy wins the day. Visit someone who is ill or someone in need of help. Do a good deed.

Monday, April 25 (Moon in Aquarius)   The moon is in your second house. Expect emotional experiences related to money and your values. It's a good day for investments, but be practical. Don't make any major purchases. You seek financial and domestic security, and you feel best surrounded by familiar objects.

Tuesday, April 26 (Moon into Pisces, 12:58 p.m.)   It's your power day and your day to play it your way. Focus on a power play. Unexpected money arrives. Expect a windfall! You have a chance to gain recognition, fame, and power.

Wednesday, April 27 (Moon in Pisces)   The moon is in your third house. Expect a lot of running around. After all, you're dealing with the everyday world. Try to group things together to cut down on your trips. You could have contact with neighbors or siblings. Something from the past comes up.

Thursday, April 28 (Moon in Pisces)   You're feeling inspired. Your imagination is strong. You have a vivid fantasy life. You respond emotionally to whatever is happening. Answers could come to you in the form of hunches, feelings, or interesting coincidences.

Friday, April 29 (Moon into Aries, 1:34 p.m.)   A partnership plays an important role. It could involve family members. Be kind and understanding. There could be some soul-searching related to a relationship, but don't make waves. Just go with the flow.

Saturday, April 30 (Moon in Aries)   Yesterday's energy flows into your Saturday. With the moon in your fourth house, stay at home or work at home. Your intuition is highlighted. Spend time with your family and loved ones. But also find time to focus inward in quiet meditation.

MAY 2011

Sunday, May 1 (Moon in Aries)   With the moon in your fourth house, spend time with your family and loved ones. Stick close to home. Work on a home-repair project. Beautify your home. You feel a close tie to your roots. A parent could play an important role.

Monday, May 2 (Moon into Taurus, 1:59 a.m.)   Your attitude determines everything, Capricorn. Spread your good news. Ease up on routines. Your charm and wit are appreciated. You're innovative and creative; you get your ideas across. You keep everyone in balance around you.

Tuesday, May 3 (Moon in Taurus)   There's a new moon in your fifth house. New opportunities related to romance and creativity come your way. They could be related to children. With Pluto forming a beneficial angle to the new moon, you're in the driver's seat related to a creative project.

Wednesday, May 4 (Moon into Gemini, 1:09 p.m.) It's a number 5 day. Change and variety are highlighted. Think freedom, no restrictions. Find a new point of view that fits current circumstances and what you know. Release old structures; get a new point of view. Take a risk; experiment. Promote new ideas.

Thursday, May 5 (Moon in Gemini) The moon is in your sixth house. It's a service day, Capricorn. Do a good deed for someone. Help others where you can. Visit someone who is ill or in need of assistance. But don't forget about your own health needs. Remember to exercise and watch your diet.

Friday, May 6 (Moon into Cancer, 10:32 p.m.) It's a mystery day as you journey into the unknown. You investigate, analyze, or simply observe what's going on. You quickly come to a conclusion and wonder why others don't see what you see. You detect deception and recognize insincerity with ease. Knowledge is essential to success. Avoid confusion and conflicts.

Saturday, May 7 (Moon in Cancer) The moon is in your seventh house. You get along well with others. You can fit in just about anywhere. However, be careful that others don't manipulate your feelings. Women play a prominent role.

Sunday, May 8 (Moon in Cancer) It's all about your home and personal life. You could be feeling moody and attracted to bodies of water—a lake or the ocean. Tend to loved ones. Do something with your children or loved ones. Beautify your home.

Monday, May 9 (Moon into Leo, 5:36 a.m.) You're at the top of your cycle. You get a fresh start. Get out and meet new people; have new experiences. You're determined and courageous. In romance, something new is developing.

Tuesday, May 10 (Moon in Leo) With the moon in your eighth house, you take an interest in a spiritual or metaphysical subject. You dig deep for information about life after death, astrology, or past lives. You could become part of a group or movement dedicated to raising people's awareness.

Wednesday, May 11 (Moon into Virgo, 10:00 a.m.)
With Mars moving into your fifth house, you're energetic, and you actively pursue the pleasures and joys of life. Romance is highlighted, and so are your creative talents. You're aggressive and competitive. Avoid any petty jealousies. Take a chance.

Thursday, May 12 (Moon in Virgo)   The moon is in your tenth house. Business dealings are highlighted. Your life is more public. You tend to be warm toward fellow workers, but avoid emotional displays in public. You're more responsive to the needs and moods of a group and of the public in general.

Friday, May 13 (Moon into Libra, 11:57 a.m.)   Freedom of thought and action is highlighted. Change your perspective. Promote new ideas; follow your curiosity. You can overcome obstacles with ease. Do something you've never done before. Variety is the spice of life.

Saturday, May 14 (Moon in Libra)   Diplomacy wins the way, especially related to your career or profession. You offer advice and support, and others appreciate you. You get along well with fellow workers. Be understanding and avoid confrontations. A domestic adjustment works out for the best.

Sunday, May 15 (Moon into Scorpio, 12:33 a.m.)
With Venus and Mercury joining Mars in your fifth house, you thrive creatively. It's also a great time for romance. You could be making a commitment for a long-term future with that special person. Try not to be overly possessive or jealous. Children could play a key role.

Monday, May 16 (Moon in Scorpio)   You work well with others and feel comfortable with a group. Friends play a surprisingly important role, especially Taurus and Virgo. Focus on your wishes and dreams. Examine your overall goals, and make sure that they're still an expression of who you are. You could become very emotionally involved with whatever effort you are undertaking with others.

Tuesday, May 17 (Moon into Sagittarius, 1:24 p.m.) There's a full moon in your eleventh house. You hear news about friends and groups, and you also gain insights into your wishes and dreams. You investigate and research a matter, possibly involving the deeper mysteries of life.

Wednesday, May 18 (Moon in Sagittarius)   The moon is in your twelfth house. You might feel a need to withdraw and work on your own. Watch what you say, and think carefully before you act. There's a tendency to undo all the positive actions you've taken. Avoid any self-destructive tendencies. Be aware of hidden enemies.

Thursday, May 19 (Moon into Capricorn, 4:17 pm) Your intuition focuses on relationships, either a new one that's developing or a current one. Cooperation is highlighted. You work well with others. Don't make waves. Don't rush or show resentment. Let things develop. Show your appreciation to others.

Friday, May 20 (Moon in Capricorn)   With the moon on your ascendant, the way you see yourself is the way others see you. Your appearance and personality shine. You get a fresh start. Your feelings and thoughts are aligned. Relations with the opposite sex flourish.

Saturday, May 21 (Moon into Aquarius, 10:32 p.m.)
Take care of your obligations. Get organized, and don't be sloppy. Try not to wander off task. Be methodical and thorough. You're building a creative foundation for your future.

Sunday, May 22 (Moon in Aquarius)   The moon is in your second house. Expect emotional experiences related to money. You feel best when surrounded by familiar objects. It's not the objects themselves that are important, but the feelings and memories you associate with them. Put off making any major purchases for a couple days. Look at your priorities in handling your income.

Monday, May 23 (Moon in Aquarius)   You have a greater sense of freedom. Your individuality is stressed. Your visionary abilities are heightened. You're dealing with new ideas, new options, originality. You get a new perspective. Group activity or social events are highlighted.

Tuesday, May 24 (Moon into Pisces, 8:24 a.m.)   It's a number 7 day, a mystery day. Look beneath the surface for the reasons others are shifting their points of view. Knowledge is essential to success. You're a spy for your own cause. Gather information, but don't make any absolute decisions until tomorrow. Make sure that you see things as they are, not as you wish them to be.

Wednesday, May 25 (Moon in Pisces)   Spend some time in meditation. Once you center yourself, you can connect with your inner guide. It's a day for deep healing. You're imaginative and inspired. Answers to your questions could come to you in the form of synchronicities.

Thursday, May 26 (Moon into Aries, 8:36 p.m.)   It's a number 9 day. Clear your desk for tomorrow's new cycle. Make room for something new. Take an inventory of where things are going in your life. Use the day for reflection, expansion, and concluding projects. Don't start anything new.

Friday, May 27 (Moon in Aries)   It's a great time for initiating projects, launching new ideas, and brainstorming. You get a new beginning. Be aware that emotions can get volatile. Remain patient, even if others are not up to your speed. You can be extremely persuasive.

Saturday, May 28 (Moon in Aries)   Spend time with your family and loved ones. Stick close to home. Work on a home-repair project, or repair any misunderstandings. You feel a close tie to your roots. A parent could play an important role.

Sunday, May 29 (Moon into Taurus, 9:02 a.m.)   Enjoy the harmony, beauty, and pleasures of life. Remain flexible. Spread your good news, and take time to listen to others. You're warm and receptive to what others say. You're intuitive, and you communicate your impressions well.

Monday, May 30 (Moon in Taurus)   The moon is in your fifth house. Your emotions tend to overpower your intellect, Capricorn. Be yourself. Be emotionally honest. Your creativity is highlighted. In love, there's great emotional depth to a relationship.

Tuesday, May 31 (Moon into Gemini, 7:57 p.m.)   Change and variety are highlighted. For example, a change of scenery would work to your advantage. You're seeking new horizons. Approach the day with an unconventional mind-set. Think freedom, no restrictions. Think outside the box. Take risks; experiment.

Wednesday, June 1 (Moon into Gemini)   There's a solar eclipse in your sixth house. New opportunities come your way related to your work. It could be something that has eluded you. It also relates to an event happening in the outside world. The new opportunities will give you structure for a project or a health maintenance plan. But you might need to complete something first before the opportunities appear.

Thursday, June 2 (Moon in Gemini)   Mercury moves into your sixth house, indicating lots of mental stimulation at work, probably related to those new opportunities coming your way. You could also be communicating about a health issue. Meanwhile, Neptune goes retrograde in your third house, suggesting that you are taking a closer look at your ideals and pondering how you can integrate them into your higher awareness.

Friday, June 3 (Moon into Cancer, 4:37 a.m.)   Let go of old, unnecessary ways of doing things; get a new point of view. Promote new ideas; follow your curiosity. Think outside the box. Variety is the spice of life. Freedom of thought and action is key. You can easily overcome obstacles.

Saturday, June 4 (Moon in Cancer)   Jupiter moves into your fifth house and stays there for one year. That means you have a chance to expand any creative project you're working on. You see the big picture. You also can go deeper into a romantic relationship. If you're single, the next twelve months would be an excellent time for a marriage.

Sunday, June 5 (Moon into Leo, 11:04 a.m.)   You launch a journey into the unknown. You pursue a mystery. Dig deep and look behind closed doors. Confidential information and secrets are involved. You're a spy for your own cause, Capricorn.

Monday, June 6 (Moon in Leo)   With the moon in your eighth house, you could attract power people to you. Your energy is more intense than usual, and drama plays a role. Your emotions could affect your feelings about belongings that you share with others. An interest in metaphysics or related rituals grabs your attention.

Tuesday, June 7 (Moon into Virgo, 3:34 p.m.)   Take care of odds and ends, Capricorn. Finish what you started. Visualize the future; set your goals, and then make them so. Look beyond the immediate. Get ready for something new. Strive for universal appeal.

Wednesday, June 8 (Moon in Virgo)   The moon is in your ninth house. If you're feeling somewhat stressed and overworked, you need to break out of your usual routine, or it could turn into a rut. Travel or higher education plays a role. Plan a trip or sign up for a seminar or workshop. A foreign country or person of foreign birth could play a role.

Thursday, June 9 (Moon into Libra, 6:32 p.m.)   Venus moves into your sixth house. You enjoy your work and get along with fellow workers. The work environment is harmonious and could be conducive to an office romance. If you were worn-out yesterday, you're feeling much better.

Friday, June 10 (Moon in Libra)   The moon is in your tenth house. You have a strong emotional commitment to your role in public life or your career. You have a keen desire for success, accomplishment, and financial security. It's a good day for sales and appearing before the public.

Saturday, June 11 (Moon into Scorpio, 8:34 p.m.)
Tear down the old in order to rebuild. Be methodical and thorough. Revise and rewrite. You're in the right place at the right time. Missing papers or objects are found. You can overcome bureaucratic red tape with ease.

Sunday, June 12 (Moon in Scorpio)   Saturn goes direct in your tenth house. That means that you can take advantage and build on past successes for the rest of the year. You get help from authorities, Capricorn. Be conservative; don't speculate or take any unnecessary risks. Maintain emotional balance. Self-discipline and structure are key.

Monday, June 13 (Moon into Sagittarius, 10:39 pm)
It's a number 6 day. Diplomacy wins the way. Focus on making people happy. Do a good deed. Be sympathetic and kind, generous and tolerant. But know when enough is enough. Avoid scattering your energies.

Tuesday, June 14 (Moon in Sagittarius)   The moon is in your twelfth house. Work behind the scenes. Reflect and meditate. Think carefully before you act. There's a tendency to undo all the positive actions you've taken. Avoid any self-destructive behavior.

Wednesday, June 15 (Moon in Sagittarius)   There's a lunar eclipse in your twelfth house. That means news comes your way related to institutions such as hospitals, government offices, the courts. Also, a doorway related to study or exploration of the paranormal or mystical realms could open.

Thursday, June 16 (Moon into Capricorn, 1:59 a.m.)
Mercury moves into your seventh house. You communicate well with a partner who plays an important role. You get your ideas across. A legal matter comes to your attention. Marriage plays a key role.

Friday, June 17 (Moon in Capricorn)   You're recharged for the remainder of the month, and this makes you more appealing to the public. You're physically vital, and relations with the opposite sex go well. The way you see yourself is the way others see you. Your feelings and thoughts are aligned.

Saturday, June 18 (Moon into Aquarius, 7:47 a.m.)
Use your intuition to get a sense of your day. Be kind and understanding. Cooperation, especially with partners, is highlighted. Don't make waves. Don't rush or show resentment. Let things develop. Collect what's owed you, and pay what you owe.

Sunday, June 19 (Moon in Aquarius)   Money and material goods are important to you and give you a sense of security. You take pride in your material possessions or whatever you value. Look at your priorities in handling your income.

Monday, June 20 (Moon into Pisces, 4:45 p.m.)   Mars moves into your sixth house. You work hard, and you don't have much tolerance for those who aren't up to your speed. Be aware that your aggressive tendencies could create problems at work. Control your temper, and try not to be overly concerned with details.

Tuesday, June 21 (Moon in Pisces)   With the moon in your third house, Capricorn, your thinking is influenced by the past, especially matters related to relatives. You also could be exploring the deep past. You communicate well, but control your emotions when you make your point.

Wednesday, June 22 (Moon in Pisces)   Your imagination is strong. You have a vivid fantasy life. You're feeling inspired. Keep track of your dreams, including your daydreams. Ideas are ripe. You're compassionate and sensitive. Watch for psychic events, synchronicities.

Thursday, June 23 (Moon into Aries, 4:24 a.m.)   It's a mystery day. You journey into the unknown and investigate something hidden that's going on behind the scenes. You dig deep. You're launching a journey into the unknown and exploring a mystery. Knowledge is essential to your success.

Friday, June 24 (Moon in Aries)   The moon is in your fourth house. Stay home, where you feel comfortable. The domestic scene plays a major role. If possible, take the day off or work at home. You're feeling closer to your roots.

Saturday, June 25 (Moon into Taurus, 4:53 p.m.)   It's a number 9 day, and that means you should finish whatever you started. Make room for something new. Clear your desk for tomorrow's new cycle, and then look beyond the immediate. Strive for universal appeal.

Sunday, June 26 (Moon in Taurus)   The moon is in your fifth house of creativity. Your love life takes off. There's an idealistic turn to whatever you do for pleasure. It's a great time for a creative project, especially fiction writing. You could be somewhat possessive of loved ones and children. Get a pet!

Monday, June 27 (Moon in Taurus)   It's a day for being practical and getting things done. Maintain your self-control. Avoid stubborn behavior if someone doesn't agree with you. Health and physical activity are highlighted. It's a good day for gardening or cultivating new ideas.

Tuesday, June 28 (Moon into Gemini, 3:57 a.m.) Partnerships and cooperation rule. Use your intuition to get a sense of your day. Be kind and understanding. Don't make waves. Let things develop. Focus on your direction and motivation. Where are you going and why?

Wednesday, June 29 (Moon in Gemini) With the moon in your sixth house, the emphasis turns to your daily work and service to others. Attend to all the details, Capricorn. Be careful not to overlook any seemingly minor matters that could take on importance. Keep up with your exercise plan, and watch your diet.

Thursday, June 30 (Moon into Cancer, 12:14 p.m.) You're restless and looking for a new perspective. You're versatile and changeable, but be careful not to overcommit yourself. Stay focused as best you can. Take risks; experiment. Pursue a new idea. Freedom of thought and action is key.

JULY 2011

Friday, July 1 (Moon in Cancer) There's a new moon in your seventh house. That indicates that new opportunities come your way related to a partnership or a friendship. Jupiter forms a nice angle, so you have a chance to expand anything you're working on with a partner. You get along well with others now.

Saturday, July 2 (Moon into Leo, 5:44 p.m.) Mercury moves into your eighth house. You investigate something that's on your mind. You look deep for answers. You could be exploring the larger mysteries, such as what happens after death.

Sunday, July 3 (Moon in Leo) You're creative and passionate, impulsive and honest. Focus on advertising, publicity, publicizing yourself. Strut your stuff. Drama is highlighted, and you're at center stage. Showmanship is emphasized.

Monday, July 4 (Moon into Virgo, 9:16 p.m.) Venus moves into your seventh house. You and your partner or friends get along well. A marriage or partnership brings success and prosperity. You can fit in just about anywhere.

Tuesday, July 5 (Moon in Virgo) The moon moves into your ninth house. You're feeling as if you need to break out of your usual routine, or it could turn into a rut, Capricorn. Travel or higher education plays a role. Plan a trip or sign up for a seminar or workshop. A foreign country or person of foreign birth could play a role.

Wednesday, July 6 (Moon into Libra, 11:54 p.m.) It's a number 9 day—your day to finish up what you've been working on and get ready for something new. Reflect on what you've been doing, and look for a way to expand. Visualize the future; set your goals, and then make them so.

Thursday, July 7 (Moon in Libra) Your hard work pays off. You get a boost in prestige; your life is more public. You're also emotional and warm toward coworkers. But it's not a good idea to get involved personally with a professional associate. If you do, you could pay a price.

Friday, July 8 (Moon in Libra)   You get along well with others and balance the energy of those around you. Go out to a cultural event, an art gallery opening, a theater to see a play, or a museum to see a new exhibition.

Saturday, July 9 (Moon into Scorpio, 2:32 a.m.) With Uranus retrograde in your fourth house until December 10, you'll be rethinking a move you're planning. You could experience an internal event in your emotional life that alters your thinking. Your family life takes on new importance. Your quest for freedom is put on hold or internalized.

Sunday, July 10 (Moon in Scorpio)   The moon is in your eleventh house. You have deeper contact with friends. You find strength in numbers and meaning through associates and groups. You work for the common good. Taurus and Virgo play a role.

Monday, July 11 (Moon into Sagittarius, 3:47 a.m.) Variety is the spice of life. Think outside the box, Capricorn. Take a risk for a change; experiment. Get a new point of view. Follow your curiosity. However, don't spread yourself too thin.

Tuesday, July 12 (Moon in Sagittarius)   The moon is in your twelfth house. Work behind the scenes, and stay out of the public view. Think carefully before you act. There's a tendency to undo all the positive actions you've taken. Avoid any self-destructive tendencies. Be aware of hidden enemies.

Wednesday, July 13 (Moon into Capricorn, 10:14 a.m.) It's a mystery day, and you look behind closed doors for answers. Avoid confusion and conflicts. Keep any secrets entrusted to you. You're a spy for your own cause. Maintain your emotional balance. Your challenge is to be independent without feeling isolated.

Thursday, July 14 (Moon in Capricorn)   You're sensitive to other people's feelings. You may feel moody one moment, happy the next, then withdrawn and sad. It's all about your emotional self. Your feelings and thoughts are aligned. Your health and your emotional self are your focus.

Friday, July 15 (Moon into Aquarius, 4:30 p.m.) There's a full moon in your first house, your ascendant. You gain insight and illumination as to how you see yourself and how others see you. Your appearance and personality shine. You're physically vital, and relations with the opposite sex go well. You reap what you've sown.

Saturday, July 16 (Moon in Aquarius)   The moon is in your second house. You could gain a financial boost that acts like a jolt of energy. You feel more secure. Determine your priorities in handling your finances. Even if you experience a sudden increase of income, put off any big purchases for a few days.

Sunday, July 17 (Moon in Aquarius)   Your individuality is stressed. You have a greater sense of freedom. You're dealing with new ideas, new options, originality. You get a new perspective. Play your hunches. Look beyond the immediate. Bust old paradigms

Monday, July 18 (Moon into Pisces, 1:13 a.m.) You're innovative and creative; you communicate well. You're also warm and receptive to what others say. Your attitude determines everything. Foster generosity. Take time to relax, enjoy yourself, and recharge your batteries.

Tuesday, July 19 (Moon in Pisces)   The moon is in your third house. You write from a deep place. It's a good day for journaling. Your thinking might be unduly influenced by the past. You could get a call or visit from a female relative. Neighbors and siblings play a role. You accept an invitation to a social event.

Wednesday, July 20 (Moon into Aries, 12:26 a.m.) Variety is the spice of life. Think outside the box. Think freedom, no restrictions. Take risks; experiment. Get a new point of view. Follow your curiosity. However, don't spread yourself too thin.

Thursday, July 21 (Moon in Aries) With the new moon in your fourth house, you find new opportunities related to your home and home life. You feel more stable in your home environment. Also, Neptune goes direct in your seventh house, indicating that your psychic abilities are enhanced over the coming weeks and months. You're also more compassionate toward others, especially partners.

Friday, July 22 (Moon into Taurus, 12:59 p.m.) It's a number 7 day, a mystery day. You investigate, analyze, or simply observe what's going on. You quickly come to a conclusion and wonder why others don't see what you see. You work best on your own. Make sure that you see things as they are, not as you wish them to be. Knowledge is essential to success.

Saturday, July 23 (Moon in Taurus) The moon is in your fifth house, Capricorn. You're emotionally in touch with your creative side. You're feeling joyous and creative. Sex for pleasure is highlighted. You feel strongly attached to loved ones, protective of children. Your emotions tend to overpower your intellect.

Sunday, July 24 (Moon in Taurus) Cultivate new ideas, but make sure that they're down-to-earth. Use your common sense in whatever you're doing today.

Your senses are highly developed. You're opinionated and highly sensual. However, avoid becoming fixed in your thoughts. Let go of any traces of stubbornness.

Monday, July 25 (Moon into Gemini, 12:35 a.m.) It's a number 1 day, and you're at the top of your cycle. You're inventive; you make connections that others overlook. You're determined and courageous. You can take the lead and get a fresh start. Don't be afraid to turn in a new direction. Trust your hunches. Intuition is highlighted.

Tuesday, July 26 (Moon in Gemini)   The moon is in your sixth house. You efficiently handle your duties. You're the one others come to for help. Your health and diet play a role, but don't get compulsive about it. You work best with a clean desk. Disorder upsets you.

Wednesday, July 27 (Moon into Cancer, 9:12 p.m.) Your attitude determines everything. Take time to relax, enjoy yourself, and recharge your batteries. Have fun in preparation for tomorrow's discipline and focus.

Thursday, July 28 (Moon in Cancer)   Mercury moves into your ninth house. Your teaching and writing abilities are strong. You express your ideas with confidence. You also might have a strong interest in foreign travel. Meanwhile, with Venus moving into your eighth house, you gain financially through a partnership, marriage, or love relationship. However, avoid any tendencies toward jealousy and possessiveness.

Friday, July 29 (Moon in Cancer)   You're feeling intuitive and nurturing. Your home life and family take on new importance. Your spouse or loved one plays a significant role. You'll probably feel moody and sensitive from time to time.

Saturday, July 30 (Moon into Leo, 2:16 a.m.)   There's a new moon in your eighth house. Get involved in a cause aimed at improving living conditions for large numbers of people. You have a strong sense of duty and feel obligated to fulfill your promises. You could be involved in managing and controlling the resources of others.

Sunday, July 31 (Moon in Leo)   You have a strong sense of duty and feel obligated to fulfill your promises. You find yourself at center stage now. You could be managing or controlling a partner's resources. Issues of the day could include matters of sex, death, rebirth, rituals, and relationships. Romance and love are highlighted, but your experiences are more intense than usual.

AUGUST 2011

Monday, August 1 (Moon into Virgo, 4:42 a.m.)   Approach the day with an unconventional mind-set. Travel and variety are highlighted. You're also more comfortable than usual in front of an audience. Freedom of thought and action is key. But so is moderation; avoid excess in whatever you're doing.

Tuesday, August 2 (Moon in Virgo)   Mercury goes retrograde in your ninth house and stays that way until August 26. Over the next three weeks, watch out for miscommunication or misunderstanding related to higher education or your plans for a long trip. You could experience some delays in plans. You also could encounter glitches with your home computer.

Wednesday, August 3 (Moon into Libra, 6:05 a.m.) Mars moves into your seventh house. Over the next six weeks, problems might flare up related to a business partner or your mate. Watch out for aggressive behavior on your part related to partnerships. You feel a need to

269

be accepted. You're looking for security, but you tend to try to force the issue.

Thursday, August 4 (Moon in Libra)   The moon is in your tenth house. Professional concerns take on more importance. You could get a promotion, a raise, or a pat on the back. You're more responsive to the needs and moods of a group and of the public in general. You move up the ladder.

Friday, August 5 (Moon into Scorpio, 7:57 a.m.)   It's a number 9 day. Clear your desk for tomorrow's new cycle. Accept what comes your way. Use the day for reflection, expansion, and concluding projects. Don't start anything new.

Saturday, August 6 (Moon in Scorpio)   The moon is in your eleventh house. Friends play an important role in your day, especially Taurus and Virgo. Focus on your wishes and dreams. Examine your overall goals for the year and beyond. Make sure those goals are an expression of who you are.

Sunday, August 7 (Moon into Sagittarius, 11:21 a.m.) It's a number 2 day. Cooperation is highlighted. You work well with others. Your intuition focuses on relationships, either a new one that's developing or a current one. Don't make waves. Don't rush or show resentment. Let things develop. Show your appreciation for others.

Monday, August 8 (Moon in Sagittarius)   The moon is in your twelfth house. You can communicate your deepest feelings to a trustworthy friend. Otherwise, it's best to keep your thoughts and your feelings to yourself. You feel comfortable working behind the scenes. Take time to reflect and meditate.

Tuesday, August 9 (Moon into Capricorn, 4:38 p.m.)
Your organizational skills are highlighted, but try not to wander off task. Keep your goals in mind; follow your ideas. Be tenacious. You tend to stay with the tried and true. It's not a day for experimentation or new approaches.

Wednesday, August 10 (Moon in Capricorn) With the sun on your ascendant, your appearance and personality shine. You're recharged for the remainder of the month, and this makes you more appealing to the public. You're physically vital, and relations with the opposite sex go well.

Thursday, August 11 (Moon into Aquarius, 11:48 p.m.)
Service to others is the theme. Diplomacy wins the way. You offer advice and support. Be understanding and avoid confrontations. A domestic adjustment works out for the best.

Friday, August 12 (Moon in Aquarius) The moon is in your second house. You feel strongly about a money issue. Finances and material goods are important to you and give you a sense of security. You identify emotionally with your possessions or whatever you value.

Saturday, August 13 (Moon in Aquarius) You gain insight and illumination related to money issues. You get a new perspective. Play your hunches. You identify emotionally with your possessions or whatever you value. You reap what you've sown.

Sunday, August 14 (Moon into Pisces, 8:55 a.m.)
Use the day for reflection, expansion, and concluding projects. Visualize the future; set your goals, and then make them so. Look beyond the immediate. Make room for something new.

Monday, August 15 (Moon in Pisces)   The moon is in your third house. Your mental abilities are strong, and you have an emotional need to express your ideas. You write from a deep place. It's a good day for journaling. Your thinking may be unduly influenced by the past. Female relatives play a role.

Tuesday, August 16 (Moon into Aries, 8:03 p.m.) Use your intuition to get a sense of your day, and focus on relationships. Be kind and understanding. Don't make waves. Don't rush or show resentment, even if other people nag. Let things develop.

Wednesday, August 17 (Moon in Aries)   Spend time with your family and loved ones. You feel close to your roots. Stick close to home, if possible. A parent plays a role. You could be getting ready for a home-improvement project. There's a good chance that you will find something that could be upgraded.

Thursday, August 18 (Moon in Aries)   Initiate projects, launch new ideas, and brainstorm. It's a good day for an outdoor adventure, hiking, climbing, biking, playing a sport, or attending a sporting event. Be careful about accidents. You're passionate but impatient. Your emotions could be volatile.

Friday, August 19 (Moon into Taurus, 8:37 a.m.) Some of yesterday's energy flows into your Friday. Promote new ideas; follow your curiosity. Look for adventure. Freedom of thought and action is key. But so is moderation; avoid excess in whatever you're doing.

Saturday, August 20 (Moon in Taurus)   The moon is in your fifth house. There could be more involvement with kids. You feel strongly attached to loved ones, particularly children. You're more protective and nurturing, but eventually you need to let go. You're emotionally in touch with your creative side.

Sunday, August 21 (Moon into Gemini, 8:53 p.m.) Venus moves into your ninth house. You love the idea of a long-distance trip for pleasure. Continuing your education also appeals to you, especially if you're pursuing a subject of interest. You could be attracted to philosophy, mythology, or religious studies. A romantic relationship with a foreign-born person is a possibility.

Monday, August 22 (Moon in Gemini) The moon is in your sixth house. It's a service day. Others rely on you for help. You improve, edit, and refine the work of others. Help others, but don't deny your own needs, and don't let your fears hold you back.

Tuesday, August 23 (Moon in Gemini) You feel a need to express yourself. It's a good time to socialize. You communicate well and get your ideas across. You're feeling restless and creative. It's a good day for a change of scenery.

Wednesday, August 24 (Moon into Cancer, 6:31 a.m.) It's a number 1 day. You're inventive; you make connections that others overlook. You're determined and courageous. Trust your hunches. Intuition is highlighted. You get a fresh start. In romance, something new is developing.

Thursday, August 25 (Moon in Cancer) The moon is in your seventh house. today. You communicate well with a spouse or partner. It's all about working together. A contract or a lawsuit could play a role. You get along well with others, but it's a challenge to remain detached and objective.

Friday, August 26 (Moon into Leo, 12:09 p.m.) Mercury goes direct in your eighth house. That means any confusion, miscommunication, and delays you've been experiencing in the past three weeks recede into the past. That's especially true related to any disagreements you've had about income or belongings that you share. If you're planning a trip, any delays you've experienced should end. Everything works better, including computers and other electronic equipment.

Saturday, August 27 (Moon in Leo) With the moon in your eighth house, your experiences are more intense than usual. Managing shared resources takes on new importance. Deal with mortgages, insurance, and investments. Other issues of the day could include matters of sex, death, rebirth, rituals, and relationships.

Sunday, August 28 (Moon into Virgo, 2:13 p.m.) There's a new moon in your ninth house. A door opens for a long journey to a foreign country. Alternately, you take new interest in worldviews, ideas, philosophy, and mythology. Sign up for a workshop or seminar. Follow whatever opportunity opens for you now.

Monday, August 29 (Moon in Virgo) Take care of details, especially related to your health. Make an appointment with a doctor or dentist. Take time to write in a journal. You write from a deep place with lots of details and colorful descriptions.

Tuesday, August 30 (Moon into Libra, 2:26 p.m.) Jupiter goes retrograde in your fifth house and stays that way until December 25. Any plans to expand what you were doing in your creative life are delayed for the next four months. You could face some misunderstandings in your romantic life. You might be somewhat possessive of loved ones, particularly children. But they might find your attention to be too controlling.

Wednesday, August 31 (Moon in Libra) The moon is in your tenth house. Professional concerns are the focus. You gain an elevation in prestige. Your life is more public. You feel close to coworkers, but don't blur the boundaries between your private and professional lives.

SEPTEMBER 2011

Thursday, September 1 (Moon into Scorpio, 2:48 p.m.) It's a number 6 day, a service day. Do a good deed for someone. Visit someone who is ill or in need of help. Focus on making people happy. Be diplomatic, but know when to say enough is enough.

Friday, September 2 (Moon in Scorpio) The moon is in your eleventh house. Friends play an important role. You find strength in numbers and meaning through friends and groups. You work for the common good, but keep an eye on your own wishes and dreams.

Saturday, September 3 (Moon into Sagittarius, 3:04 p.m.) It's a number 8 day, your power day and your day to do it your way. You're in the power seat. So look for a power play. You have a chance to gain recognition, fame, and power. Be courageous. Be yourself; be honest.

Sunday, September 4 (Moon in Sagittarius) The moon is in your twelfth house. Withdraw and work behind the scenes. Think carefully before you act. There's a tendency to undo all the positive actions you've taken. Avoid any self-destructive tendencies. Be aware of hidden enemies.

Monday, September 5 (Moon into Capricorn, 10:04 p.m.) It's a number 1 day. You're at the top of your cycle. You take the lead in something new, and you get a fresh start.

You're inventive; you make connections that others overlook.

Tuesday, September 6 (Moon in Capricorn) Your moon is on your ascendant. It's a great day for starting something new. Your appearance impresses; your personality shines. Your feelings and thoughts are aligned. You're physically vital, and relations with the opposite sex go well.

Wednesday, September 7 (Moon in Capricorn) Your ambition and drive to succeed are highlighted. Your responsibilities increase. You may feel stressed, overworked. Don't ignore your exercise routine. Self-discipline and structure are key.

Thursday, September 8 (Moon into Aquarius, 5:43 a.m.) It's a number 4 day. Persevere to get things done. Don't get sloppy. It's a time for hard work and fulfilling obligations. Put off any impulses to wander off task. It's not a good day for romance. You're building a foundation for the future.

Friday, September 9 (Moon in Aquarius) The moon is in your second house. You tend to react emotionally to an event in your life related to money or your values. You identify emotionally with your possessions or whatever you value. Look at your priorities in handling your income. Watch your spending.

Saturday, September 10 (Moon into Pisces, 3:27 p.m.) A domestic adjustment works out for the best. You could face emotional outbursts or someone making unfair demands. Be understanding and avoid confrontations. Offer advice and support, but do it in a diplomatic way.

Sunday, September 11 (Moon in Pisces) You're creative and imaginative. Turn inward for inspiration.

Universal knowledge, eternal truths, and deep spirituality are the themes. Keep track of your dreams. Watch for synchronicities, those meaningful coincidences.

Monday, September 12 (Moon in Pisces)   There's a full moon in your third house. You gain insight, illumination, or news related to matters of the past. Your mental abilities are strong, and you have an emotional need to reinvigorate your studies, especially regarding matters of the past. You're attracted to historical or archaeological studies.

Tuesday, September 13 (Moon into Aries, 2:50 a.m.) Look beyond the immediate. Finish what you started. Visualize the future; set your goals, and then make them so. Complete a project, and make room for something new.

Wednesday, September 14 (Moon in Aries)   Venus moves into your tenth house, your native house, Capricorn. So you have a three-week window in which things go smoothly with your career. Women are helpful, especially in the arts, and they could be an opportunity for a raise, a grant, or a bonus.

Thursday, September 15 (Moon into Taurus, 3:25 p.m.) It's all about partnerships, cooperation, working together to get things done. A new relationship could be forming. Use your intuition to get a sense of how it will work out. Help comes through friends. Collaborate with a coworker.

Friday, September 16 (Moon in Taurus)   Pluto goes direct in your first house. That means that you could be dealing with a power issue. There's more intensity in the personality you project. You're more magnetic and transformative, but you could also be seen as egotistical and power hungry.

Saturday, September 17 (Moon in Taurus)   With the moon in your fifth house, take a chance and experiment. Your creativity is emphasized. Your originality is highlighted. Be aware that your emotions tend to overpower your intellect. Alternately, you are more protective and nurturing toward children.

Sunday, September 18 (Moon into Gemini, 4:06 a.m.) Mars moves into your eighth house, indicating that over the next three weeks you could be aggressively pursuing an important investigation or research. Your experiences are more intense. You could be putting lots of energy into a matter related to taxes, insurance, or a mortgage. Alternately, you could be delving into the realm of the weirdness and strange: ghosts, past lives, or communication with the dead.

Monday, September 19 (Moon in Gemini)   With the moon in your sixth house, the emphasis turns to your daily work, health, and service to others. Look to the big picture. Be careful not to overlook any seemingly minor matters that could take on importance. Keep up with your exercise plan, and watch your diet.

Tuesday, September 20 (Moon into Cancer, 2:54 p.m.) It's a number 7 day, a mystery day. Confidential information plays a role. You dig deep for information by looking behind closed doors. You're a spy for your own cause. You detect deception and recognize insincerity. Just make sure that you see things as they are, not as you wish them to be.

Wednesday, September 21 (Moon in Cancer)   The moon is in your seventh house of partnerships and contracts. Loved ones and partners are more important than usual. A legal matter could come to your attention. Be careful that others don't manipulate your feelings.

You're looking for security, but you have a hard time going with the flow.

Thursday, September 22 *(Moon into Leo, 9:56 p.m.)* It's a number 9 day. It's time to complete a project. Clear your desk, and make room for the new, but don't start anything new until tomorrow. Spend some time in deep thought. Consider how you can expand your base.

Friday, September 23 *(Moon in Leo)*   The moon is in your eighth house. You attract powerful people. Your experiences are more intense, especially related to belongings that you share with someone. An interest in metaphysics plays a role.

Saturday, September 24 *(Moon into Virgo, 10:50 p.m.)* Cooperation is highlighted. Use your intuition to get a sense of your day. Be kind and understanding. Show your appreciation for others. There could be some soul-searching related to relationships.

Sunday, September 25 *(Moon in Virgo)*   Mercury moves into your tenth house. That means you communicate well. Your speaking and writing abilities are in tune, and you can use them to move ahead in your career. You can address the public and get your ideas across.

Monday, September 26 *(Moon into Libra, 12:51 a.m.)* Get things organized for the week, Capricorn. Revise and rewrite. Clear your desk or clean a closet or storage area. Be methodical and thorough. Be practical with your money.

Tuesday, September 27 *(Moon in Libra)*   There's a new moon in your tenth house. A new opportunity to move ahead in your career comes your way, possibly an advancement, a raise, or a new project. You get along well with fellow workers, but be careful not to mix your personal and professional lives.

Wednesday, September 28 (Moon into Scorpio, 12:06 a.m.) Service to others is the theme. You offer advice and support. Do a good deed for someone. Focus on making people happy. Domestic purchases are highlighted.

Thursday, September 29 (Moon in Scorpio) The moon is in your eleventh house. Your friends support you in whatever you're doing. You could be involved with a group of people working for a social cause. Pay attention to your wishes and dreams, and make sure they are still a reflection of who you really are.

Friday, September 30 (Moon into Sagittarius, 12:42 a.m.) It's a number 8 day, your power day. You attract financial success. Open your mind to a new approach that could bring in big bucks. Be aware that fear of failure, or fear that you won't measure up, will attract tangible experiences that reinforce the feeling.

OCTOBER 2011

Saturday, October 1 (Moon in Sagittarius) The moon is in your twelfth house. Work behind the scenes, and avoid any conflict. You could be dealing with a matter from the past that has returned to haunt you. Keep your feelings secret. Follow your intuition.

Sunday, October 2 (Moon in Sagittarius) You see the big picture, not just the details. You could be hearing news about a publishing project, or a legal matter could play a role. You're feeling restless, impulsive, and inquisitive. Travel is on your mind, but don't limit your options.

Monday, October 3 (Moon into Capricorn, 4:16 a.m.)
It's a number 9 day and a good day to complete a project. Clear your desk and make room for the new, but don't start anything new until tomorrow. Spend some time in deep thought. Consider how you can expand your base.

Tuesday, October 4 (Moon in Capricorn)   The moon is on your ascendant, and you're at the top of your cycle. Begin something new. You're recharged for the month ahead, and this makes you more appealing to the public. Your appearance and personality shine. Your feelings and thoughts are aligned.

Wednesday, October 5 (Moon into Aquarius, 11:19 a.m.)   Use your intuition to get a sense of the day. Don't make waves. Don't rush or show resentment. Let things develop. The spotlight is on cooperation. Show your appreciation to others.

Thursday, October 6 (Moon in Aquarius)   The moon is in your second house. Deal with money issues. Pay what you owe, and collect what others owe you. You equate your financial assets with emotional security. Look at your priorities in handling your income.

Friday, October 7 (Moon into Pisces, 9:14 p.m.)   It's a number 4 day. So tear down the old in order to rebuild. Be methodical and thorough. Revise and rewrite. Persevere to get things done. Romance goes onto the back burner.

Saturday, October 8 (Moon in Pisces)   The moon is in your third house. Your mental abilities are strong, and you have an emotional need to reinvigorate your studies, especially regarding matters of the past. You're attracted to historical or archaeological studies. You write from a deep place. It's a good day for journaling. Female relatives play a role.

Sunday, October 9 (Moon in Pisces)   With Venus moving into Scorpio, your eleventh house, you could experience an emotional romantic interlude. You're also very good at getting friends together to help you with your plans, especially if you're working for the common good. You attract artistic people to your cause.

Monday, October 10 (Moon into Aries, 8:57 a.m.) It's another 7 day, a mystery day. You launch a journey into the unknown. Secrets, intrigue, and confidential information play a role. You work best on your own. Knowledge is essential to success. Gather information, but don't make any absolute decisions until tomorrow.

Tuesday, October 11 (Moon in Aries)   There's a full moon in your fourth house. You gain insight and illumination related to your home life, possibly related to a home-remodeling project, the sale of your home, or the purchase of a new one. You're open to new ideas, highly motivated, and looking for adventure. Be aware that you can be somewhat pushy, especially in your dealings with your home or loved ones.

Wednesday, October 12 (Moon into Taurus, 9:35 p.m.) Finish whatever you've been working on. Clear up odds and ends. Be practical and down-to-earth. Maintain your self-control. Take an inventory of where things are going in your life. Make room for something new. Get ready for your new cycle.

Thursday, October 13 (Moon in Taurus)   Mercury moves into Scorpio, your eleventh house. You investigate something that puzzles you; you dig deep for information. Friends play a role in helping you get to the bottom of the matter. You and friends pledge secrecy about what you found out.

Friday, October 14 (Moon in Taurus)   The moon is in your fifth house. You're emotionally in touch with your creative side. You feel strongly attached to loved ones, particularly children. But eventually you need to let go. Take a chance; experiment.

Saturday, October 15 (Moon into Gemini, 10:15 a.m.) Your charm and wit are appreciated. You're adaptable and versatile; you communicate well. Make time to listen to others. Relax, enjoy yourself, and recharge your batteries. In business dealings, diversify. Insist on all the details, not just bits and pieces.

Sunday, October 16 (Moon in Gemini)   You're emotionally adaptable; you get your ideas across. You're also well grounded and practical, Capricorn. Take care of any health issues. Watch your diet, and don't forget to exercise.

Monday, October 17 (Moon into Cancer, 9:39 p.m.) Promote new ideas; follow your curiosity. Freedom of thought and action is key. Think outside the box. Take risks; experiment. Variety is the spice of life. You can overcome obstacles with ease.

Tuesday, October 18 (Moon in Cancer)   You're full of ideas, yet well grounded, Capricorn. You can accomplish whatever you've set out to achieve. You're emotionally adaptable; you communicate your ideas well. You're also practical and stable.

Wednesday, October 19 (Moon in Cancer)   The focus turns to relationships, business and personal ones. You get along well with others. Don't be afraid to ask them for advice and to involve them with what you're doing. You can fit in just about anywhere. You feel a need to be accepted. You're looking for security, but you have a hard time going with the flow.

Thursday, October 20 (Moon into Leo, 6:07 a.m.)
It's your power day, so focus on a power play, Capricorn. Business discussions go well. You pull off a financial coup. Buy a lottery ticket. Unexpected money arrives.

Friday, October 21 (Moon in Leo) Yesterday's energy flows into your Friday. You're a powerhouse among your peers. You're friendly and popular; you're ready to step to center stage. You tend to be somewhat material-oriented and more interested in people than ideas or ideals. You're loyal but practical and willing to change course if necessary.

Saturday, October 22 (Moon into Virgo, 10:42 a.m.)
You're at the top of your cycle. Trust your hunches. Intuition is highlighted. You're inventive; you make connections that others overlook. You're determined and courageous. Stress originality.

Sunday, October 23 (Moon in Virgo) The moon is in your ninth house. You have a strong emotional urge to expand your mental abilities. The intellect is highlighted, balancing yesterday's intuitive visions. You tend to make moral and philosophical decisions based on emotions, not on logic.

Monday, October 24 (Moon into Libra, 11:50 a.m.)
It's a number 3 day. You're innovative and creative; you communicate well. You keep everyone in balance. Your artistic talents are highlighted.

Tuesday, October 25 (Moon in Libra) Your emotions and ideas get all mixed up. You have an imaginative and creative perspective, but you might lack the drive to carry out your vision. You're also impatient, which makes it harder for you to clearly communicate your unusual ideas.

Wednesday, October 26 (Moon into Scorpio, 11:09 a.m.) There's a new moon in your eleventh house. You find strength in numbers, and new opportunities through friends and members of a group. You work for a social cause, but keep an eye on your own wishes and dreams. Examine your overall goals, and make sure that they are still an expression of who you are.

Thursday, October 27 (Moon in Scorpio) You're intuitive with a keen understanding of how others feel. Pay attention to first impressions. Although you're loyal and trustworthy, you feel a need to work on your own. You're working hard to attain whatever you set out to achieve.

Friday, October 28 (Moon into Sagittarius, 10:46 a.m.) It's a number 7 day, a mystery day. Like yesterday, you work best on your own. Secrets, intrigue, and confidential information play a role. You investigate, analyze, or simply observe what's going on. You detect deception, and recognize insincerity with ease. Maintain your emotional balance.

Saturday, October 29 (Moon in Sagittarius) You're a doer, a thinker, and a tireless worker. You've got lots of energy. You're multitasking, studying or researching, browsing the Internet, and then working around the house. Your compassion runs deep, and you have a need for comfortable surroundings.

Sunday, October 30 (Moon into Capricorn, 12:39 p.m.)
Visualize for the future. Set your goals, and then make them so. Strive for universal appeal. You're up to the challenge. Complete a project, and get ready for something new coming up.

Monday, October 31 (Moon in Capricorn)   You're dedicated, and serious; you exhibit amazing self-control. You succeed at whatever you attempt. You're also all about following the rules and regulations. The way you see yourself is the way others see you. You're fully recharged for the month ahead.

NOVEMBER 2011

Tuesday, November 1 (Moon into Aquarius, 6:08 p.m.)
It's another power day, and your chance for a power play. You can expand what you're doing and attract financial success. You pull off a financial coup, and you gain recognition for your efforts. Remember that you're playing with power, so be careful not to hurt others.

Wednesday, November 2 (Moon in Aquarius)   With Venus and Mercury moving into your twelfth house, you're comfortable remaining behind the scenes and working on your own. Work on a writing project. You're independent and versatile, and you have a strong love of personal freedom.

Thursday, November 3 (Moon in Aquarius)   The moon is in your second house. You identify emotionally with your values or whatever you value. You tend to equate your assets to emotional security. You feel best when surrounded by familiar objects, especially in your home. It's not the objects themselves that are impor-

286

tant, but the feelings and memories you associate with them.

Friday, November 4 (Moon into Pisces, 3:18 a.m.) Use your intuition to get a sense of your day. Be kind and understanding, sympathetic and sensitive toward others. Don't make waves. Don't rush or show resentment. Let things develop.

Saturday, November 5 (Moon in Pisces) You're capable of delving deeply into anything that you want to know more about. You're reliable, and others trust you implicitly and willingly confide in you. You're also imaginative, compassionate, and inspired. It's a day for deep healing.

Sunday, November 6—Daylight Saving Time Ends (Moon into Aries, 2:02 p.m.) Your organizational skills are called upon. Be methodical and thorough. Do things like cleaning your closet, clearing your desk, and straightening up your garage. Something lost turns up as if by magic. Stay focused.

Monday, November 7 (Moon in Aries) You're impatient and restless, but your mind is strong. You're tactful but fearless. You're looking for something new that challenges you. You abide by the rules, but you don't like being cajoled or tricked into doing something.

Tuesday, November 8 (Moon in Aries) Start a new project, especially one related to your home. You move ahead quickly with whatever you're working on; you have little patience for those who aren't up to your speed. Spend time with your family and loved ones. Get out and enjoy the fall, and take time to smell the proverbial roses.

Wednesday, November 9 (Moon into Taurus, 2:46 a.m.)
Neptune goes direct in your second house and stays that
way until April 5. That means you'll be intuitive and
highly sensitive over the coming months, especially related to money issues. You'll feel most comfortable with
your values and possessions you cherish. You also might
deal with your finances in an unusual way that raises
eyebrows.

Thursday, November 10 (Moon in Taurus) There's
a full moon in your fifth house. You reap what you've
sown related to a creative project. You also gain insight
and illumination related to a romantic relationship.
Children could play a role.

Friday, November 11 (Moon into Gemini, 3:11 p.m.)
With Mars moving into Virgo, you plan and organize
before charging ahead, Capricorn. You put much energy into helping others, and you're tireless in that task.
When you're not thinking about helping others, you're
considering how you can learn more about a subject
that interests you. You could also be planning a long
trip.

Saturday, November 12 (Moon in Gemini) Some
of yesterday's energy flows into your Saturday. You're
full of ideas and versatile, but also well grounded. Help
others, but don't ignore your own needs. You're compassionate and sensitive. You tend to feel very strongly
about whatever you're involved in, Capricorn. Go with
the flow. Diplomacy wins the way.

Sunday, November 13 (Moon in Gemini) You're
emotionally adaptable; you communicate your ideas
well. You're also practical and stable, Capricorn. Your
curiosity drives you forward. You quickly absorb ideas
and put them to use. However, you tend to avoid digging
very deep into any subject.

Monday, November 14 (Moon into Cancer, 2:20 a.m.)
It's a number 3 day. Your attitude determines everything.
Spread your good news. You're innovative and creative;
you communicate well. Enjoy the harmony, beauty, and
pleasures of life. Beautify your home.

Tuesday, November 15 (Moon in Cancer) You're
sensitive and intuitive, but you're also well-centered.
You're fond of your home life; you feel secure there. Try
not to quarrel. If the environment gets too hostile, put
up a protective shield. You tend to be somewhat overly
introspective. Your challenge is to avoid being overly
secretive.

Wednesday, November 16 (Moon into Leo, 11:18 a.m.)
Approach the day with an unconventional mind-set.
Change and variety are highlighted. You're seeking new
horizons. Think freedom, no restrictions. Think outside
the box. Take risks; experiment.

Thursday, November 17 (Moon in Leo) The moon
is in your eighth house. You pursue a mystical matter. It
could involve life after death or past lives, even hauntings or ghost hunting. You dig deep for information. You
could become part of a group or movement dedicated to
raising people's awareness.

Friday, November 18 (Moon into Virgo, 5:20 p.m.)
It's another mystery day. Secrets, intrigue, and confidential information play a role. Be aware of decisions
made behind closed doors. You work best on your own.
You're a spy for your own cause. Knowledge is essential
to success. Go with the flow, and maintain your emotional balance.

Saturday, November 19 (Moon in Virgo) You
have a sharp mind and an intuitive side that comes out.
Ideas come to you easily, and you find ways to put them

to use. When you're confident that you're right about a matter, don't hesitate. You could miss your opportunity. Act while the time is right. You get along well with the opposite sex. Your emotions are important to you.

Sunday, November 20 (Moon into Libra, 8:17 p.m.) Complete a project. Clear up odds and ends. Take an inventory of where things are going in your life. Use the day for reflection, expansion, and concluding projects. Accept what comes your way now. It's all part of a cycle.

Monday, November 21 (Moon in Libra) The moon is in your tenth house. You get along well with coworkers, Capricorn. It's a good day for sales and dealing with the public. You're good at problem solving, but you're also versatile and adaptable, a nice combination.

Tuesday, November 22 (Moon into Scorpio, 8:59 p.m.) Cooperation is highlighted. You work well with others. Your intuition focuses on a relationship, either one that's developing or a current one. Don't make waves. Don't rush or show resentment. Let things develop. Show your appreciation for others.

Wednesday, November 23 (Moon in Scorpio) Secrecy is your middle name. There are things you don't want to talk about with just anyone. However, you might confide in a trusted friend. You're looking deep for answers, trying to get to the heart of a matter. Write in a journal or a file on your computer in which you can put down your thoughts.

Thursday, November 24 (Moon into Sagittarius, 8:58 p.m.) Mercury goes retrograde in your twelfth house and stays that way until December 13. The energy shifts. You can expect some delays regarding your plans. Your feelings are more powerful than your logic. Group activities can be particularly challenging over the next three weeks. You feel best working behind the scenes, keeping your thoughts to yourself.

Friday, November 25 (Moon in Sagittarius)   There's a solar eclipse and new moon in your twelfth house. That means a new opportunity comes your way, and it could lead to working at home, on your own, or behind the scenes. It could involve a connection from the past or something that has previously eluded you. Your reaction to the offer could bring success and help you deal with rejection or failure.

Saturday, November 26 (Moon into Capricorn, 10:05 p.m.)   With Venus moving into your first house, your personal grace and pleasing manner put others at ease. You're socially outgoing; you have a pleasant, upbeat outlook on life. Your personality shines, and your appearance attracts positive comments.

Sunday, November 27 (Moon in Capricorn)   The moon is in your first house. You're sensitive to other people's feelings. You may feel moody one moment, happy the next, then withdrawn and sad. It's all about your health and your emotional self. It's difficult to remain detached and objective.

Monday, November 28 (Moon in Capricorn)   As the week begins, you're driven, serious, and ambitious, Capricorn. You're intent on succeeding. You won't give up. Your challenge is to open yourself to others, stay positive, and let others follow their own paths.

Tuesday, November 29 (Moon into Aquarius, 2:02 a.m.) It's a number 9 day. Finish what you started. Clear up odds and ends. Make room for something new, but don't start anything new until tomorrow. Look beyond the immediate. Take an inventory of where things are going in your life. Strive for universal appeal.

Wednesday, November 30 (Moon in Aquarius) The moon is in your second house. Expect emotional experiences related to money. Be yourself; be emotionally honest, especially when dealing with money issues. You identify with your possessions or whatever you value. Look at your priorities in handling your income. Put off making any major purchases.

DECEMBER 2011

Thursday, December 1 (Moon into Pisces, 9:46 a.m.) You express yourself well, especially through writing, and you're also very helpful and giving. Your challenge is to avoid moodiness or acting overly possessive. Don't scatter your energies.

Friday, December 2 (Moon in Pisces) Your mental abilities are strong, and you have an emotional need to express your ideas. However, when you do so, control your emotions, especially when you're dealing with relatives or neighbors. You also could be dealing with something from the past.

Saturday, December 3 (Moon into Aries, 8:52 p.m.) You're adaptable, considerate of others, and sensitive to their needs. You're also diplomatic and cooperative; and you work best with a partner. Avoid drowning yourself in details. Remain positive, and try to be a little more outgoing.

Sunday, December 4 (Moon in Aries) The moon is in your fourth house. Spend time with your family and loved ones. Stick close to home. You're dealing with the foundations of who you are and whom you are becoming. Take time to retreat to a private place for meditation. It's also a good day for dream recall.

Monday, December 5 (Moon in Aries)   You're open to new ideas, highly motivated, and looking for adventure. It's a great day for initiating projects and brainstorming. You're extremely persuasive, especially if you're passionate about what you're doing or selling or trying to convey.

Tuesday, December 6 (Moon into Taurus, 9:36 a.m.) It's all about freedom and no restrictions, but also about acting responsibly. Travel and variety are highlighted. Release old structures; get a new point of view. Be careful not to spread yourself too thin. All things in moderation.

Wednesday, December 7 (Moon in Taurus)   The moon is in your fifth house. Put your personal style into whatever you're doing. Express yourself creatively. Go to a concert, out on a date, or pursue a hobby. A gamble could pay off. Children could play a role, or maybe you just act in a childlike manner.

Thursday, December 8 (Moon into Gemini, 9:54 p.m.) You evaluate what's going on and detect deception and insincerity with ease. Knowledge is the key to success. You rely heavily on your experiences, but you're also intuitive. Your hunches are on the mark. Avoid being overly secretive or quarrelsome. Try to maintain your balance, and don't make any decisions on what you've learned until tomorrow.

Friday, December 9 (Moon in Gemini)   You're articulate and witty as well as adaptable and versatile. Look for a change of scenery. You tend to get along well with others, and you see both sides of a matter. Others see you as well grounded.

Saturday, December 10 (Moon in Gemini)   There's a lunar eclipse in your sixth house. That could mean that you have an emotional reaction to an issue related to your daily work or your health. Your efforts to help others are affected. Meanwhile, with Uranus direct in your fourth house, sudden events related to your home life are positive.

Sunday, December 11 (Moon into Cancer, 8:27 a.m.)
It's a number 1 day and you're at the top of your cycle. Get out and meet new people; have new experiences. Explore and discover. Creativity is highlighted. Express your opinions dynamically. In romance, a flirtation turns more serious.

Monday, December 12 (Moon in Cancer)   You're sensitive and intuitive, but also stable. You enjoy your home life and feel comfortable with friends and family. A partner plays an important role. Try to avoid being too secretive. If you're dealing with a contract, don't be afraid to ask for help.

Tuesday, December 13 (Moon into Leo, 4:49 p.m.)
Mercury goes direct in your twelfth house. That means any confusion, miscommunication, and delays that you've been experiencing, especially related to whatever you're keeping hidden, recede into the past. Things move smoothly. You can communicate your deepest feelings to a trustworthy friend. Pursue a spiritual or mystical discipline.

Wednesday, December 14 (Moon in Leo)   You're friendly; you get along well with others much better. Your popularity is on the rise, and you're ready to step to center stage. Get involved in a cause aimed at improving living conditions for large numbers of people. You have a strong sense of duty, you feel obligated to fulfill your promises.

Thursday, December 15 (Moon into Virgo, 10:59 p.m.)
Promote new ideas; follow your curiosity. Look for adventure. Freedom of thought and action is key. Pursue self-employment. You're courageous and adaptable. You're versatile and action-oriented, but try not to be impatient with others.

Friday, December 16 (Moon in Virgo)   Stick close to home, if possible. Take care of details, especially related to your health. Start exercising; watch your diet. Stop worrying and fretting. Take time to write in a journal. You write from a deep place with lots of details and colorful descriptions.

Saturday, December 17 (Moon in Virgo)   Your mind is active, and you yearn for new experiences. Plan a long trip. Sign up for a workshop or seminar. Your thoughts run wild. You're a dreamer, a thinker, and your thoughts tend to rattle the status quo. You jump easily from one idea to another.

Sunday, December 18 (Moon into Libra, 3:07 a.m.)
You can handle power and authority with ease. You're decisive and commanding. You gain recognition. But control your impatience, and watch where the money is going. Be courageous. Be yourself; be honest.

Monday, December 19 (Moon in Libra)   With the moon in your tenth house, yesterday's energies move into your Monday. Professional concerns and business dealings are highlighted. You gain an elevation of prestige for all your hard work. Your life is more public. You're emotional and warm toward coworkers.

Tuesday, December 20 (Moon into Scorpio, 5:33 a.m.)
Venus moves into your second house, which suggests that you're feeling very comfortable about finances or

you're fervently wishing that were the case. Whether it has happened or not, you have a very strong desire to make money and gain financial security. Artistic talents could play a role.

Wednesday, December 21 (Moon in Scorpio)
Friends play an important role in your day, especially Taurus and Virgo. You find strength in numbers. You find meaning through friends or a group of like-minded people. Social consciousness plays a role in your day. You could be working for a social cause.

Thursday, December 22 (Moon into Sagittarius, 7:03 a.m.)   You keep everyone in balance around you. You're creative; you express yourself well. Your artistic talents are highlighted. Enjoy the harmony, beauty, and pleasures of life. Expect an invitation from a friend, but remain flexible.

Friday, December 23 (Moon in Sagittarius)   Think carefully before you act. There's a tendency to undo all the positive actions you've taken. Avoid any self-destructive behavior. Be aware of hidden enemies. Unconscious attitudes can be difficult. Keep your feelings secret.

Saturday, December 24 (Moon into Capricorn, 8:48 a.m.)   There's a new moon in your first house. That means you get a new opportunity to put yourself out in front of the public. Your appearance and personality shine. Your feelings and thoughts are aligned. You have an opportunity to pursue something that has eluded you.

Sunday, December 25 (Moon in Capricorn)   Jupiter goes direct in your fifth house. Romance is highlighted. You have the opportunity to expand a creative endeavor. You're also in quite a romantic mood on this holiday, Capricorn. Merry Christmas!

Monday, December 26 (Moon into Aquarius, 12:15 p.m.) It's a number 7 day. You journey into the unknown and explore a mystery. Investigate something that's going on behind the scenes. You dig deep. Knowledge is essential to your success.

Tuesday, December 27 (Moon in Aquarius) The moon is in your second house. You come up with lots of moneymaking ideas. You're very vocal; you get your ideas across, especially the ones that deal with personal finances and investments. You communicate values that emphasize financial security.

Wednesday, December 28 (Moon into Pisces, 6:46 p.m.) Finish what you started. Make room for something new. Clear your desk for tomorrow's new cycle, and then look beyond the immediate. Strive for universal appeal.

Thursday, December 29 (Moon in Pisces) You're highly intuitive, Capricorn, and sensitive to others. You're sympathetic and understanding. Others confide in you, and you feel good when you can help others. But avoid trying to make others change their ways.

Friday, December 30 (Moon in Pisces) You're busy interacting with neighbors or relatives in a social gathering. You get your ideas across, but try not to get too emotional. A female relative plays an important role.

Saturday, December 31 (Moon into Aries, 4:49 a.m.) Ease up on your routines, and spread your good news. You communicate well. You're warm and receptive to what others say. Your imagination is keen. You're curious and inventive. Enjoy the harmony and pleasures of life. Beautify your home.

HAPPY NEW YEAR!

Appendix 1

Jupiter Ephemeris

Locate where your birth date falls in the ephemeris and find the sign for your natal Jupiter. Then look up the description in chapter 5.

01-01-1930 Ju Gemini
06-26-1930 Ju Cancer
07-17-1931 Ju Leo
08-11-1932 Ju Virgo
09-10-1933 Ju Libra
10-10-1934 Ju Scorpio
11-08-1935 Ju Sagittarius
12-02-1936 Ju Capricorn
12-19-1937 Ju Aquarius
05-14-1938 Ju Pisces
07-29-1938 Ju Pisces
12-29-1938 Ju Pisces
05-11-1939 Ju Aries
10-29-1939 Ju Aries
12-20-1939 Ju Aries
05-16-1940 Ju Taurus
05-26-1941 Ju Gemini
06-10-1942 Ju Cancer
06-30-1943 Ju Leo
07-25-1944 Ju Virgo
08-25-1945 Ju Libra

```
09-25-1946 Ju  Scorpio
10-23-1947 Ju  Sagittarius
11-15-1948 Ju  Capricorn
04-12-1949 Ju  Aquarius
06-27-1949 Ju  Aquarius
11-30-1949 Ju  Aquarius
04-15-1950 Ju  Pisces
09-14-1950 Ju  Pisces
12-01-1950 Ju  Pisces
04-21-1951 Ju  Aries
04-28-1952 Ju  Taurus
05-09-1953 Ju  Gemini
05-23-1954 Ju  Cancer
06-12-1955 Ju  Leo
11-16-1955 Ju  Virgo
01-17-1956 Ju  Virgo
07-07-1956 Ju  Virgo
12-12-1956 Ju  Libra
02-19-1957 Ju  Libra
08-06-1957 Ju  Libra
01-13-1958 Ju  Scorpio
03-20-1958 Ju  Scorpio
09-07-1958 Ju  Scorpio
02-10-1959 Ju  Sagittarius
04-24-1959 Ju  Sagittarius
10-05-1959 Ju  Sagittarius
03-01-1960 Ju  Capricorn
06-09-1960 Ju  Capricorn
10-25-1960 Ju  Capricorn
03-15-1961 Ju  Aquarius
08-12-1961 Ju  Aquarius
11-03-1961 Ju  Aquarius
03-25-1962 Ju  Pisces
04-03-1963 Ju  Aries
04-12-1964 Ju  Taurus
04-22-1965 Ju  Gemini
09-20-1965 Ju  Cancer
11-16-1965 Ju  Cancer
```

```
05-05-1966 Ju Cancer
09-27-1966 Ju Leo
01-15-1967 Ju Leo
05-23-1967 Ju Leo
10-19-1967 Ju Virgo
02-26-1968 Ju Virgo
06-15-1968 Ju Virgo
11-15-1968 Ju Libra
03-30-1969 Ju Libra
07-15-1969 Ju Libra
12-16-1969 Ju Scorpio
04-30-1970 Ju Scorpio
08-15-1970 Ju Scorpio
01-14-1971 Ju Sagittarius
06-04-1971 Ju Sagittarius
09-11-1971 Ju Sagittarius
02-06-1972 Ju Capricorn
07-24-1972 Ju Capricorn
09-25-1972 Ju Capricorn
02-23-1973 Ju Aquarius
03-08-1974 Ju Pisces
03-18-1975 Ju Aries
03-26-1976 Ju Taurus
08-23-1976 Ju Gemini
10-16-1976 Ju Gemini
04-03-1977 Ju Gemini
08-20-1977 Ju Cancer
12-30-1977 Ju Cancer
04-11-1978 Ju Cancer
09-05-1978 Ju Leo
02-28-1979 Ju Leo
04-20-1979 Ju Leo
09-29-1979 Ju Virgo
10-27-1980 Ju Libra
11-26-1981 Ju Scorpio
12-25-1982 Ju Sagittarius
01-19-1984 Ju Capricorn
02-06-1985 Ju Aquarius
```

02-20-1986 Ju Pisces
03-02-1987 Ju Aries
03-08-1988 Ju Taurus
07-21-1988 Ju Gemini
11-30-1988 Ju Gemini
03-10-1989 Ju Gemini
07-30-1989 Ju Cancer
08-18-1990 Ju Leo
09-12-1991 Ju Virgo
10-10-1992 Ju Libra
11-10-1993 Ju Scorpio
12-09-1994 Ju Sagittarius
01-03-1996 Ju Capricorn
01-21-1997 Ju Aquarius
02-04-1998 Ju Pisces
02-12-1999 Ju Aries
06-28-1999 Ju Taurus
10-23-1999 Ju Taurus
02-14-2000 Ju Taurus
06-30-2000 Ju Gemini
07-12-2001 Ju Cancer
08-01-2002 Ju Leo
08-27-2003 Ju Virgo
09-24-2004 Ju Libra
10-25-2005 Ju Scorpio
11-23-2006 Ju Sagittarius
12-18-2007 Ju Capricorn
01-05-2009 Ju Aquarius
01-17-2010 Ju Pisces
06-06-2010 Ju Aries
09-08-2010 Ju Aries
01-22-2011 Ju Aries
06-04-2011 Ju Taurus

Saturn Ephemeris

Locate where your birth date falls in the ephemeris and find the sign for your natal Saturn. Then look up in the description in chapter 7.

03-15-1929 Sa Capricorn
02-23-1932 Sa Aquarius
08-13-1932 Sa Aquarius
11-19-1932 Sa Aquarius
02-14-1935 Sa Pisces
04-25-1937 Sa Aries
10-17-1937 Sa Aries
01-14-1938 Sa Aries
07-06-1939 Sa Taurus
09-22-1939 Sa Taurus
03-20-1940 Sa Taurus
05-08-1942 Sa Gemini
06-20-1944 Sa Cancer
08-02-1946 Sa Leo
09-18-1948 Sa Virgo
04-02-1949 Sa Virgo
05-29-1949 Sa Virgo
11-20-1950 Sa Libra
03-07-1951 Sa Libra
08-13-1951 Sa Libra
10-22-1953 Sa Scorpio

01-12-1956 Sa Sagittarius
05-13-1956 Sa Sagittarius
10-10-1956 Sa Sagittarius
01-05-1959 Sa Capricorn
01-03-1962 Sa Aquarius
03-23-1964 Sa Pisces
09-16-1964 Sa Pisces
12-16-1964 Sa Pisces
03-03-1967 Sa Aries
04-29-1969 Sa Taurus
06-18-1971 Sa Gemini
01-09-1972 Sa Gemini
02-21-1972 Sa Gemini
08-01-1973 Sa Cancer
01-07-1974 Sa Cancer
04-18-1974 Sa Cancer
09-16-1975 Sa Leo
01-14-1976 Sa Leo
06-05-1976 Sa Leo
11-16-1977 Sa Virgo
01-04-1978 Sa Virgo
07-26-1978 Sa Virgo
09-21-1980 Sa Libra
11-29-1982 Sa Scorpio
05-06-1983 Sa Scorpio
08-24-1983 Sa Scorpio
11-16-1985 Sa Sagittarius
02-13-1988 Sa Capricorn
06-10-1988 Sa Capricorn
11-12-1988 Sa Capricorn
02-06-1991 Sa Aquarius
05-20-1993 Sa Pisces
06-30-1993 Sa Pisces
01-28-1994 Sa Pisces
04-07-1996 Sa Aries
06-09-1998 Sa Taurus
10-25-1998 Sa Taurus
02-28-1999 Sa Taurus

08-09-2000 Sa Gemini
10-15-2000 Sa Gemini
04-20-2001 Sa Gemini
06-03-2003 Sa Cancer
07-16-2005 Sa Leo
09-02-2007 Sa Virgo
10-29-2009 Sa Libra
04-07-2010 Sa Libra
07-21-2010 Sa Libra

Appendix 3

Uranus Ephemeris

Locate where your birth date falls in the ephemeris and find the sign for your natal Uranus. Then look up the description in chapter 8.

03-31-1927 Ur Aries
06-06-1934 Ur Taurus
10-09-1934 Ur Taurus
03-27-1935 Ur Taurus
08-07-1941 Ur Gemini
10-04-1941 Ur Gemini
05-14-1942 Ur Gemini
08-30-1948 Ur Cancer
11-12-1948 Ur Cancer
06-09-1949 Ur Cancer
08-24-1955 Ur Leo
01-27-1956 Ur Leo
06-09-1956 Ur Leo
11-01-1961 Ur Virgo
01-10-1962 Ur Virgo
08-09-1962 Ur Virgo
09-28-1968 Ur Libra
05-20-1969 Ur Libra
06-24-1969 Ur Libra
11-21-1974 Ur Scorpio
05-01-1975 Ur Scorpio

```
09-08-1975 Ur Scorpio
02-17-1981 Ur Sagittarius
03-20-1981 Ur Sagittarius
11-16-1981 Ur Sagittarius
02-14-1988 Ur Capricorn
05-26-1988 Ur Capricorn
12-02-1988 Ur Capricorn
04-01-1995 Ur Aquarius
06-08-1995 Ur Aquarius
01-12-1996 Ur Aquarius
03-10-2003 Ur Pisces
09-14-2003 Ur Pisces
12-30-2003 Ur Pisces
05-27-2010 Ur Aries
08-13-2010 Ur Aries
```

Appendix 4

Neptune Ephemeris

Find the sign that Neptune occupied at your birth, then read its description in chapter 10.

09-21-1928 Neptune Virgo
10-03-1942 Neptune Libra
04-17-1943 Neptune Virgo
08-02-1943 Neptune Libra
12-24-1955 Neptune Scorpio
03-11-1956 Neptune Libra
10-19-1956 Neptune Scorpio
06-15-1957 Neptune Libra
08-06-1957 Neptune Scorpio
01-04-1970 Neptune Sagittarius
05-02-1970 Neptune Scorpio
11-06-1970 Neptune Sagittarius
01-18-1984 Neptune Capricorn
06-22-1984 Neptune Sagittarius
11-21-1984 Neptune Capricorn
01-28-1998 Neptune Aquarius
08-22-1998 Neptune Capricorn
11-27-1998 Neptune Aquarius
04-04-2011 Neptune Pisces
08-04-2011 Neptune Aquarius
02-12-2012 Neptune Pisces

Appendix 5

Lunar Nodes Ephemeris

Locate your date of birth, find the sign of your north node, then read the description in Chapter 12.

07-04-1930 NN Taurus
12-29-1931 NN Aries
06-25-1933 NN Pisces
03-09-1935 NN Aquarius
09-14-1936 NN Capricorn
03-04-1938 NN Sagittarius
09-11-1939 NN Scorpio
05-23-1941 NN Libra
11-19-1942 NN Virgo
05-13-1944 NN Leo
12-01-1945 NN Cancer
12-10-1945 NN Cancer
12-14-1945 NN Cancer
07-31-1947 NN Gemini
01-22-1949 NN Taurus
07-26-1950 NN Aries
03-29-1952 NN Pisces
10-10-1953 NN Aquarius
04-02-1955 NN Capricorn
10-04-1956 NN Sagittarius
06-16-1958 NN Scorpio
12-15-1959 NN Libra

```
06-08-1961 NN  Virgo
12-21-1962 NN  Leo
08-25-1964 NN  Cancer
02-18-1966 NN  Gemini
08-20-1967 NN  Taurus
04-20-1969 NN  Aries
11-04-1970 NN  Pisces
04-27-1972 NN  Aquarius
10-27-1973 NN  Capricorn
07-11-1975 NN  Sagittarius
01-08-1977 NN  Scorpio
07-04-1978 NN  Libra
01-11-1980 NN  Virgo
09-23-1981 NN  Leo
03-16-1983 NN  Cancer
09-13-1984 NN  Gemini
04-01-1986 NN  Taurus
04-14-1986 NN  Taurus
04-22-1986 NN  Taurus
11-30-1987 NN  Aries
05-24-1989 NN  Pisces
11-19-1990 NN  Aquarius
08-03-1992 NN  Capricorn
02-01-1994 NN  Sagittarius
08-01-1995 NN  Scorpio
01-25-1997 NN  Libra
10-19-1998 NN  Virgo
04-12-2000 NN  Leo
10-11-2001 NN  Cancer
04-11-2003 NN  Gemini
12-24-2004 NN  Taurus
06-19-2006 NN  Aries
12-15-2007 NN  Pisces
08-22-2009 NN  Aquarius
02-28-2011 NN  Capricorn
```

SYDNEY OMARR

Born on August 5, 1926, in Philadelphia, Pennsylvania, Sydney Omarr was the only person ever given full-time duty in the U.S. Army as an astrologer. He is regarded as the most erudite astrologer of our time and the best known, through his syndicated column and his radio and television programs (he was Merv Griffin's "resident astrologer"). Omarr has been called the most "knowledgeable astrologer since Evangeline Adams." His forecasts of Nixon's downfall, the end of World War II in mid-August of 1945, the assassination of John F. Kennedy, Roosevelt's election to a fourth term and his death in office ... these and many others are on the record and quoted enough to be considered "legendary."

ABOUT THE SERIES

This is one of a series of twelve *Sydney Omarr® Day-by-Day Astrological Guides* for the signs of 2011. For questions and comments about the book, go to www.tjmacgregor.com.

COMING SOON

SYDNEY OMARR'S®
ASTROLOGICAL GUIDE
FOR YOU IN 2011

These expert forecasts for 2011 offer valuable insights about the past and extraordinary predictions for the future. Brimming with tantalizing projections, this amazing guide will give you advice on romantic commitment, career moves, travel, and finance. Along with year overviews and detailed month-by-month predictions for every sign, you'll learn everything that's new under the stars, including:

- What to expect from relationships with family and partners
- New career opportunities for success in the future
- Global shifts and world forecasts
- And much more!

Available wherever books are sold or at
penguin.com